THIS BOOK CONTAINS
GRAPHIC LANGUAGE

Also available from Continuum

THIS BOOK CONTAINS GRAPHIC LANGUAGE

COMICS AS LITERATURE

ROCCO VERSACI

continuum

NEW YORK • LONDON

2007

The Continuum International Publishing Group Inc
80 Maiden Lane

The Continuum International Publishing Group Ltd
The Tower Building, 11 York Road, London SE1 7NX

www.continuumbooks.com

Portions of Chapter 1 appeared, in slightly different form, in Doug Fisher and Nancy Frey (eds.), *Picture This: The Role Visual Information Plays in Literacy Learning*, copyright 2007 by Corwin Press. Reprinted with permission.

Portions of Chapter 6 appeared, in slightly different form, in *The English Journal* v. 91, n. 2, copyright 2001 by the National Council of Teachers of English. Reprinted with permission.

All efforts have been made by the author to determine and contact the copyright holders of the illustrations within this book and to obtain their permission to reprint these illustrations.

Printed in the United States of America

Library of Congress Cataloging-in-Publication Data

Versaci, Rocco.
  This Book contains graphic language : comics as literature / Rocco Versaci.
     p. cm.
  Includes bibliographical references and index.
  ISBN-13: 978-0-8264-2877-6 (hardcover : alk. paper)
  ISBN-10: 0-8264-2877-0 (hardcover : alk. paper)
  ISBN-13: 978-0-8264-2878-3 (pbk. : alk. paper)
   ISBN-10: 0-8264-2878-9 (pbk. : alk. paper) 1. Comic books, strips, etc.--History and criticism. 2. Literary form. I. Title.

PN6714.V47 2007
741.5--dc22

                                                2007031995

CONTENTS

To the ones I love

ACKNOWLEDGMENTS

Every so often during my days as a somewhat nerdy high school student who spent way too much time inside of his own head, I used to envision a future me: a somewhat nerdy writer toiling away at his word processor in a log cabin tucked away in the Maine woods. Why Maine? I have no idea; I had never even set foot in the state (and still haven't). But there's something about the northeastern-most state that suggests austerity, remoteness, and solitude—all features that I imagined were part and parcel of the authentic writer's life. Despite my conviction back then that my imagination was unique, I now know that there are many of us who entertain this vision of the writer as reclusive creative genius whose only companions are his words, a bottle of scotch, and a large faithful dog—preferably a German Shepherd or Labrador Retriever.

I also know that this image is largely a fiction. The experience of writing this book has taught me that an undertaking of this sort does not exist in a vacuum. So naturally, some thanks are in order.

First, I would like to extend my gratitude to my editors at Continuum, David Barker and Gabriella Page-Fort, for their belief in this project and for their advice and guidance during the revision stage.

One of the tasks that emerged during this state was to obtain permissions for the many illustrations that appear in the following pages. This task was formidable, but the process was aided mightily by several individuals whose efforts went above and beyond the call of duty. I'm thinking especially of Eric Reynolds and Cathy Gaines Mifsud, both of whom coordinated the permissions of many illustrations from books published by Fantagraphics Books, Inc. and William M. Gaines (EC), respectively.

Also helpful on the permissions front were Jaak Jarve at Jack Lake Productions, Jamie Quail at Drawn and Quarterly, Terry Nantier at NBM, Chris Staros at Top Shelf Productions, Sarah Serafimidis at North Atlantic Books, Carol Pinkus at Marvel Comics, Thomas King of DC Comics, and Nick Wylie of the Wylie Agency.

What made the task of obtaining permissions so important was the artwork itself, which I feel brilliantly represents the wonder of this medium. Therefore, I would like to extend special thanks to those artists whose generosity in sharing their art has made this book and its argument more engaging and persuasive: Harvey Pekar, Joe Sacco, Phoebe Gloeckner, Lynda Barry, Paul Hornschemeier, Al Davison, Robert Sikoryak, Jaime Hernandez, Gilbert Hernandez, Dan Clowes, Chris Ware, Catherine Doherty, Ted Rall, Craig Thompson, Debbie Drechsler, Peter Bagge, Dean Haspiel, Carol Lay, and Sue Coe.

I am also greatly indebted to the many comics scholars and archivists whose work has come before mine. More specifically, my project benefited from the work of those individuals who helped to document the rich history of this medium. In print, these writers include William B. Jones (*Classics Illustrated: A Cultural History, with Illustrations*) and Fred von Bernevitz and Grant Geissman (*Tales of Terror! The EC Companion*); on the Internet, these individuals include Michael Rhode and John Bullough, architects of the Comics Research Bibliography (www.rpi.edu/~bulloj/comicsbib.html), and the Grand Comics Database Team, creators of the best comics reference resource, period: the Grand Comics Database (www.comics.org). All of these individuals are important comics advocates who enable other supporters of the medium—like myself—to do a better job.

Closer to home, I would like to thank those at Palomar College—the college where I teach—who support and sustain the various leave programs that rightly recognize faculty as professionals and encourage us to develop as thinkers, writers, and teachers. In addition, I wish to thank my colleagues in the English Department and the Palomar College Library who have supported my efforts to introduce comics to our students.

My deep thanks also go out to various friends and colleagues who have helped me at the various stages of thinking about and completing this project: Brent Gowen, John Lucas, Carlton Smith, and Jack Quintero. Jack, especially, deserves thanks for his generous donation of time to provide me with close, close readings of my chapters despite the fact that he is not a fan of comic books. I'm still waiting to hear if that's changed . . .

Special thanks are due to my close friend Pat Gonder, whose love of comics reinvigorated my own when we were graduate students together at Indiana University. Many of the ideas in the pages that follow have benefited from our long talks (too long, if you ask our wives) about comics, film, and teaching. It's safe to say that if not for Pat, this book would not have been written—at least not by me.

I also must thank my students—an important group of people who share credit for this book. Their engagement with the comics that I have set before them has encouraged me to continue to bring this medium into my classes, and our conversations there have helped inspire me to clarify my thoughts on paper.

Finally, my unending thanks go to my wife, Laura, and my two sons, Nick and Tony. Laura's penchant for finding projects for me to do if I sat idle too long ensured that I kept working on this book. Of course, her support and eye for detail are invaluable. As for Nick and Tony, their excitement and energy are infectious, and they were always willing to give me a break from writing by playing baseball with me.

1.
WHY COMICS?
An Introduction with Several Digressions

My mother reads magazines—usually *Us* or *Star*. My father reads the *Chicago Tribune* and the occasional biography of people like Frank Sinatra, Joe Dimaggio, or some other Italian-American that he admires. When he was younger, my brother read Ellery Queen mysteries and *Mad* magazine; now, he reads dental journals and every word in every issue of *Backstreets*, the official fan magazine for Bruce Springsteen. My two sons will read anything with an athlete or something resembling a ball on the cover. This is also true of their coach (my wife), who reads widely but prefers nonfiction—especially books like H. G. Bissinger's *Friday Night Lights* or Darcy Frey's *The Last Shot*. Unlike her daughter, my mother-in-law reads novels that typically feature a gold-foil embossed title overlaying a Fabio look-alike, and she always insists on reading the last page first so that she won't have to worry about what's going to happen—a practice that still drives me to deliver the most absurd lectures on the sanctity of narrative, even after knowing her for almost twenty years. As for me, I prefer to read graphic language. Not "graphic" as in "explicit" (though I'm certainly not averse to coarse language—just ask my neighbors), but "graphic" as in "illustrated," which is a roundabout way of saying that I read comic books.

Of course, I don't read only comic books. I earn my living as an English professor who teaches composition, creative writing, and literature, so my bookshelves are stuffed with a wide variety of reading material. But over the last several years, I have noticed that my graphic novels—or, as Art Spiegelman puts it, "comic books that need bookmarks" (quoted in McGrath 26)[1]—are incrementally edging out my more "reputable" fiction, nonfiction, drama, and poetry. More and more often, as packages of graphic novels from Amazon.com arrive on my doorstep, I find myself carting displaced books to my office at school in the hopes of finding a home for them there. This colonization by characters like Maggie and Hopey, Mr. Natural, the Fantastic Four, and Swamp Thing of the prime real estate once occupied by Richard Ford, Jane Austen, and Arthur Miller has been met with more than a few raised eyebrows—at least two of which belong to my wife. These eyebrows silently wonder if the changes on my bookshelves constitute a step back in literacy.

Given common perceptions of comic books—that they are juvenile, disposable trash—such concerns are unsurprising and perhaps even expected. These perceptions, in fact, are something that every serious comic book reader over a certain age has had to deal with. Matthew Pustz, author of *Comic Book Culture: Fanboys and True Believers*, argues that the people who read comic books form a very interesting, productive, but largely marginalized community. A major reason for this marginalization, he states, is due to the fact that ". . . most Americans view comic books with contempt, especially when read by adults. Adult fans and collectors are seen as geeks and worse. Reading material supposedly aimed at children is somehow seen as a sign of psychological maladjustment or arrested development" (208–9). Few who wander into my office at school would disagree; after all, it's hard to mount a case against arrested development when the first thing people notice is an eighteen-inch-high action figure of Galactus (flanked by a six-inch-high Silver Surfer and Thing, no less) standing tall atop the file cabinet by my door.

So why would an adult have so many comic books? Or, more to the point: why would a seemingly well-adjusted adult have so many comic books?

In many ways, this entire book is an attempt to answer this question (and, indirectly, to defend myself as a well-adjusted adult). But before laboring in earnest at this task, I am going to assume that you're a reader and ask you to put this down and take a good look at your own bookshelves. What kinds of books are there? How has your reading changed over the years, and why? Are there places on your bookshelves that you visit more than others?

Why do you read what you read?

We read for a variety of needs and desires, and sometimes several of these reasons operate at the same time: to be informed, entertained, instructed, challenged, or transported. I wish to focus briefly on this last motivation—to be transported—because it is often associated with a certain kind of reading that is usually not held in high regard: escapism. By and large, "escapism" is associated with the most "pop" of our popular culture: the entertainment that is designed for mass appeal and minimal thinking. Such examples include "Chick Lit," horror, and other "genre" novels; big budget action films; most of what is on television, but especially sitcoms, sci-fi dramas, and so-called "reality" shows; Internet role playing games; and of course, comic books. Connotations of escapism are generally negative. Such entertainment is not "high" or even "good" art, or so the thinking goes; it's the kind of material that we engage with when we simply want to shut down our thinking centers. Unsurprisingly, creative works that fall under the banner of escapism are regarded with great suspicion by those who like to refer to themselves as "well-read." In their view, these works are to the "literary" what the corn dog is to cuisine: an indulgence that certainly does more harm than good to whoever consumes it. Why? Because from this perspective, escapist entertainment is all about "hiding" from what really matters—namely, the real world, the people in it, and the important ideas that we should be grappling with there.

Interestingly, some comic book creators embrace the "escapist" label for their work. Carl Barks, the legendary writer and artist of Walt Disney's Donald Duck and Uncle Scrooge comics, makes this position plain:

> I was writing escapist entertainment. The plots that so often featured the "far away and long ago" were staged in those areas and times because they took the reader out of his present world. The comic books of the "golden years" of the 40s, 50s, and 60s were all escapist reading in my opinion. The kids who read Superman, Plastic Man, and Tales from the Crypt were all taking a trip. (np)

Here, Barks implies that the term "escapism" holds no shame, and this sentiment is echoed by Michael Chabon in *The Amazing Adventures of Kavalier and Clay* (a wonderful novel that still has, and will have for some time to come, a choice location on my shelves). In this book, Chabon's two protagonists—Joe Kavalier and Sam Clay—find their fortune in the new world through the nascent comic book industry thanks to Clay's business sense and Kavalier's imagination, both of which produce their greatest creation, the Escapist. This hero, whose main power is the ability to break free from any constraints, owes his existence to Joe's personal history, which includes his own narrow escape from Nazi-occupied Prague. Over the years, Joe suffers many losses, and his pain fuels his affection for the comic book. Chabon writes, "Having lost his mother, father, brother, and grandfather, the friends and foes of his youth, his beloved teacher Bernard Kornblum, his city, his history—his home—the usual charge leveled against comic books, that they offered merely an easy escape from reality, seemed to Joe actually to be a powerful argument on their behalf" (575). Later, Chabon describes, in lyrical prose, how Joe has been able to forget his troubles via this escape:

> He would remember for the rest of his life a peaceful half hour spent reading a copy of Betty and Veronica that he had found in a service-station rest room: lying down with it under a fir tree, in a sun-slanting forest outside of Medford, Oregon, wholly absorbed into that primary-colored world of bad gags, heavy ink lines, Shakespearean farce, and the deep, almost Oriental mystery of the two big-toothed, wasp-waisted goddess-girls, light and dark, entangled forever in the enmity of their friendship. The pain of his loss—though he would never have spoken of it in these terms—was always with him in those days, a cold smooth ball lodged in his chest, just behind the sternum. For that half hour spent in the dappled shade of the Douglas firs, reading Betty and Veronica, the icy ball had melted away without him even noticing. That was magic—not the apparent magic of the silk-hatted card-palmer, or the bold, brute trickery of the escape artist, but the genuine magic of art. (575–76)

For Joe—and Chabon—the great achievement of comic books, or of any art, is to successfully transport readers elsewhere, allowing them to "escape."

At this point, I hope that readers will allow me a brief autobiographical aside (in fact, readers of this book should probably get used to this sort of thing). Unlike Chabon's protagonist, Joe Kavalier, my own insight into the "magic art" of comic books did not arrive via Betty and Veronica, though I do remember pawing through copies of *Archie*, *Richie Rich*, and *Looney Toons* in Sam's Barber Shop, where my dad and I would get our hair cut back when I was a kid. These books were barely held together, having suffered the eager rubbing of hundreds, maybe thousands, of oily, sticky, and—above all—small fingers. Those read-to-within-an-inch-of-their-lives comic books were just about all that I looked forward to on haircut Saturdays (every six weeks on the button), which were characterized by Sam's excruciating tugs with the thinning shears during the haircut and a free chunk of rock hard Bazooka gum wrapped in its own mini-comic from Sam's candy box afterward.

At home my comic book tastes were a bit more exotic. As a child in the 1970s, I naturally gravitated toward the Marvel superheroes. Because my favorite heroes were born of the atom, their bodies undergoing strange mutations at the hands of science gone awry, I was also drawn toward monsters. And not just the mostly lame attempts to resurrect the once-dominant horror genre in titles like

Ghost Rider, Man-thing, and *Tomb of Dracula;* my tastes ran to the larger scale monster stories—the reprints of the Jack Kirby and Stan Lee creatures in titles like *Where Monsters Dwell, Where Creatures Roam,* and *Creatures on the Loose.* Like Joe Kavalier, I was transported by these stories to a more brightly colored world where the most fantastic things could happen. If I needed to be coerced to dust my room, put away my green plastic soldiers, or go on yet another shopping trip to the K-Mart, my mother knew that my price was a comic book.

Eventually, I moved away from these books. Having my mom throw out my entire collection (twice!) might have had something to do with it. I did remain an avid reader, though, eventually becoming an English major who amassed some ninety-plus hours in literature classes on my way to an undergraduate degree. It was as a PhD student in English when I rediscovered comic books via two sources: an on-campus lecture by Art Spiegelman and a friendship with someone who never stopped reading them. Inspired by both, I read as much as I could and discovered a fascinating world of stories and storytelling that looked quite a bit different from what I remembered. And although I didn't know it at the time, I started down a path that would eventually lead to my current set of sagging, overstuffed bookshelves.

What weighs them down is undoubtedly "escapist" fare, but I want to examine this term—particularly as it relates to comics—in order to recapture it from those cultural critics who denigrate such entertainment generally, and to complicate its "magic" as articulated by artists like Barks and Chabon. In response to the critics, I contend that "escapism" and "literature" are not mutually exclusive, and that the former term does not have to mean, pejoratively, either hiding or retreat. On the contrary, the notion of escape lies at the heart of our engagement with all texts—not just those that fail to stimulate our thinking centers. For, despite the great diversity among the many texts that surround our lives, they nevertheless have a common thread: however beautifully or ineptly or movingly or lifelessly conveyed, these works are someone's interpretation of how the world in which we live either is or was or should be or might be or might have been. So when we "escape" into a novel, poem, essay, television show, article, video game, or comic book, we enter into an authored representation of the world. Every time. And the number of versions of the world is exactly equal to the number of texts that ever were or will be created. Seen in this light, "escape" does not have to preclude thinking; escape into these diverse worlds might mean, paradoxically, that we encounter meanings that are often lost in the chaotic din of our lives. In his memoir *Stop-Time* (1967), Frank Conroy voices this very situation when he writes, "I could not resist the clarity of the world in books, the incredibly satisfying way in which life became weighty and accessible" (143). Thus, our escape into different representational forms is not always a retreat from things that matter; on the contrary, such "escape" can often be a movement to the very things that do matter.

But just as the equating of "escape" to "mindless" is reductive, so too is the equating of comics with magical transportation—the belief that comic books provide easy passage to other worlds. This idea is tempting because the worlds that are commonly associated with comic books—the worlds of superheroes, talking animals, spaceships, ghouls, Archie, and the like—are clearly fantastical and suggest a place far removed from our own location. What is more, the notion that a particular medium gives us unfettered access to such imaginative realms is both romantic and powerful. But one of my main contentions that will reappear later in this chapter and throughout this book is that one can never completely "escape" into a comic book because its form—impressionistic illustrations of people, places, and things—reminds us at every turn (or panel) that what we are experiencing is a representation. While comics are very adept at engaging us with their creators' representations of the world, they never allow us to escape completely, and this, I hope to show, is a source of their great strength as a sophisticated medium.

I focus on escapism in order to deepen that term and free it from its traditional role as the arch-nemesis of Literature. Having attempted this, I now return to an earlier question: why would a seemingly well-adjusted adult have so many comic books? My most direct answer is that comic books are not a mindless but a mindful form of escapism that uses a unique kind of language—"graphic language"—to invite us into different worlds in order to help us better understand our own. Yet there are those who look at the medium and scoff at comics' obvious inferiority to the novel or film. To those individuals, I respond with the words of science fiction writer Theodore Sturgeon, who so eloquently stated that "Ninety percent of anything is crud."[2] As Sturgeon well knows, novels and films (and plays and poems, for that matter) also have their crud, but that fact does not tarnish those forms, and neither should it tarnish comics. The real challenge lies in how to distinguish the crud from the non-crud—the "low" from the "high," the mediocre (and worse) from the "literary." The methods of doing so vary from person to person and, as a literature teacher, I spend most of my time helping students develop their own means of making such distinctions. Of course my own biases factor in to this process, so I'll present them as such. First, as I'm sure is the case with many others, I find that noncrud is filled with interesting and complicated (and therefore compelling) characters, which in turn leads to engaging narratives. In addition, I see the noncrud as being that which challenges us to see the world differently. This challenge is mounted in a number of ways: by using exceptional and unique representational strategies, by subverting commonly held beliefs and assumptions, and by calling attention to both how texts represent the world and what is at stake in those representations. Certainly these are not the only means by which art challenges us to see the world differently, but they are important means, and they are the means that will factor into my analyses throughout the chapters that follow.

Before getting to a more thorough discussion of how comics accomplish these feats, a little history is in order.[3] Storytelling with pictures existed as early as prehistory, when tales of the hunt were documented in cave-paintings. Since then, this form has continued to develop in both Eastern and Western cultures. In fact, before literacy extended beyond the privileged classes, pictures were an effective way to communicate information, as evidenced by seventeenth-century British "broadsheets"—woodcut images of then-current events (Sabin 1996 11). Comic books are often (and arguably erroneously) referred to as an "American" art form because the comic book as we now recognize it first appeared in the US in 1934 with the release of *Famous Funnies* #1 (Goulart 18). Comic books themselves were an outgrowth of the newpaper comics in that early comic books simply reprinted newspaper strips. Before long, however, comic books like *Famous Funnies* began to feature original material, and with the first appearance of Superman in 1938's *Action Comics* #1, the industry was changed forever. In the 1940s, also known as the "Golden Age" of comics, this medium enjoyed a popularity that has never been equaled; by mid-decade, ninety percent of kids aged eight to fifteen were regular comic book readers (Benton 41).

The size and age of this readership prompted sharp criticism, the first shot being fired by Sterling North, who wrote, in a column entitled "A National Disgrace" that ran in newspapers across the country, that comics amounted to "cultural slaughter of the innocent" (quoted in Jones 168–69). North concluded that comics were a "poison" whose antidote lay in bookstores and libraries and that any "parent who [did] not acquire that antidote [was] guilty of criminal negligence" (quoted in Nyberg 4).[4] Predictably, the main charges were that comics negatively impacted literacy, that "comic-book readers [were] handicapped in vocabulary building because in comics all the emphasis is on the visual image and not on the proper word" (quoted in Giddins 89). Despite several studies that determined that "reading comic books, even to the exclusion of other activities, seemed to make little difference in reading skills, academic achievement, or social adjustment" (Nyberg 11), the comic book retained its reputation as something that could cause only harm to young readers.

This "harm" took on a decidedly sociological cast in the 1950s, when comic books were cited as a primary cause of juvenile delinquency (Nyberg 18). One of the main forces behind this accusation was Dr. Fredric Wertham, who in 1953 published his anticomic crusade *Seduction of the Innocent*—a "study" based largely on anecdotal evidence and questionable logic. His conclusion, in essence, was that comic books caused delinquency because imprisoned juvenile delinquents had read them (Sabin 1993 158). The very next year, 1954, saw the beginning of the "Kefauver Hearings," which were nationally televised Senate hearings designed to investigate the issue of comics' negative effects on children. One of the witnesses was Wertham himself, who in typical overstated fashion declared that "'Hitler was a beginner compared to the comic book industry'" (quoted in Sabin 159).

These hearings, fueled by negative public sentiment, led publishers to create the Comics Magazine Association of America (CMAA), whose sole mission was to enforce the "Comics Code," widely regarded as the most restrictive ratings code that any entertainment medium in this country has faced (Benton 53).[5] In order for a title to receive the "Seal of Approval," it had to adhere to the Code, which meant, in part, that it had to avoid complex characterization—especially as regarded "official" figures like police officers and judges—and topics that might be of interest to older readers (Sabin 1993 251–53). The end result of the Code and the publishers' conformity was the mainstream juvenilization of the medium, which in turn caused the general public to equate comic books as a form suitable only for children.

This misapprehension persists today. One of the clearest recent examples comes in rhetoric surrounding the August 2006 release of Sid Jacobson and Ernie Colon's *The 9/11 Report: A Graphic Adaptation*. This comic book adaptation of *The 9/11 Commission Report* (2004)—a book that details the events leading up to and including the attacks on September 11, 2001—was profiled in the *Washington Post* by Bravetta Hassell, who asks at one point, "can a topic as massive and sobering as Sept. 11 be dealt with effectively in the pages of a comic book?" (D1). The assumption here is that the weight of the topic is simply too much for the medium to bear. In response to her question, one reader—a pilot for a major airline—writes that he is "outraged by the attempt to depict the horrific events of Sept. 11 in a comic book format" and that "while shielding children from the details of this horrific tragedy is appropriate, telling the rest of society about it in a comic book isn't" (Villani A14). The fact that the letter-writer has only seen the book through the limited scope of Hassell's article (and has probably not picked up a comic book in the last twenty years) is largely beside the point. What is important to note here is the assumption he makes that comic books are a juvenile medium that can only trivialize serious matters.

Certainly, the attention that *The 9/11 Report: A Graphic Adaptation* garnered has been fueled by this assumption. Interestingly enough, the creators themselves attempt to distance themselves from the negative connotations of the term "comic book" and any perceived inappropriateness between that form and the World Trade Center attacks. Jacobson, who created *Richie Rich*, "'never felt it was a comic book. . . . What we do is graphic journalism'" (quoted in Smith F7). This kind of name-game playing is nothing new where comic books are concerned.[6] I am not writing to defend *The 9/11 Report: A Graphic Adaptation*; rather, I am writing to defend the medium itself, which is more than capable of tackling tough issues and subject content, as its history has shown. Critics of the very idea of the adaptation might be surprised to know that comic books have very ably depicted controversial subjects. In the chapters that follow, in fact, I will be examining comic book representations of incest, homosexuality, cancer and other physical challenges, the Holocaust, the Palestine conflict, World Wars I and II, the Korean War, the Vietnam War, and the Bosnian War, just to name a few. Most people tend to associate comic books with superheroes—not that there's anything wrong with that—but there are many more comic book stories being told than those about men and women in tights. In fact, it is probably safe to say that whatever your interests, there is a comic book out there somewhere for you.

Despite the prevailing assumption that comics are an inferior medium, the tide has been (slowly) turning. Every several years since the mid-1980s, some critic writes an article brandishing a title like "Zap! Pow! Comics Aren't for Kids Anymore!" as if the or she were the first person to recognize this fact. The first wave of such articles began appearing on the heels of Alan Moore's *Watchmen* (1986), Frank Miller's *The Dark Knight Returns* (1987), and Art Spiegelman's *Maus* (1986). These three works and their reception in the mainstream media were instrumental in the "maturation" of comic books in terms of both art and commerce. Suddenly, there was grittier superhero fare! Suddenly, there was a comic book taking on a "serious subject"! In actuality, the "suddenly" part was more a product of perception than reality: superhero comics had been dealing with more mature subject matter as early as the 1970s,[7] and independent comics in the 1980s had many more practitioners than Art Spiegelman.[8] Yet the impact of these three books was substantial. *Watchmen* and *Dark Knight* proved to be powerful templates for a new breed of comic book antihero that was far darker than earlier incarnations, and *Maus*, for its part, showed the non-comic-book-reading public that alternative comic book creators could produce interesting work. The real issue was that this work lacked an easy way to get into the hands of readers.

This situation changed somewhat with the rise of the "direct market," a means of organizing sales whereby publishers began dealing with an increasing number of comic shops, thus bypassing the traditional distributors. Because this system allowed publishers to fill specific needs, this new system had the effect of cutting overhead costs for publishers (in the form of overprints) while at the same time putting creators in closer touch with the reading interests of comic shop denizens. Not surprisingly, these new opportunities led to a proliferation of publishers—both mainstream and alternative—and comic shops (Sabin 1993 66). As comic book purchasing moved from the newsstands and into these specialty shops, enforcement of the Comics Code became much more difficult (Nyberg 161), thus allowing a large percentage of comic book creators more freedom in pursuing previously verboten subject matter.

The new arrangements also fostered changes in creative ownership and control, as well as marketing, and these led to the rise of the "collector culture," which for a short time boosted sales of comics as speculators bought up titles in excessive numbers (Sabin 1993 67). The end result of all of this was that in the late 1980s and early 1990s comics enjoyed a state of popularity unmatched since the 1950s (Sabin 1993 68). Eventually, however, the bubble burst, and comics entered a state of decline. Many houses like Marvel and DC overestimated the endurance of comic book collecting, and a suddenly saturated market met with readers' (i.e., non-collectors') increasing dissatisfaction over inflated prices and obvious marketing ploys like crossover storylines and multiple covers of the same issue. Declining sales inevitably led to financial hardships for comic shops (many of which closed) and publishers (some of which, including Marvel, filed for bankruptcy).

More recently, however, comic books have enjoyed a renewed surge in popularity. In part, this popularity has been due to the impact of the Internet on fan communities of all kinds: readers with the most idiosyncratic reading interests have been able to find others of like mind and participate in discussions about their favorite titles and characters; similarly, with online comic book stores and auction houses, the ability of readers to obtain previously hard-to-find books has markedly increased.

Perhaps most significantly, the relatively higher profile that comics are now enjoying is, in no small part, due to the film industry. Of course the mainstream superhero films have received the most press (and Marvel's sale of the rights to many of its most popular characters helped rescue it from bankruptcy), but lesser known, edgier mainstream comics have also been adapted into high-profile films. The movies *Sin City* (2005), based on Frank Miller's comic, and *V for Vendetta* (2005), based on Alan Moore's graphic novel, have called attention to the fact that the mainstream is comprised of more than just superheroes. In addition, alternative comics have benefited with the release of acclaimed films like *Crumb* (1994), *Ghost World* (2000), and *American Splendor* (2003), all of which have drawn new attention to this medium.

Reflecting and extending the zeitgeist, the popular press has responded with articles about and reviews of serious graphic novels; such pieces have appeared in the *New York Times Book Review*, Time.com, and *Entertainment Weekly* (which, it should be noted, is owned by Time Warner, the same conglomerate that owns DC Comics). The work of these publications is certainly helping the cause, as is the fact that "real" book publishers like Knopf, Random House, and Houghton Mifflin are publishing graphic novels; the latter publisher, in fact, has added a new addition to its "Best American" series: *The Best American Comics 2006* (only time will tell if this title becomes an annual event).

Also helping is the fact that many teachers and librarians have embraced this form and are introducing them into classrooms and libraries. In fact, it is not at all difficult to find resources for librarians who are interested in creating or improving their graphic novels collections. The Association of College and Research Librarians published, in their February 2005 issue of the *C&RL News*, an article entitled, "Comic Books and Graphic Novels: Digital Resources for an Evolving Form of Art and Literature." What would Fredric Wertham's response be, I wonder, to the fact that this article was written by Leslie Bussert—an actual (gasp!) librarian?

Like Bussert, I have no problem mentioning comic books and literature in the same sentence. The reasons for this opinion are certainly interrelated and will continue to develop throughout this book, but I can enumerate the main three here. The first reason has to do with comics' position in our culture. As I mentioned earlier, comic books have, throughout their history, been seen as a disposable medium that is meant primarily for children. As a result of this view, they have been relegated to the margins of representational media. That is, comic books by and large are not accorded the same status as other forms such as novels or film. On the surface, such outsider status would seem to have a negative impact on the medium—and I suppose it has. But the marginality of comics has also allowed comic book creators to take advantage of others' (dis)regard for them in order to create representations that can be both surprising and subversive. If one characteristic of good literature is that it challenges our way of thinking, then comics' cultural position is such that they are able to mount these challenges in unique ways.

The second reason that I see comics as a sophisticated literary art form has to do with the self-consciousness that lies at the heart of comics' "graphic language," which always prevents us from "escaping" completely. Fredric Jameson contends that historical events—both large and small, public and personal—are available to us only indirectly through representations; he writes that "our approach . . . to the Real itself necessarily passes through its prior textualization" (35). In other words, we can "know" the past only through various representations. Whether we are dealing with fiction or nonfiction, these representations of the world come to us is some form of narrative, and "any narrative presents a selection and an ordering of material" (Brooks 13). In turn, narratives have authors with their own perspectives, biases, and agendas. Because the representation of the "Real" can be politically charged, and because I distrust authors who represent the past (and present) by remaining hidden or by making false claims to realism, I am intrigued by those creative works that in some way call attention to their own making. I have argued and will continue to argue that comic books do exactly this, for it is impossible for a comic book creator either to hide entirely or to project complete realism because of the medium's use of illustrations. That is, the comic book aesthetic projects unreality to some degree because every comic book is a drawn version of the world and, therefore, not "real."

In addition to this innate self-consciousness, comics have a history of overtly underscoring their own artifice, and in so doing, they call necessary attention to the spaces between "the Real" and its "textualization." George Herriman's long-running strip *Krazy Kat* (1913–44), for instance, has often been praised for its self-reflexivity. This comic featured a cast of anthropomorphized animals, but the main three were Krazy Kat, Ignatz Mouse, and Offisa Pup—all of whom were involved in a bizarre and counterintuitive "love triangle": Krazy loved Ignatz, Pup loved Krazy, and Ignatz beaned Krazy with bricks. This ongoing narrative was bolstered by Herriman's multiple and complex plays on words and his exploration (and demolition) of comics conventions. Critic M. Thomas Inge likens this strip to the Dadaist art movement, for both make us "aware that it is an artifice we are viewing, and the violation of conventions becomes a technique itself to further its own ends" (51). Similarly, American comics pioneer Winsor McCay was fond of reminding readers of the fact that the comic possessed its own structure separate from reality. In one of his *Little Sammy Sneeze* strips, for example, the very framework of the six-panel comic is blown apart by the force of Sammy's sneeze. McCay was, even in the form's infancy, highlighting that comics traffic in unreality. In later years, comics' bread and butter would become the "unreal" worlds of super beings and talking animals and whatnot, and the dominance of these genres over the medium's history all but ensures that people come to comics today hyperaware of their artificiality. Yet my belief is that rather than compromising their ability to be a powerful form of representation, this perceived artificiality makes comic books an ideal medium to call attention creatively and insightfully to how the world is represented in texts of all kinds.

My third and final reason for seeing comics as a sophisticated representational form is that their graphic language operates with a unique poetics that I will begin to discuss here in some detail and return to throughout this book. While acknowledging that "the comics form is infinitely plastic [and that] there is no single recipe for reconciling the various elements of the comics page" (Hatfield xiv), I will argue that some broad conclusions can and should be drawn (so to speak) about this medium. That is, comic narration blends and modifies features shared by other art forms—especially literature, painting, photography, and film. Like literature, comics contain written narrative and dialogue, and they employ devices such as characterization, conflict, plot, and all of those components of well-written fiction that we learn about in school. Unlike literature, comics are able, quite literally, to "put a human face" on a given subject. That is, comics blend words and pictures so that, in addition to reading text, readers "see" the characters through the illustrations. Like painting and photography, a comic's illustrations can be both highly expressionistic or

realistic, and individual static panels incorporate principles of composition, perspective, shading, and (if the publishing budget allows)
color. Unlike these two artistic forms, however, comics use multiple
images in succession to create narrative. Like film, the transitions
between panels in comics function much the same as editing cuts,
resembling film's ability to manipulate time and space. Unlike film,
comics do not rely on photographic representation but on illustration.
Also unlike film, the images in comics are "read" more like paintings
and photographs rather than "watched" like movies. And while film
and comic narrative both rely on a succession of still images, the
transitions between those still images in film are far less visible than
between those in comics. That is, we do not notice the still images
in a film (they move too fast at twenty-four frames per second); in
comics, because the still images are laid out before us, we are free
to examine how one illustration moves to the next.

All of these characteristics funnel into a core attribute of comics'
graphic language: the unique ways in which one "reads" this language. More specifically, the interplay between the written and visual is a complicated process; a comic "does not 'happen' in the words,
or the pictures, but somewhere in-between, in what is sometimes
known as 'the marriage of text and image'" (Sabin 1993 9). Because
this "in-between" space is difficult to identify and varies from title to
title, reading comic books requires an active though largely subconscious participation on the part of the reader. Such participation has
been referred to as "closure," whereby the reader fills in the details
of the empty spaces between the panels, and the result of this
process is to "foster an intimacy . . . between creator and audience"
(McCloud 64, 69). One significant outcome of closure is that readers
are able to sympathize and empathize with comic book characters in
unique ways. Another significant outcome is that we read the combination of words and pictures differently than we do either words
exclusively or pictures exclusively.

The nature of this reading is somewhat unusual.[9] On the one
hand, comics are read, as are literature and film, in a linear fashion,
meaning that the reading progresses from point A to point B and so
on. Part of comics' graphic language is the alteration of panel size
and shape to influence, for various purposes, the pace of reading.
But because these panels form page-length and sometimes multi-
ple-page-length layouts, reading a comic is not always linear. That
is, unlike film, which unspools at a more or less predetermined (and
from the viewer's perspective, uncontrollable) pace, comics creators
can play with the design of an entire page by manipulating the visuals within panels and the panels themselves within the page to cre-

Figure 1.1. Copyright Jaime Hernandez.
Image appears courtesy of Fantagraphics Books, Inc.

ate additional layers of meaning. Thus, a comic, in addition to unfolding temporally, also exists "all at once," and this existence is a feature unique to this medium.

One of my favorite examples of this principle is the first page of Jaime Hernandez's story, "Flies on the Ceiling" (1989). The story recounts his character Isabel (Izzy) Ortiz's strange experiences in Mexico, but the first page presents her struggle to write as unpleasant memories from the past—her divorce, abortion, suicide attempt—crowd her consciousness (see Figure 1.1). The page is what is referred to by industry practitioners as a standard nine-panel page, and it is virtually text-free. Read in a linear fashion, we see how Izzy's tension increases along with the severity of her memories. If we consider the page as a whole, however, new meanings come to light. For example, the page's central panel (a position that often carries the greatest visual weight because of its prime placement) is the only panel of Izzy's memories in which she does not appear in some way. One interpretation of its placement and her absence could be that this is her most difficult memory. Also, another interesting meaning arises by looking at the page as a whole. The panels containing Izzy's memories form an X shape over the entire page, suggesting that her past is "crossing out" any possibility for peace in her present. Such meanings abound in comics.

As this example suggests, comics are a unique form of narrative. Other features of the medium—the wide variety of available narrative points of view, the physical texture of the comic, the nature of comics' publishing, and the malleability of comic narrative—allow for additional methods of narrative that are highly sophisticated and unavailable in other media. To give some sense of how complicated and unique storytelling in comics can be, let's look briefly at two works: issue #22 of *Eightball*, by Daniel Clowes, and *Love and Rockets*, by Gilbert and Jaime Hernandez.

Eightball #22 (2001) is one of the latest issues in Daniel Clowes's series, which he began in 1989 and has published sporadically (as is typical of many independent comic book artists) since then. This comic book has been the main showcase for Clowes's work, ranging from short, standalone "gag" strips to long, serialized narratives. In fact, the graphic novels that Clowes is best known for—*Ghost World* (1997) and *David Boring* (2000)—originally appeared in installments within the pages of *Eightball*. *Eightball* #22 represents a departure of sorts for the title insofar as it is a self-contained narrative comprising twenty-nine more or less interrelated stories.[10] The main narrative thread of *Eightball* #22 involves the seemingly unmotivated kidnapping of young David Goldberg in a town not used to such dramatic events. In fact, the kidnapping itself is a bit of a narrative MacGuffin, for Clowes's real intent is to explore the psychologies of the town's oddball citizens—particularly the self-proclaimed (and self-deluded) "Poet Laureate of Ice Haven," Random Wilder; Vida, granddaughter of Random Wilder's literary nemesis; Violet, a lovelorn high schooler who can't stand her mother and new stepfather; and Charles, a classmate of the kidnapped David and stepbrother to Violet, whom he loves.

One significant achievement by Clowes in *Eightball* #22 is the demonstration of the different ways that comics can present a variety of narrative perspectives within a single work. Clowes presents three of his first person narrators—Wilder, Vida, and Violet—in largely different ways. For example, we know Wilder mainly through stories in which he delivers extended monologues, via word balloon, to the reader. Clowes uses no thought bubbles or text boxes with Wilder; all of the failed writer's views come to us through direct address. In the case of Vida, most of her thoughts come to us through her writing (she is the founder and sole contributor of *The Weekly*, an idiosyncratic 'zine in which she offers her views on humanity). Thus, she addresses us directly—as her readers— through text box narration. Violet's narration is different yet; specifically, Clowes presents her thoughts not in the conventional method of thought balloons but instead in diary entries (in "Seventeen") and text boxes (in "Violet in Love"). Each of these methods creates a slightly different first person narration that fosters different relationships between character and reader. Wilder's word balloons—where he speaks aloud, to no one in particular—makes him self-important, odd, and somewhat pathetic. In Vida's case, however, her direct address is naturalized insofar as she is obviously speaking to fans of *The Weekly*. This positioning fosters a conspiratorial—but still distanced—relationship with the reader. Violet's narration, because it arrives to us through her diary and because her thoughts are of a more intimate nature, comes off as voyeuristic, and as a result she is a far more sympathetic character than either Wilder or Vida.

Clowes also shows how comics can present a third-person narrative point of view in different ways, and he does this mainly through his varied presentations of Charles. In "Our Children and Their Friends," Charles is presented from a distanced third-person perspective that contains no interiority save for what he reveals in dialogue to others (see Figure 1.2). In "David Goldberg Is Missing," by contrast, Charles's thoughts are revealed through cutaway panels. At this particular point in the narrative, Charles is afraid that his classmate Carmichael might have been telling the truth when he told him

Figure 1.2. Copyright Daniel Clowes.
Image appears courtesy of Fantagraphics Books, Inc.

that he killed David Goldberg. Clowes represents these fears completely through the visuals; specifically, he presents separate panels that interrupt images of Charles fretting in bed (see Figure 1.3). In "Charles," Clowes presents Charles's point of view through a mixture of dialogue and thought balloons (see Figure 1.4), allowing us to apprehend a contrast between Charles's external and internal world. Because of the numerous permutations between word and image available in the comics form, the answer to the always important question of who tells the story can become both layered and complex.

In addition to exploring the variety of narrative perspectives possible in comics, Clowes also manipulates his images to show how comics have a kind of physical "texture" that can create added layers of meaning to a story. Consider three different "versions" of Charles that appear within *Eightball* #22. In the aforementioned story, "Our Children and Their Friends," Charles is rendered in full color as a passive character insofar as he barely speaks and we have no access to his thoughts. In another story—"Charles"—he is rendered more stylistically, in a pinkish hue and spewing comically overwrought lamentations about his unrequited love for Violet. Both the images and characterizations here provide a stark contrast to "Charles." In yet another story—"Charles and His Therapist"—the

Figure 1.3. Copyright Daniel Clowes.
Image appears courtesy of Fantagraphics Books, Inc.

Figure 1.4. Copyright Daniel Clowes.
Image appears courtesy of Fantagraphics Books, Inc.

final panel represents an amalgam of the previous two: the image is visually stylized in a similar fashion to the previous one—Clowes replaces pink with blue here—but in terms of text, we are given a contrast between what he says and what he thinks. This particular presentation is at once more revelatory of Charles's character than the first panel and more realistic than the second. Taken together, Charles becomes a model for the complex characterization possible in comics as Clowes exploits part of the medium's formal elements.[11] Again, this is a method of character presentation that is simply not available to artists and writers in other media.

Other dimensions of a comic book's "texture" lie in its presentation and physical aspects, and throughout *Eightball* #22, Clowes exploits these features to create a wholly original presentation of his characters and stories. Within the context of this comic, some of these twenty-nine stories are more realistically visual than others. Some stories, by contrast, are quite self-consciously presented as comics. For example, "Julie Patheticstein," "Mrs. Ames," "Kim Lee," and "Officer Kaufman" are all in the format of a four-panel newspaper strip. In addition, one story, "Blue Bunny," features an anthropomorphic rabbit—a mainstay of cartoons and "funny animal" comics—as the main character, and another story, "Rocky 100,000 B.C.," stars a sociopath caveman who resembles Fred Flintstone.[12] In addition, Clowes manipulates the very texture of the page by placing some stories—like "David Goldberg Is Missing" and "Charles"— on off-white pages that call to mind yellowing newspaper. Through all of these methods, Clowes reminds us that we are reading a comic, and this reminder creates an ongoing and interesting tension between our engagement with and estrangement from the stories and their characters. This tension is intensified in the book's last story, "Harry Naybors Explains Everything," in which one of the previously introduced characters—a comic book expert, no less— deconstructs *Eightball* #22 while at the same time hawking Clowes's other books and products. What is truly amazing about these stories that call attention to their constructed nature is that they do not render *Eightball* #22 incoherent; instead, such manipulation of text and texture allows a reader to enter the narrative at several levels. Like the French New Wave filmmakers and the metafictionalists of the 1960s, Clowes makes the texture of his medium apparent to us with directness and variety. And, just as those media had their own unique methods of deconstructing their work, so too do comics.[13]

Love and Rockets (1982–present) by brothers Gilbert and Jaime Hernandez demonstrates other important dimensions of the unique poetics of comics. Since their very first issue, Gilbert and Jaime

Hernandez—and sometimes their brother, Mario—have been writing a sprawling narrative featuring a multitude of characters and locales. Gilbert's stories are set primarily in the fictional Central American village of Palomar, while Jaime's characters inhabit Hoppers, a barrio that bears a striking resemblance to Oxnard, where the Hernandez brothers grew up. In contrast to the single-issue *Eightball #22*, *Love and Rockets* is a massive, continuing work; it was published by Fantagraphics Books from 1982 to 1996, and then again from 2000 to the present. While *Love and Rockets* took a four-year hiatus, Gilbert and Jaime did not. The two continued to produce comics featuring their characters and introducing a few new ones.[14] Both brothers write, draw, and ink their own work, and there is no significant crossover—save thematic—between their sets of characters and stories. When published as individual issues, *Love and Rockets* generally features the work of both brothers. These issues have also been collected in trade paperbacks, which to date number twenty-two volumes. The early volumes of these trade paperback collections, like the comics themselves, feature the work of both brothers. Since the late 1980s, however, the collections have been separated.[15] In addition to the regular publication of both the comic and the trade paperbacks, two massive hardcovers have been released: *Palomar: The Heartbreak Soup Stories* (2003), a 512-page collection of most of Gilbert's Palomar stories, and *Locas: The Maggie and Hopey Stories* (2004), a 780-page collection of brother Jaime's Hoppers stories. As a whole, *Love and Rockets* is a character-driven saga in which Gilbert and Jaime's main—and strongest—characters are women.[16] What drives all of these narratives are the relationships among the characters, and if forced to reduce *Love and Rockets* to its very essence, I would say that the entire work is a study of the many dimensions of love. But discussing this entire work is not my intent here; instead, I wish to highlight features of this comic book that help to establish comics' unique representational strategies.

First, *Love and Rockets* demonstrates how comics are the ideal medium in which to examine characters over a long period of time. Unlike other media, comics allow characters to age—almost in real time—over the duration of a particular book, which in the case of *Love and Rockets* is approaching twenty years. Gilbert and Jaime have embraced the naturalistic possibilities of this feature: unlike most mainstream titles, where the superheroes are ageless, Los Bros. Hernandez have aged their characters not only in the maturation of their perspectives and attitudes, but in their physical features as well. In Gilbert's stories, his main character, Luba, has obtained more wrinkles and weight as the years have passed (see Figure

Figure 1.5. Copyright Gilbert Hernandez.
Images appear courtesy of Fantagraphics Books, Inc.

Figure 1.6. Copyright Jaime Hernandez.
Images appear courtesy of Fantagraphics Books, Inc.

1.5). Jaime's main character, Maggie Chascarillo, has similarly aged (see Figure 1.6). Such naturalism over an extended period of time is possible only because comics are both serialized and drawn. Thus, creators have much more freedom with their characters than do authors of more traditional literature. One important effect of this feature is that comics can foster close connections with their readership. As one longtime *Love and Rockets* reader writes, "I started reading L&R as I said when I was 11 and the characters were in their late teens. Now, I'm in my mid-20s and they're in their mid-30s, and I love it that I see the way my life & attitudes have slightly changed mirrored in the way theirs have. I don't find it depressing that they're ageing, but again, beautiful" (Shamsavari 31). Another reader writes, "I'm continually amazed at how I can always learn something new about your characters when I've watched them for over 15 years. It's like real people in that you never know everything about them" (Leroy 8). These readers' connections to *Love and Rockets* bear out the views of one critic, who writes, "Graphic art is the artistic medium perhaps most suited to chronicling life as it is lived: as a visual record of physical action and change, and an emotional record of people as the sum parts of their speech, interactions, and relationships with the outside world" (Benfer). Not surprisingly, the subject of this article is the portrayal of women by the Hernandez Brothers in their long-running series.

A second feature demonstrated in *Love and Rockets*, and one that is a crucial component of comics' graphic language, is the malleability of comic narrative. In part, this malleability is reflected in the multiplicity of perspectives and layering of form evident in *Eightball* #22, but it also emerges in the ability of comic book creators to revisit and reopen unexplored smaller narratives within a larger one with a freedom that is all but impossible in other media. In volume eight of the complete *Love and Rockets—Blood of Palomar* (1989)— Gilbert tells the story "Human Diastrophism," a multichapter saga that interweaves several narrative threads, including one that centers on Tonantzin, a woman who undergoes a political awakening over the course of the book. Eventually, she and her lover, Khamo, leave Palomar, and the two of them travel to their country's capital in order to participate in some unspecified political demonstration. At the end of *Blood of Palomar*, we learn from news reports that Tonantzin has immolated herself as part of the protest. Khamo, unaware of her intentions, attempted to save her and was burned beyond recognition. He survived, returning to Palomar to marry Luba, with whom he had previously fathered two children. Twelve years and eleven volumes later, in *Luba in America* (2001), Gilbert returns to the story of Tonantzin and Khamo. One story in that volume, "Poseur," is an eight-page chronicle of Khamo's life, which has been characterized by constant redefinition. On the penultimate page of the story, Gilbert delivers an extended scene between Khamo and Tonantzin on the eve of her self-immolation. Readers of the earlier story know that Khamo was unaware of what she was going to do, and this part of the story remains consistent here. What we gain through this revisitation, however, is a new understanding of Tonantzin. At the end of *Blood of Palomar*, her sacrifice was both sudden and shocking, and our last impression of her in that previous book was as an impassioned but somewhat naïve revolutionary. As she tells her sister, "me and Khamo are going to join groups from one side of a serious political battle and then later join the opposite side, so we can find out the truth of matters" (101). In "Poseur," however, we get a new insight into Tonantzin as she both forces Khamo to be a responsible father and searches earnestly for some way to make a difference (124). Throughout the history of *Love and Rockets*, the Hernandezes constantly play with chronology and return to the past to re-explore old narratives by opening up new ones within them.[17] The point here is that with comics, as Gilbert and Jaime Hernandez have shown, the characters are never finished developing, the story is never over; unlike other media, one of the defining characteristics of comics is that narrative structure is infinitely malleable, and earlier points of narrative may be reopened, added to, or altered.[18]

Clowes and the Hernandez Brothers are but two examples of the exemplary talent today that is using the comic book to create highly original and expressive works. And they are certainly not alone. Noteworthy contemporaries of these three individuals include Alison Bechdel, Debbie Drechsler, Charles Burns, Phoebe Gloeckner, Alex Robinson, Joe Sacco, Adrian Tomine, Chris Ware, and many others, any of whom I could have used to explore comics' graphic language. In addition, there are the comic book creators who have influenced these individuals (e.g., Robert Crumb, Art Spiegelman), and the generation that influenced those creators (e.g., Carl Barks, Jack Kirby, Harvey Kurtzman) and so on and so on. This outstanding work is not limited to the United States. Comics are a global literary form, with talented writers and artists emerging from all over the world: Japan (Hideshi Hino, Yoshihiro Tatsumi, Hayao Miyazaki, Keiji Nakazawa), Israel (Rutu Modan), Iran (Marjane Satrapi), Norway (Jason), Finland (Tove Jansson), France (David B., Dupuy & Berberian, René Goscinny, Hergé, Jacques Tardi), Canada (Chester Brown, Julie Doucet, Joe Matt, Seth), the United Kingdom (Warren Ellis, Garth

Ennis, Neil Gaiman, Alan Moore, Grant Morrison, Sue Coe), Southeast Asia (Lat), Central and South America (Enrique Breccia, Antonio Prohias, Eduardo Risso), Africa (Marguerite Abouet, Joe Daly) and elsewhere. Looking ahead, there are young and promising comic book creators who are already making their own unique marks in this medium: Jessica Abel, Ellen Forney, Paul Hornschemeier, Kevin Huizenga, R. Kikuo Johnson, Craig Thompson, Brian K. Vaughan, and many others. Indeed, this medium is so replete with talent, promise, and accomplishment that it is impossible to be exhaustive. Even attempting to be exhaustive—as with my name-dropping above—carries with it the danger of trivializing the medium by assuming that everything important can be listed, that all of the "noncrud" can be contained.

As with any literary study, choices must be made. I chose Clowes and the Hernandezes for two main reasons. First, their work demonstrates the wide variety possible in comic narrative: like Clowes, some creators use a single issue as their tableau; others, like Gilbert and Jaime Hernandez, choose a more "grand" narrative that spans many novel-length books; and still others—in fact, most others—fall somewhere in between. And second, these three creators and their works serve nicely as an introduction to discussing my main point, which I will continue to develop in the chapters that follow: comic books are a true "literature." Certainly arguments have been made, both implicitly and explicitly, on behalf of the artistic merit of comic books, but what would be useful—and what has been missing from critical writing on this medium—is a close comparative analysis between comics and other media whose literary value most people would not argue. For this book, I have chosen memoir, Holocaust memoir and photography, journalism, film, and "literature" (you know, the "classics"), and I have chosen these particular types of works because they are the ones that I teach, talk about, and return to again and again for any number of reasons—in short, they represent, along with comics, the literature that I love. But in addition to being forms that I admire a great deal, they are all—relative to the history of letters and literary studies—newcomers whose worth had to be demonstrated, argued and debated. It is easy to forget that university departments and programs focusing on autobiography, Holocaust studies, journalism, or film—now plentiful and present in any major institute of higher education—have been in existence only for the last forty years or so. These literatures—today considered worthy of literary study—had to move out of their own margins and did so with the aid of motivated advocates.

In the following chapters, I discuss each of these literatures in terms of what makes them interesting—their history, their artistic approaches to their subjects, their key issues—and then I look closely at their comic book "counterparts" to show how comics are a unique and sophisticated representational medium that can express formal, thematic, and political issues in ways directly attributable to either their poetics or their cultural positioning or some interesting combination of the two. What follows is a brief synopsis of each chapter.

In Chapter Two, the "legitimate" writing against which I position comic books is the memoir. In recent years, this genre of writing has become one of the most popular literary forms, garnering attention among academics, the popular press, and the general reader. Taken as a whole, memoirs have raised several important issues, including the variety of ways in which one may present his or her life story, the tricky exploration of what constitutes an "identity" or "self," and the troublesome relationship between autobiographical writing and "truth." Not surprisingly, one of the richest genres in comic books—particularly among alternative comic book creators—is autobiography, and the best of these works raise the very same issues as their prose counterparts, but given the unique formal principles of comics, they animate these issues in slightly different, no less sophisticated, and just as interesting ways. In fact, the very nature of the medium allows comic book memoirists to explore various issues of self-representation in ways not fully available to writers of prose memoirs.

In Chapter Three I continue my study of memoir, but in a more focused way. One of the most interesting (and distressing) subgenres of autobiographical writing is Holocaust memoir—the writing about their experience by people associated with the Holocaust. Among this group of works, issues about writer identity and representational strategies become particularly acute given the extremity of the history in question. In this chapter, I examine how Art Spiegelman's *Maus* adeptly reflects key issues in Holocaust memoir as well as another important representation of that history: photography. While this latter category might not be, technically, a "literature," photography is nevertheless a form of representation that is taken more seriously than comic books. My argument here is essentially twofold: first, that using the comic book form allows Spiegelman to approach this difficult topic in ways unavailable to those recounting their Holocaust experiences in traditional prose, and second, that Spiegelman uses comic book art to rethink what has become the Holocaust's defining—and silencing—representational feature: its photographic images. What Spiegelman's *Maus* gives to readers, I will argue, is a new model for understanding this particular history, which so often defies understanding.

In Chapter Four, I turn my attention to journalism and, indirectly, the politics of representation. Admittedly, "journalism" is a broad term that encompasses many different media, approaches, and attitudes. One of the most common associations that people make with journalism is objectivity; that is, the journalist must, above all else, be a neutral observer. In the 1960s, however, several writers challenged this notion and wrote in a style that called attention to the subjectivity inherent in all journalism. These "New Journalists" raised questions about how we represent the world in print, and their work—and, certainly, their personalities—were both radical and controversial. Over time, however, the subversive promise of their work has been incorporated into the mainstream to the extent that "creative nonfiction" now stands, unironically, as a true literary genre. My argument in this chapter is that comic book journalists have taken up the cause of the New Journalists and are revitalizing the once-trenchant questions about subjectivity and representation that have since become obscured. As with the previous chapters, my argument largely centers on how comics' graphic language and their cultural positioning makes such invigoration possible.

In Chapter Five, this issue of how comic books are positioned culturally and politically becomes more pronounced. In the first three chapters—and especially in Chapter Three—I imply that comic books, due to the conflict between their sophisticated representational strategies and popular (mis)conceptions about their lack of sophistication, are able to recreate the world in provocative and, at times, politically charged ways. In this chapter, I move that implication to direct argument by focusing on the 1940s and 1950s, when both comics and film were hard at work representing war. This period is especially revealing given the similarities and differences between the two industries and their representations of war. My overall argument is that despite being denigrated as a largely juvenile medium, the work done in certain comic book titles in the 1940s and 1950s was more visually and politically sophisticated than war films of the same era. In making this argument, I continue to develop the idea of "powerful marginality": that comics, precisely because they are considered a marginal form, are a viable vehicle for subversive and even incendiary political messages.

In Chapter Six, I look at "Literature" in a more focused manner, concentrating on the "canon." More specifically, I examine how comic books have positioned themselves in relation to "the classics" and how they force us to rethink the question, "What is literature?" The works that I consider begin with the early line of *Classics Illustrated* and end with more contemporary comics, including the work of two mainstream masters—Alan Moore and Neil Gaiman—all of which reinterpret literary works through the lens of comics. Over the history of these comics, there is a marked progression of this reinterpretation. Early on, comic book adaptations of canonical literature sought to efface their own medium while introducing readers to the "great works"; more recently, these types of comic books embraced their medium's poetics with greater energy; yet another recent approach by comic book artists has been to meld comic book and literary sensibilities in such a way as to argue that comics are indeed an important form of literature. In light of ongoing debates about the literary canon, these works—along with the others that I have discussed throughout this book—invite us to think more deeply about how literary merit is accorded and why this is a question worth pursuing.

When I discuss writing with my students, I always tell them to emphasize depth over breadth, to narrow their focus to a smaller number of materials so that they may analyze more deeply. In writing this book, I have found myself sometimes guilty of ignoring my own advice. While of course my aim is to achieve both depth and breadth, I have also tried to incorporate as many comic book works as I could reasonably handle. With the exception of Chapter Three, where my focus is primarily on Art Spiegelman's *Maus*, I have attempted to offer a large sampling of relevant comic book titles. I could have very easily focused Chapter Two entirely on, say, Harvey Pekar's *American Splendor* or Craig Thompson's *Blankets*; likewise, there was probably no need, in Chapter Four, to look much beyond the work of Joe Sacco to make my points. But my striving for breadth is reflected in my book's main objective. That is, I am making an argument here that excellence in comic books is not isolated to a few titles but is much more prevalent. I do not want interested readers of this book to seek out one or two authors; I want them to want to track down many. Even so, my study is by no means exhaustive. Truly, such a goal is impossible: there are simply too many good comic books currently available, and more are being published all the time. I find that I have been writing this book with a steadily growing anxiety about the number of new releases that could quite easily fit into one (or several) of these chapters.

I have watched the colonization of my bookshelves by these inviting and troublesome works, and as I have investigated this passion and obsession of mine further, it has become clearer to me why these books are often the first thing I reach for when I am looking to escape—and not escape—from the world in which I live.

These books and their graphic language have rewarded me with engaging narratives, memorable characters, and ideas and per-spectives that stay with me long after I replace the book either on the shelf or to its protective polyethylene bag. If, after reading this book, you begin to appreciate the complexity of which comics are capable and begin to reconsider what it means to be "literary," then I have accomplished my goal. And if you're not already the kind of person who can name all of the different Green Lanterns since his first appearance in 1948's *All-American Comics* #16—that is, the kind of person who is predisposed to agree with me—then I will claim an even greater success.

Notes

1. To a large extent, I use the terms "comics," "comic book," and "graphic novel" somewhat interchangeably throughout this and subsequent chapters. "Comics" is a somewhat generic term that often refers to both comic books and comic strips. There are, of course, important differences between these two forms, but my use of the word "comics" is meant to indicate the general aesthetic feature that is present in both—the interplay of word and image—and the more specific aesthetic and cultural features that are present in comic books—page layout, longer narratives, separately published issues, readers' attitudes, and others. Different terms have been proposed to better denote this form, the most famous of which is probably Will Eisner's "sequential art." Comics scholars who have taken up this term have done so, in part, to "sidestep associations with the burlesque and the ridiculous" (Witek 6), but several points of my larger argument depend on just these types of associations. As for "graphic novels," this term at times refers to multi-issue story arcs that have been collected into one volume and essentially tells the same story that originally appeared in serialized form. In other cases, graphic novels are original publications, having never appeared before in the comic book form. This latter situation was once pretty rare, but is now becoming more common. In terms of comics' "graphic language," a term that I will use throughout this book and explain in some detail in this introduction, there is little difference between the comic book and the graphic novel; both engage the same set of formal principles. In terms of culture and commerce, however, there are important differences between a comic book and a graphic novel. For one thing, graphic novels are more "acceptable" forms of reading—particularly by adults. The word "novel," of course, calls to mind the form of choice for Dickens, Wharton, and Hemingway—you know, "real" literature. In addition, bookstores prefer to carry graphic novels rather than comic books because, in part, they have a thick spine, sit nicely upon a shelf, and, overall, look more like "real" books. On a recent trip to Borders—who much to their credit carry both graphic novels and comic books—I saw that the former group had their own bookshelf while the latter were on a wire rack alongside the magazines (other "disposable" reading). Another important difference involves the production and packaging of these forms. In most comic books there is a "letters" column, which is a forum where readers engage with the book's creator(s). These columns form a central component to comics culture and are the prime example of how uniquely interactive this community is. Several comic book writers, such as Marv Wolfman, began as fans writing letters; in addition, the storylines of many comic books have been influenced by fan input through these letter columns and other venues. However, when individual comic books are collected into a graphic novel, these columns are the first to be jettisoned. Also given the ax are the advertisements, which are valuable for cultural critics who study a particular era and use comic books as part of their source materials. The relatively privileged status of the graphic novel is evident in my own method as well: throughout this book, when given the choice to cite an individual comic book or its graphic novel incarnation, I tend to opt for the latter, mainly because the graphic novel versions are the ones that will be most accessible commercially to interested readers. Books remain in print; comic books wind up in dusty "back issues" boxes in hard-to-find comic book stores.

2. This little gem is known affectionately as "Sturgeon's Law."

3. Although I address portions of the history of the development of the comic book in this and other chapters, a complete survey lies far beyond the scope of this book. Besides, such histories already exist in several excellent studies. My personal favorites are Mike Benton's *The Comic Book in America* (1993), Ron Goulart's *Over 50 Years of American Comic Books* (1991), and Roger Sabin's *Comics, Comix & Graphic Novels: A History of Comic Art* (1996). All three of these books discuss comic art generally and comic books specifically. For a complete and cogent study of comic strips, I recommend Judith O'Sullivan's *The Great American Comic Strip* (1990) and, for the early years of the comic strip, Coulton Waugh's *The Comics* (1947).

4. What a difference sixty or so years can make: today's bookstores and libraries are excellent places to find comics.

5. Today, the Comics Code is largely irrelevant, but at the time, it was quite serious. In effect, if a publisher wanted to sell a particular comic book at either a newsstand, drugstore, or grocery store, then the book needed to have the imprimatur of the Comics Code—the "Seal of Approval." At the time, these retail locations represented the only venue in which to sell a comic book. Thus, if a comic did not conform to the strictures of the Code, then for all intents and purposes it could not be sold.

6. When I first proposed my course "Comic Books as Literature" to the Curriculum Committee at the college where I teach, there was excitement, but a couple of members did ask if I wanted to change the name to "Graphic Novels as Literature." I declined, and the course went forward as I originally named it.

7. See Stan Lee's *The Amazing Spider-Man: The Death of Gwen Stacy* (2001), which reprints the 1971 comics in which Peter Parker's friend, Harry Osborne, becomes addicted to pills. Also relevant is Dennis O'Neill and Neal Adams's *Green Lantern/Green Arrow* Volumes I and II (2004), which reprint the two creators' landmark run from 1970 to 1974; during this period, their heroes deal with racism, drug addition, child abuse, and other important social issues.

8. In fact, many of these practitioners, such as Lynda Barry, Charles Burns, Krystine Kryttre, and Gary Panter, all appeared in the pages of Spiegelman's anthology periodical *Raw*, in which *Maus* was originally serialized. Others self-published, and the most successful practitioner of this route is probably Harvey Pekar, whose revolutionary autobiographical series, *American Splendor*, first appeared in 1976. It is currently being published by DC Comics.

9. Readers interested in a theoretical examination of the complexities of reading comics should take a look at Chapter Two of Charles Hatfield's *Alternative Comics: An Emerging Literature* (2005).

10. Interestingly enough, though this issue is self-contained (i.e., is not a portion of a longer narrative) and runs thirty-eight pages (including inside covers), *Eightball* #22 was reformatted and expanded by Clowes and published as the graphic novel *Ice Haven* by Pantheon Books in 2005. This and the other titles by Clowes are emblematic of a unique feature of comics: the tendency for a given narrative to exist in several different formats. Revised texts of novels are

pretty rare—John Fowles's *The Magus* (1965 & 1977) and Stephen King's *The Stand* (1978 & 1990) are the only examples that spring immediately to mind (I'm sure there are others) and the advent of DVD and its showcasing of "director's cuts" and "bonus features" is fairly recent, certainly postdating the "repackaging" of comic book narratives into trade paperback collections and graphic novels.

11. The principle of character mutability is continually enacted in mainstream comics through the common practice of changing writers and artists over the course of a given comic book's existence. That is, each new writer and artist add dimension to an already existing character by "remaking" him or her in their narratives. The closest analogy from another medium might be the James Bond franchise and the several different actors who have played that character with their own particular inflections. The most pointed and self-conscious illustration of this principle in comics is Warren Ellis and John Cassaday's *Planetary/ Batman: Night on Earth* (2001), in which the Planetary team of Elijah Snow, Jakita Wagner, and the Drummer Boy chase a killer through various iterations of Gotham City, where they encounter different versions of Batman. Ellis and Cassaday have a keen sense of Batman's history and they show both the complicated nature of this character and the strength of this particular medium in exploring such complexity.

12. One may be wondering how "Blue Bunny" and "Rocky" fit in with the other stories. In the case of "Blue Bunny," the title character is a bizarre version of a stuffed rabbit toy belonging to George, the younger, silent chum of Charles who serves mainly as audience for Charles's angst-filled soliloquies. As for Rocky, he may have been Ice Haven's earliest resident; during his wanderings, he comes across a huge, knob-shaped rock, which is Ice Haven's natural landmark. Both stories demonstrate how far Clowes is willing to stretch the boundaries of his narrative and its characters.

13. The latest issue of *Eightball* (as of this writing) is #23, and in it, Clowes continues the experimentation reflected in *Eightball* #22: #23, known as *The Death Ray*, is at once a deconstruction of the superhero mythos and an exploration of the comic book form. In my mind, these two issues taken together represent the most economical and thorough exploration of a given medium ever delivered by an artist or writer.

14. Beginning with this four-year period, Gilbert produced *Luba* and *Luba's Comics and Stories* while Jaime produced *Penny Century*. The stories from these comics have also been included in the *Love and Rockets* trade paperbacks.

15. The first six volumes of the collected *Love and Rockets* featured work by both Gilbert and Jaime. Beginning with volume seven, Jaime's *The Death of Speedy* (1989), the trade paperbacks have featured one of the two brothers exclusively. The two exceptions have been volume nine, *Flies on the Ceiling* (1991), and volume fifteen, *Hernandez Satyricon* (1997).

16. Along with Neil Gaiman's *Sandman* (1988–96), *Love and Rockets* boasts as many female as male readers (Bender 117)—a significant achievement in comic books.

17. One of the most interesting of these "new" narratives has not yet been written. It comes to me anecdotally, but from a pretty good source: the author himself.

In the spring of 2001, I taught the first version of my Comic Books as Literature class. One of the books that I assigned was Jaime Hernandez's *The Death of Speedy*. The titular event of this book is ambiguously rendered; it is unclear whether Speedy has been killed by rival gang members or died by his own hand. This ambiguity enhances the story and allows for good classroom discussion. That semester, I was fortunate to have convinced Jaime (who lives about an hour and a half away from the college where I teach) to visit my class. He didn't know me, so getting him to come required stalkerlike diligence on my part. Prior to class, I asked him about Speedy's death—did he kill himself or was he killed? Jaime's earnest response was that he didn't know, and he liked that because it left the door open for him to go back at some later time and tell that story.

18. Comics did not invent the desire to open "pockets" in pre-existing narrative; rather, it is a method that comics can achieve with greater ease than any other single media. There have been examples of this sort of opening taking place between different media, the most entertaining of which might be Robert Coover's short story, "You Must Remember This" (1985), which tells the story of what took place in the film *Casablanca* (1942) when Ilsa and Rick reconcile. Fans of the film might remember that there is a fade to black after Ilsa falls into Rick's arms, and when we return, they are both much calmer as Rick asks her, "And then . . . ?" We never really find out what has transpired during that time or, for that matter, how long that "time" was. In his story, Coover delivers an explicit love scene between the two of them. The main difference between this situation and that of *Love and Rockets* is that the comic represents the work of a single artist revisiting and exploring his own creation. In the case of Coover, I highly doubt that *Casablanca*'s screenwriters would appreciate his vision.

2.
CREATING A "SPECIAL REALITY"
Comic Books vs. Memoir

Imagine that you are an aspiring young author who also happens to be a recovering addict and alcoholic. Because you have a some-what checkered past and because you can read a bestsellers chart, you decide to pen a memoir. But not just any memoir. Your aim is to create a distinctive voice that pulls your reader into the horrifying maw that is the addict's life and recovery process. Of course, com-municating this vision requires—or so you tell yourself—that a few details be fudged. Or invented completely. Okay, maybe more than a few. But still and all, these inventions are meant to serve the story. And, hell, don't all memoirists do this very thing? There's no way that Frank McCourt's childhood was that bad, right? So you forge ahead, creatively recounting your past, and lo and behold, your book gets published. It enjoys mostly positive reviews with the exception of a few critics who question the veracity of your more inventive details. Despite these killjoys, your book appears on several respectable publications' "Year's Best" lists, and it is selling well enough for you to get a second book deal. And then lightning strikes: the queen of talk shows chooses your memoir for her television book club. Fame and fortune in the guise of astronomical sales, movie deals, and more media exposure opportunities than you can shake a syringe at lie just over the horizon.

Experiencing something like this scenario, James Frey must have thought he hit the jackpot. His memoir, *A Million Little Pieces*, was published in 2003, and in it he details the six weeks that he spent in Hazelden, the renowned drug and alcohol rehab center where he attempted to overcome his substance addiction and right his life's disastrous course, which according to his account included several outstanding arrest warrants, including one felony. Despite some doubts voiced in the media about Frey's details,[1] his potent mix of content and style—an electric stream-of-conscious delivery that eschews most punctuation and paragraph indentations—continued to attract admirers, the most important of whom was Oprah Winfrey, who selected *A Million Little Pieces* as the September 2005 title for her book club. The immediate effect was to increase sales of Frey's book almost exponentially.[2] Because he wrote about addiction and recovery—topics that are valuable currency in the American reading market—and because his followup, *My Friend Leonard*, had just been released in hardcover, Frey's potential to reap the benefits of membership in Oprah's book club seemed almost limitless.

But one potential pitfall to all of the attention that Oprah's imprimatur brings—especially as regards a "memoir" and its pesky sidekick, the "truth"—is that more people get curious about the claims you make. A few such readers happened to run The Smoking Gun, a website devoted to chipping away the thin veneer that often protects celebrities' lives. According to their report, they set out to find a mug shot of Frey to add to their collection ("A Million Little Lies" 2), but the deeper they dug, the faster Frey's carefully constructed image of his lawbreaker past began to crumble away. As it turned out, Frey was not a fugitive from justice who was wanted for hitting a police officer with his car, attempting to incite a riot, and being in possession of an obscene amount of crack cocaine. Nor had he been forced to spend three months in jail as part of a deal worked out among him, lawmakers in Ohio, and two fatherly, influential friends from his rehab program—one a shadowy Mafioso and the other a federal appeals judge ("A Million Little Lies" 3–4). In addition, a key episode from his past involving his role in—and subsequent guilt over—the death of a high school classmate turned out not to involve him at all ("A Million Little Lies" 5–6). As these revelations gave way to others, the media pounced, and Frey appeared again with Oprah on her show to respond to the charges. He essentially admitted that The Smoking Gun revelations were true, and his previous position that a memoir is "an individual's perception of what happened in his own life" (quoted in Grossman 58) was less forcefully held as he sat four feet away from Oprah and before millions of viewers.

There are those, like Joe Woodward, who responded to the Frey incident by stating that "a fake is fine in fiction, but not in a genre that is meant to purvey the truth—no matter how many writers like Frey . . . may sully that term's definition" (11). And it is easy to dismiss the whole affair as a simple case of an author who lied about his life pure and simple, was unmasked, and punished.[3] Yet there are others, like Sara Nelson, who have a more nuanced perspective. In her view, a memoir "has to have a narrative and development and denouement.

And sometimes that means the story might sacrifice small accuracies for larger 'truth'" (5). My own response lies closer to Nelson's, for she recognizes that even though a memoir represents something real—a person's life—it is nevertheless an artistic representation, and as such, its "truth" is not as easily defined as Frey's most vocal critics would like to believe. To my mind, the Frey controversy throws a sharp light on some key questions about the genre of memoir[4]: How can one best express the true nature of his or her self? What exactly is a "self"? In a memoir, what does it mean to be "true"? The ambiguity of the answers to such questions in no small part contributes to the memoir's enduring popularity among writers and readers. Since 1960—when Roy Pascal's seminal study, *Design and Truth in Autobiography*, appeared—numerous other critical studies of this genre have been published (Adams 1),[5] and many colleges and universities have added to their curricula classes in memoir and the "literature of the self" (Atlas 27). In addition, several memoirs have been nominated for and received major literary awards, and, commercially, the memoir is viewed as "the blue-chip performer in the literary stock market" (Rust 19). It is no accident that memoirs continue to garner critical attention from a variety of quarters; they do so because of the artistry they are capable of displaying and the epistemological questions they are capable of raising.

On the face of it, the comic book would seem like an unlikely source of either this art or this philosophy. As mentioned in Chapter One, popular opinions of this form gravitate toward the juvenile or superheroic, the conventions of which include broad humor, excessive emotion, physical action, and large but digestible conflict—in short, elements that do not easily lend themselves to the study and writing of the delicate relationship between our inner and outer lives. But in fact, autobiographical comics—a huge and ever-growing genre of comics—address the aforementioned key questions of the memoir, and they do so in ways that are wholly unique to their medium. Like their prose counterparts, comic memoirs take a variety of shapes and forms, but comics are capable of demonstrating a broader and more flexible range of first-person narration than is possible in prose. In addition, while many prose memoirists address the complex nature of identity and the self, comic book memoirists are able to represent such complexity in ways that cannot be captured in words alone. Finally, as scholars and critics have pointed out, the best prose memoirs complicate the issue of truth-telling both implicitly and explicitly; for their part, autobiographical comics undermine simplistic notions of "truth," and they do this through their unique formal elements, coupled with popular assumptions about comics in general. As a representation of the life of its author, the comic book memoir achieves what Will Eisner calls a "special reality" (2000 3) that explores issues of autobiographical writing in ways unavailable in prose alone.

This is not to suggest that prose memoir is lacking. Quite the contrary. In fact, prose autobiographical writing has reached great artistic heights, and one of this body of work's accomplishments is to reveal the many different maps that writers have used to explore the roads of the self. Indeed, a quick survey of the memoir reveals that this "genre has always been defined by formally experimental works" (Gilmore 18). Such experimentation has included different forms, such as diaries and letters (both of which reveal their authors but do so in different ways than conventional narrative), short essays, and book-length memoirs. And within these subgenres, writers have stretched the boundaries. After all, what should we make of *The Education of Henry Adams* (1918), a memoir in which Adams writes in the third person? Or of Gertrude Stein's *The Autobiography of Alice B. Toklas* (1933), in which she delivers her own story through the eyes of her lifelong partner? Innovation has continued in works like Vladimir Nabokov's *Speak, Memory* (1967), a text that works simultaneously as an autobiography and as a parody of autobiography; Maxine Hong Kingston's *The Woman Warrior* (1976), which delivers five dreamlike stories that delve into her family and cultural history in order to reveal her own; and David Eggers's *A Heartbreaking Work of Staggering Genius* (2000), in which the narrative proper—the story of how he raised his brother Toph after the sudden death of both their parents—is continually interrupted by tongue-in-cheek asides and digressions that, among other things, question the very idea of memoir and our interest in it.[6]

There have also been fictional works that are temptingly read as autobiographical. One writer who has invited such readings more than any other is, arguably, Ernest Hemingway; in fact, academics are fond of scrutinizing his more famous characters as facets of the man himself.[7] Tobias Wolff, a great admirer of Hemingway, addresses this situation in his own novel, *Old School* (2002). Wolff's unnamed narrator—a private boys' school student and aspiring writer whose literary model is Hemingway—reflects at one point on the Nick Adams stories. He thinks,

> We had been taught not to confuse the writer with the work, but I couldn't separate my picture of Nick from my picture of Hemingway. And I had a sense that I wasn't really supposed to, that a certain confusion of author and character was intended....

Knowing that readers like me would see him in Nick, he had given us a vision of spiritual muddle and exhaustion almost embarrassing in its intimacy. (96–97)

The trick of Wolff's novel is that he invites the very same comparisons between himself and his own narrator: both discovered that their fathers were Jewish, leading to a certain identity crisis; both came from blue-collar backgrounds in the Pacific Northwest; both were "asked to leave" prestigious boys' schools in the Northeast; and both became writers after a stint in the military. Like *Old School*, Tim O'Brien's collection of stories, *The Things They Carried* (1990), invites autobiographical interpretation. In spite of its designation as "a work of fiction," this book contains scenes that bear a resemblance to those in O'Brien's memoir, *If I Die in a Combat Zone* (1973). In addition, the author names his "fictional" protagonist "Tim O'Brien," and this O'Brien tells us information that we know to be true, such as the fact that he has written a book entitled *Going After Cacciato*.

A less playful example is Kathryn Harrison's novel *Thicker than Water* (1990), in which the main character, Isabel, has a sexual relationship with her father. The author's later memoir, *The Kiss* (1996), would generate controversy because of the same subject matter: Harrison's consensual sexual relationship with her father. In the novel, Isabel's father tells her, "you'll never be able to get close to someone other than me, because you won't be able to resist telling them what we've done. . . . And once they know, they'll leave you, all of them" (237). In her memoir, her own father tells her "and now you'll never be able to have anyone else, because you won't be able to keep our secret. You'll tell whoever it is, and once he knows, he'll leave you" (188). To some extent, all of these so-called fictional works—the Nick Adams stories, *Old School*, *The Things They Carried*, *Thicker than Water*—have significant autobiographical content.

My point here is that one of the defining characteristics of autobiographical writing is the variety of first-person perspectives used by memoirists. Comic book memoirs are also varied in this regard, yet because of the comics' unique graphic language, these memoirists—rather than simply mimicking the approaches of prose writers—have additional ways to express and layer the first-person perspective. One method of creating an "I" is through direct address, where the narrator delivers information through a word balloon (see Figure 2.1). This particular method, in a comic book memoir, is effective at achieving an immediate intimacy with the reader. While gifted

Figure 2.1. From *The Quitter*, copyright Harvey Pekar and Dean Haspiel.
All rights reserved. Used with permission of DC Comics.

prose memoirists also know how to create this relationship,[8] it is difficult to match the directness of an author appearing amid the panels of his narrative, looking us in the eye, and delivering heartfelt testimony about him- or herself. Another device used by comic book memoirists is the thought bubble. With this element, the comic book creator creates an immediate scene where we are given a "secret window" into the character's thoughts. Still another way to deliver first-person narration is the text box. This method allows for a disjunction between narrator and character as the visual image recreates the narrator in the past, but the text may deliver the voice of the narrator at any number of points in time, including a "present" voice that reflects upon the incidents of the past.

These elements are not mutually exclusive; comic book memoirists often use them together to create not only a more flexible first person perspective, but a more complicated one as well. In his memoir *I Never Liked You* (1994), Chester Brown demonstrates this principle. Throughout the book, which details the troubled relationships he had with female friends during his adolescence, Brown blends all of these traditional expressions of the first-person perspective in comics: thought bubbles (31), text boxes (48), and word balloons/direct address (124). By combining these devices, Brown creates several layers of narrative: the thought bubbles suggest immediacy, as we see Chester's thoughts as they occur to him dur-

Figure 2.2. Copyright Phoebe Gloeckner. Used with permission.

ing the narrative proper; the text boxes suggest reminiscence, as they are clearly the thoughts of Chester the comic book creator, delivering interjections as he recreates his past; and the direct address implies another level of reality, as Chester "steps outside" the narrative proper to confide in his reader. Such various approaches, if they had equivalents in prose memoir, would no doubt render the narrative incoherent, but in a comic, the visuals act as a unifying force that allows for a more flexible first-person narrator.

Another way in which the unique features of the comics medium allows greater flexibility by avoiding potential incoherence is with the "alter ego"—a type of first-person narrator that works more effectively in comic book memoir than in prose. The use of an alter ego suggests distance between writer and character, but the visual dimension of comics allows these memoirists to communicate to the reader that the narrative is memoir as opposed to fiction. The most notable—and perhaps notorious—instance of such an approach is Justin Green's "Binky Brown Meets the Holy Virgin Mary" (1972), a comic that Art Spiegelman credits with inventing "confessional autobiographical comix" (1995 4). On the story's very first page, Green depicts himself, bound and gagged, as he writes this "confession": "O, my readers, the saga of Binky Brown is not intended solely for your entertainment, but also to purge myself of the compulsive neurosis which I have served since I officially left Catholicism on Halloween, 1958" (10). With this opening, he eliminates the possibility that we will regard Binky Brown as anyone other than Green's stand-in.

Other notable comic book memoirists have followed suit, such as Harvey Pekar and Phoebe Gloeckner, both of whom also use visual clues to indicate that their characters are clear extensions of themselves. In Pekar's case, most of his *American Splendor* stories feature himself, but he also writes stories that use a number of other characters who share distinctive physical and behavioral characteristics with the author and are, in fact, unmistakable versions of Pekar (Witek 123).[9] Gloeckner's alter ego is "Minnie," who has appeared in many of her stories, the most unsettling of which is "Minnie's Third Love" (1995). This story documents Gloeckner's troubled adolescent as a girl whose sexuality is abused by others—including her "best friend," who gets Minnie drunk and allows different men to have sex with her in exchange for drugs. As is the case with several of her "Minnie" stories, Gloeckner begins this one with an image of herself à la Green (see Figure 2.2), and there is an unmistakable resemblance between her and Minnie. She takes a similar approach in *The Diary of a Teenage Girl* (2002), where her own photograph adorns the front cover. This is no standard author photograph; instead,

Figure 2.3. Copyright 1990 Chester Brown. Used with permission.

Gloeckner's eyes are closed and her head is tilted back as she affects a dreamlike pose typical of the "teenage girl" of the title. The effect in both cases is to collapse the distance between author and narrator, a move that Gloeckner reinforces in interviews, where she has a tendency to "shift arbitrarily between referring to 'Minnie' and 'me'" (Orenstein 28).

The comic book has additional visual elements that provide different avenues for memoirists to express their interior thoughts, and these elements are unique to the medium. In another of Chester Brown's memoirs, *The Playboy* (1992), he depicts how he became guiltily obsessed with *Playboy* magazine and portrays himself as an essentially passive, emotionally withdrawn individual who has a history of poor relations with women. He also employs a unique method to get us "inside" his head: a winged "mini-Chester" who flies about and delivers Chester's thoughts and other information to the reader. In one scene, Chester is disposing of a *Playboy* in a nearby forest only to discover that he is not alone out there. Rather than convey his thoughts directly to us, Brown has the winged Chester do so (see Figure 2.3). Here, Brown is able to externalize his thoughts in a way that is understandable to the reader and that still maintains the distance that this particular self-portrayal requires. Though this winged figure may be startling at first, we quickly understand that he is a visual representation of Brown's conscience. More important, this device is one that has no equivalent in prose memoir.

The great flexibility of first person narration that comics allows is but one way that this medium enriches the "I" perspective. Like their counterparts working in prose, comic book memoirists recognize that one's style of writing is a powerful tool to evoke the first-person perspective. After all, what better way to understand a person than to "hear" not only a person's thoughts but how he or she frames them? Early in her prose memoir *Fat Girl* (2005), Judith Moore writes, "narrators of first-person claptrap like this often greet the reader at the door with moist hugs and complaisant kisses. I won't. I will not endear myself. I won't put on airs. I am not that pleasant. The older I get the less pleasant I am" (2). Here, it is impossible not to get a sense of Moore's personality: she is pugnacious, direct, and refuses to feel sorry for herself. Similarly, Lynda Barry, in her comic book memoir *One Hundred Demons* (2002), reveals herself through language. In one part, "Lost Worlds," Barry reminisces about the kickball games she played when she was a child and wonders why we remember certain things but not others. She writes,

> Who knows which moments make us who we are? Some of them? All of them? The ones we never really thought of as anything special? How many kickball games did I play? And what would I give to have just one more ups. What would I give to see them all again. Chuckie, roll the ball this way. Chuckie, roll me a good one. (36)

Here, Barry conveys not only that she is inquisitive, but also that she nurtures close connections with her past. At the start of this short excerpt, Barry's rhetoric is philosophical; by the end of it, she is standing ready at home plate, waiting for a good roll from Chuckie. That she moves so seamlessly in her text between present and past and that she ably captures the language ("ups") and cadences of her childhood reveal how close she is to that time, and this style is a trademark of her work as a whole.

Figure 2.4. Copyright Lynda Barry. Image appears courtesy of Darhansoff, Verrill, Feldman Literary Agents, New York.

But comic book memoirists have an additional "signifier" at their disposal—the artistic style of their images—and this important visual element allows them to present the first person narration in ways unique to the comics medium.[10] As a representational device, images present the world through a third-person perspective; by contrast, the text of comic book memoir is typically written in the first person. Thus, the words achieve interiority through the "I," yet the pictures suggest exteriority because we "see" the first-person narrator and are therefore positioned "outside" of him or her. However, the visual dimension of comics allows comic book memoirists to overcome this potential paradox. More specifically, both the hand lettering of the text and the drawn images encourage readers to see the story as the author's personal expression, and these devices represent how a given memoirist "sees" the world. In the case of the Lynda Barry excerpt above (see Figure 2.4), the "handcrafted" elements of her story are evident. The text is very "visual," containing a childlike mixture of block letters and cursive writing that evokes Barry's youth. Also evocative are the images themselves: in the first panel we see young Lynda and her friends arguing, and in the second panel we see Chuckie getting ready to pitch. These visuals work to reinforce and deepen Barry's evocation of childhood, and their presence makes the ephemeral nature of the past about which Barry writes more poignant: her drawings are, after all, her imperfect recreations of that "lost world."

Thus, by their very nature, comic book memoirs present the world as seen through their artists' eyes, and those "visions" become the memoirists' powerful and evocative worldviews. Underground comics legend Robert Crumb, for example, sees the world with a caricaturist's eye, and he conveys that perspective largely through his visuals. In his story "I Remember the Sixties" (1982), Crumb's attitude toward this particular past is clearly embedded in his illustrations. In one sequence of panels, he describes in the text how the lightheartedness of the times began to dissipate in the late sixties, and he complements these words with metaphorical renditions, including people represented as animals, a drooling beast as the personification of paranoia, and a literal spinning wheel meant to represent how the times were becoming less stable for the so-called "counter" culture (2000 160). While the content of Crumb's observations is not necessarily unique (he is but one in a long line of writers to express disillusionment with the sixties), his visual expression of those ideas is highly personal, an extension of his first-person perspective. As Witek points out, "Crumb cannot resist transforming his personal stories into self-parodies and shameless fantasies" (129). While this is true, it is important to remember that "self-parody" and "fantasy" are key to the worldview that Crumb presents; these qualities are a direct extension of his personality, the protean nature of which is reflected in the varied visual strategies that he employs throughout his large body of work. Throughout "Uncle Bob's Mid-life Crisis" (1982), for example, Crumb never deviates from a twelve-panel page, where the panels are all uniform in size and laid out, gridlike, in four rows of three panels each. This structural choice creates a visual rigidity and repetition that mirrors the ennui haunting him in this particular story. By contrast, "Footsy" (1987) is heavily shaded and features asymmetrical, jagged panels that are visual expressions of the story's subject: young Crumb's sexual confusion and energy.

David B.'s *Epileptic* (2004) also uses visuals to convey a particular worldview, although his perspective is more grim than Crumb's. This arresting book, which was originally published in serialized form in France, recounts the author's relationship with his brother, who suffers from epilepsy. David (born Pierre-Francois Beauchard) delves deeply and painfully into his family's dynamics as his parents search in vain for one cure after another. In the face of this situation and fueled by the stories from history told to him by his parents, young David begins to draw, first as a diversion and then as an escape. Success does not come easily for him, and a portion of the narrative is devoted to David's search for a way to translate his own pain and fear through his art. The artistic style that he decides on is highly expressionistic and dreamlike, characterized by extensive use of black space and various "monster"-type figures meant to represent different feelings that have haunted him throughout his life. On one page, for example, David appears with his favorite "ghosts" as he tells them that he must go to Paris alone, and the page, which is almost entirely black with heavy shading, becomes a visual reflection of his pessimism (275). His artwork throughout confirms that illustration is an important—perhaps the most important—means of expression for the comic book memoirist, and that drawing the painful past is every bit as difficult as writing it.

One of the most recognizable uses of images to express the memoirist's worldview is in comic book memoirs of childhood, where artists deliver "childlike" drawings in order to mimic the perspective of a young person, not unlike how a fiction writer will create a young first-person narrator by mimicking the voice of a child. Lynda Barry's work, as discussed earlier, is but one example of this approach. Another is Debbie Drechsler's *Daddy's Girl* (1995), a disturbing book in which the author recreates her past with a visual frankness that distinguishes itself among comic book memoirs. In it she recalls her sexual molestation by her father, and she expresses her depression and disorientation through her art. Her style is characterized by heavy shading and almost surreal perspectives, and Drechsler evokes a younger point of view by creating visuals that resemble a child's artwork where the characters are improbably long and bendy, their eyes huge and round (see Figure 2.5). This general strategy of conveying a child's perspective has also been successfully used by Marjane Satrapi in *Persepolis* (2003), a memoir of her childhood in Iran in the 1970s and 1980s. In this book, Satrapi presents herself as a child with a vivid imagination and fantasy life, and to evoke this perspective, Satrapi presents fanciful panels, including several where she appears with God (8, 13–4, 70). In all of these cases, the visual styles form a crucial part of the comic book memoirist's first person narration.

So powerful is this visual element in creating a personal point of view that these memoirists still "reveal" themselves even when they provide little or no interiority with their text. One of the primary practitioners of this model is Jeffrey Brown, who has chronicled his relationship ups and downs (but mainly downs) in *Clumsy* (2002), *Unlikely* (2003), *Any Easy Intimacy* (2005), and *Every Girl Is the End of the World for Me* (2005). Brown's defining narrative strategy is in constructing short scenes, typically between himself and a girlfriend, with nary a thought bubble or text box in sight. Neither does he

Figure 2.5. Copyright Debbie Drechsler.
Image appears courtesy of Fantagraphics Books, Inc.

address us directly; the only indication we get of his thoughts is through his actions and words. In one particular scene in *Clumsy*, Brown and his girlfriend Theresa share the reactions that they had about each other when they first met. When asked his thoughts, Brown adopts a Cheshire grin, and we have no idea what is going through his head until he says, "I thought you were kind of a dirty hippy" (76–77). The lack of interiority does not estrange readers from Brown; on the contrary, the "scratchiness" of Brown's drawings and lettering actually works in his favor here as one cannot read his stories without getting a sense of the author's shaping hand. His stories unfold visually in very expressionistic ways that ensure we remain close to his perspective. In addition, Brown frequently puts us in the same position as Theresa and his other girlfriends—as someone who is in the process of discovering who he is. And in this way, Brown creates a more realistic kind of autobiography in that he suggests that we can never really know other people's thoughts; we can only judge them based on what they say and do.

In addition to standing as evidence of the myriad ways in which writers present their lives and ways of seeing the world, memoirs also address the complex nature of identity and the "self"—its origins, nature, and expressions. Over the course of the twentieth century, various movements have challenged the long-standing Western ideal of the self as a unified, coherent individual. One of these movements is certainly Poststructuralism, which seeks to examine the "ways in which cultures shape the individual subject" (Eakin 1999 14). That is, each one of us has many characteristics that are more or less beyond our control—gender, ethnicity, sexuality, class, education, and so on—and these characteristics define us insofar as they influence how we view ourselves and how others view us. What is more, these viewpoints interweave with and impact each other in ways both conscious and subconscious, and they are constantly shifting as our "selves" exist in a web of complicated social relationships that entangle us on an almost ongoing basis.

At several points over the course of a given day, for example, I adopt the personae of husband, father, teacher, colleague, coach, writer, customer, neighbor, and several others (especially if it is a busy day). Each of these roles is in no small part dependent on how others see me; in fact, one could argue that many if not all of these roles are meaningless without a larger social context. That is, how I view myself often becomes a function of how others view me and vice versa—two processes that R. D. Laing has distinguished as "self-perception . . . [and] 'other-perception'" (quoted in Bruss 13). At times, these perceptions and the various social and cultural factors in which they are steeped may conflict with one another, creating potential and actual instabilities.[12] In short, the latest development in the "over two thousand years of deliberation on and celebration of the subjective self" (Gergen 6), is that who we are is complicated indeed. In the arena of autobiographical theory and criticism, the "trend has been steady retreat from the idea of the self as an embodiment of the attributes of the first-person singular pronoun" (Couser 18)—a retreat, in other words, from a unified entity that unproblematically unites author, narrator, and protagonist (Lejeune 5).

This retreat is certainly warranted, for the landscape of the "self," as explored in memoir, is a rocky, uneven surface where the best writers will acknowledge the complexity of who we are. In her introduction to *Survival Stories: Memoirs of Crisis* (1997), a collection of personal writings that deal with tragic experiences, editor Kathryn Rhett contends that autobiography is about, at least in part, the construction of a "literary self." She writes, "constructing an 'I' is part of surviving—to take a narrative stance at all, to adopt a point of view, is to step away from the experience. As much as writers evoke and reenter life through writing, they also stand apart from it" (10). Here, Rhett identifies at least one important rift between the writer and protagonist of any given memoir. There are others as well, but sifting through the various "selves" that critics and scholars have identified and discussed is really outside of this chapter's scope. I wish to focus instead on the general idea that the "self" is ever-shifting, socially impacted, and multifaceted. More to the point is my argument that comic book memoirs are able to present these complexities in unparalleled fashion.

For example, the visual component of comics allows comic book memoirists to represent the complicated and shifting nature of the self. In his story "Just Another Day" (1991) Dan Clowes presents an economical presentation of the shifting self as only comics can. The story begins as we watch a man—presumably Clowes—performing his morning rituals before a bathroom mirror. Eventually, this scene is interrupted by the "real Clowes" (so denoted by a helpful text box), who explains his motives in showing such a mundane scene. This Clowes, an insensitive "wheeler-dealer," gives way to "the real real Clowes" (again denoted by a text box), who questions his previous self-depiction. By the story's fourth and final page, we are introduced to five more "Cloweses," each of whom promises to be the "actual" Clowes until the final panel, whose text box contains a simple "Etc., Etc." (see Figure 2.6). Here, the visuals and their details—the slightly altered images of Clowes, the objects of each Clowes's background—are tangible representations of the idea not only that we are different people—different "selves"—at different times, but that there is no "true" self; identity is a rapidly shifting thing, impossible to pin down from one moment to the next. To present radically different selves in prose narrative would, in all likelihood, be incoherent. However, because visuals are an effective communicator of identity and because they are bound together by the text boxes, this potentially incoherent concept achieves formal unity in the comics medium.

Comic book memoirists are able to use visuals to express the complicated nature of identity in other ways as well. Catherine Doherty's memoir, Can of Worms (2000), is all about the search for identity. In this nearly wordless book, Doherty, who was adopted, recounts her search for her birth mother. Because Doherty communicates the narrative almost exclusively through her illustrations, she is adept at developing visual clues to reinforce the separation she feels from others. More specifically, she graphically represents her-

Figure 2.6. Copyright Daniel Clowes.
Image appears courtesy of Fantagraphics Books, Inc.

Figure 2.7. Copyright Catherine Doherty.
Image appears courtesy of Fantagraphics Books, Inc.

Figure 2.8. Copyright Joyce Brabner and Harvey Pekar.
Used with permission.

self as being different from those around her (see Figure 2.7). While the other individuals in her life—her adoptive parents, a couple on the street, the doctors who delivered her—are depicted more or less realistically, Doherty presents herself as a more "cartoony" image, visually expressing the difference she feels in her identity. Only her birth mother, whose story Doherty must imagine at one point, is depicted in the same style. Here and throughout *Can of Worms*, Doherty mines the possibility of the comics form in order to discover a way of representing the complexities of self.

Comics are also unique in their ability to capture an important concept in identity theory alluded to earlier—the Social Constructivist view, which maintains that "the self is not an essence, but a socially created construction—a cultural artifact fashioned collaboratively and publicly out of ready-made materials, like a quilt patched together at a quilting bee" (Couser 16). To be "socially created"—where our "self" is, at least in part, dependent on the perception of others—is not a terribly comforting prospect. In his novel *Immortality* (1990), Milan Kundera captures the unattractiveness of this situation quite adeptly through his character, Paul. He says,

> "Our self is a mere illusion, ungraspable, indescribable, misty, while the only reality, all too easily graspable and describable, is our image in the eyes of others. And the worst thing about it is that you are not its master. First you try to paint it yourself, then you want at least to influence and control it, but in vain: a single malicious phrase is enough to change you forever into a depressingly simple caricature." (127)

The speaker here, Paul, takes a resignedly dim view of this circumstance, but regardless of one's view on the matter, the comic book is uniquely adept at reflecting this idea that our identities are collaborative, as evidenced mainly by the work of Dennis Eichhorn and Harvey Pekar, both of whom write autobiographical comics that are illustrated by others.

In terms of content, Eichhorn and Pekar could not be more different: where Eichhorn's stories are full of action—typically violence, drug use, and sex—Pekar's are concerned instead with the more mundane aspects of life, such as forgetting to buy coffee at the store, running into someone he knows at the bank, or steeling himself for another day of work as a file clerk at a V.A. hospital. Yet reading several stories by both authors is a revelatory experience because, as with the Clowes comic, their physical identities—and, therefore, how we "see" the two men—are constantly shifting in accordance with a given artist's style. In effect, the very approach of Pekar and

Eichhorn—to use multiple artists' depictions of their "selves"—underscores the important point that the comics "medium embodies in its material form the collaboration of other people in the construction of individual identity" (Witek 137). The idea here that we are dependent, in part, on others for our identity becomes literal in the cases of comics by Eichhorn and Pekar, where who they are (or appear to be) is partially created by their artists.

One of Pekar's longer narratives, *Our Cancer Year* (1994)—a powerful documentation of his diagnosis of and recovery from cancer—makes brilliant use of visuals to show how comics can uniquely depict how our identities are, at least in part, determined by how others see us. In one sequence, Pekar is disoriented and having trouble remembering who he is, and in his confusion, the only image that comes to his head is the logo for his comic *American Splendor*. As his wife enters the bathroom, he asks her, "Am I some guy who writes about himself in a comic book called *American Splendor*? Or am I just a character in that book?" (see Figure 2.8). Of course, we know that Pekar is a real person, but what does that mean to us? After all, we who read *American Splendor* know Pekar only through that book, so his identity, as far as we are concerned, is "just a comic book character." This point is emphasized by Stack through his "double framing" on this page, the effect of which is to contain Pekar in a panel within a panel and highlight his presence as a character in a comic book. This self-conscious presentation of Pekar's image reminds us of the layers of identity we all possess.

That one's "self" is multifaceted is a concept that most people can appreciate. So, too, is the idea that one of these facets is undoubtedly our physical "self," and some scholars of autobiography have turned their attention to the role that our bodies play in who we are. As autobiography scholar Paul John Eakin argues, "it is possession of a body image that anchors and sustains our sense of identity" (1999 11), and he develops his theory that both "self and memory . . . are grounded in the body and the body image" (1999 20) by examining memoirs that focus on the writers' physical identities—memoirs like Oliver Sacks's *A Leg to Stand On* (1984), Lucy Grealy's *The Autobiography of a Face* (1994), and Robert Murphy's *The Body Silent* (1987).

This latter memoirist, Robert Murphy, was an anthropology professor at Columbia when he was diagnosed with an inoperable tumor growing in his spine, a particularly cruel situation which gradually turned him into a quadriplegic. His book documents this illness, but he also offers many anthropological observations of the culture of the handicapped and its relation to the larger, able-bodied culture, and these insights establish the importance of one's physical identity to sense of self. Murphy writes, "whatever the physically impaired person may think of himself, he is attributed a negative identity by society, and much of his social life is a struggle against this imposed image" (113). Murphy goes on to say that "the disabled person's radical bodily difference, his departure from the human standard, dominates the thoughts of the other and may even repel him" (122).

That we are defined, in part, by how others regard our body is certainly borne out in Grealy's *Autobiography of a Face*. As a child, Grealy was diagnosed with Ewing's Sarcoma, a bone cancer in her jaw. The treatment was to remove a large portion of her jaw, and this surgery led to many, many others as Grealy sought to reconstruct her face, which she refers to as her "self" (170). Each of these surgeries rendered her face swollen, bandaged, and in the end not much different, and along with the vicious taunting that she routinely received from classmates, Grealy was left with the sense that she was "ugly," which led to worse consequences. She writes, "by equating my face with ugliness . . . I separated myself even further from other people" (180). Despite these harrowing surgeries, she could not resist, even as an adult, the hope offered by one more procedure: "how could I pass up the possibility that it might work, that at long last I might finally fix my face, fix my life, my soul?" (215). Grealy's memoir attests to the fact that we see ourselves largely through the eyes of others. That is, other people's opinions of our appearance influence, often detrimentally, our self image.

Murphy, Grealy, and others write about the importance of our physical identities, and, like these writers, several comic book memoirists are interested in addressing this issue. What is unique about comics, however, is that creators may represent and manipulate those physical identities in much more direct ways—that is, visually. Although writers like Marya Hornbacher, in *Wasted: A Memoir of Anorexia and Bulimia* (1998), and Judith Moore, in *Fat Girl*, focus on their weight and the ways in which their body images have defined their lives, their ability to represent their physical selves—other than an author's photo on the book jacket—never extends beyond the "I" of first person narrative.

Comic book memoirs, by contrast, provide memoirists with another level of representation that can influence meaning. One artist who uses the visual dimension of comics to this end is Al Davison, whose memoir *The Spiral Cage* (1990) tells of his struggles with spina bifida, a birth defect characterized by the incomplete formation of the spinal cord. The result of this affliction is often lifelong paralysis

Figure 2.9. *The Spiral Cage* is copyright 2007
Al Davison/The Astral Gypsy. Used with permission.

below the waist, and Davison's memoir chronicles growing up with
this condition, suffering the prejudices of others, and ultimately finding peace. What is remarkable about Davison's narrative is the variety of artistic styles that he uses, ranging from the childishly iconic to
almost photographically realistic. Also, Davison's particular condition
has an outward manifestation (incompletely developed legs, wheel-
chair), and he uses his comic's visuals to display his body in all of its
awkwardness and (as he feels early on) shame. His visual depictions of himself are unsparing (see Figure 2.9), and at these
moments, Davison uses a more realistic style of art so that we are
confronted with his physical self; he challenges us to look at his body
without turning away—a challenge that is made possible only
through the visuals.

Davison continues to manipulate these visuals throughout. One
poignant episode is when, as a young child, he is reading Mary
Shelley's *Frankenstein*, and he reaches the part where the creature
discovers that he is "ugly." Davison presents this sequence in a
series of panels that alternate between images of the monster and
his own younger self, eventually settling, at the end of the page, on
his thin legs (see Figure 2.10). The visuals here allow Davison to jux-
tapose, in a quite direct manner, the "monstrosity" of the beast with
his own physical image. As readers, we see a clear distinction
between the monster and the boy, but we also understand that the
young Davison does not. In prose narration, this dual meaning would

Figure 2.10. *The Spiral Cage* is copyright 2007
Al Davison/The Astral Gypsy. Used with permission.

have to be directly stated to the reader, but in comics, more subtlety is possible: Davison uses the visuals to show—rather than tell—the tension between his earlier and later perceptions of his body.

The final issue central to the memoir that finds unique expression in comic books is the idea that the "facts" of a life are altered by their translation into some representational medium, that "telling the truth" in memoir is not always a straightforward process. Scrutinizing the "truth" of so-called factual texts has its origins in the 1960s, when deconstruction theory first took hold. One of the most significant thinkers on this issue, Hayden White, argued that various historical texts were mediated by different narrative models and, thus, by the narrators themselves. To White's mind, historical narratives are always influenced by subjective forces—the writers' own biases, perspectives, interests, and agendas chief among them. He writes,

> the facts do not speak for themselves, but . . . the historian speaks for them, speaks on their behalf, and fashions the fragments of the past into a whole whose integrity is—in its representation—a purely discursive one. Novelists might be dealing only with imaginary events whereas historians are dealing with real ones, but the process of fusing events, whether imaginary or real, into a comprehensible totality capable of serving as the object of representation is a poetic process. (125)

Here, he links the historian and the novelist inasmuch as both use language to communicate and create events, and this process, being "poetic," is influenced by the storyteller. The upshot of this view is that history always has narrators, and narrators have subjective perceptions that influence how historical "truth" is presented.[13] Some individuals have transferred White's basic idea from historical to autobiographical writing: Eakin writes that "autobiography is nothing if not a referential art; it is also and always a kind of fiction" (1990 131); even more directly, comic book creator Jason Lutes writes that "imposing retroactive order on the messy unfolding of experience may be unavoidable in autobiography" (24).

Yet the outcry against James Frey and *A Million Little Pieces* suggests that many people hold fast to the notion that memoir is pure "nonfiction" in that it contains unvarnished truth and provides unfiltered access to an individual's past. In large part, such a notion provides the main appeal of the memoir to readers, for they "tend to enjoy a story more when they think it's true" (Long 30). In the case of those memoirs that document hardship and suffering, the reactions that we feel are certainly grounded in our belief that the details actually took place in the life of the writer whose name is on the book's cover. During Frey's penitent second visit with Oprah, the talk show host held nothing back in taking both Frey and his publisher, Nan Talese, to task: she repeated (three times) to the latter, in reference to whether a book is classified as fiction or nonfiction, "I'm trusting you" ("James Frey and the *A Million Little Pieces* Controversy"). Agreeing with Oprah that a distinct line can be drawn between fiction and nonfiction is novelist Anna Quindlen, who voices the importance of truth and accuracy in autobiographical writing when she proclaims that she "will never write a memoir . . . [because she's] got a lousy memory" and that she would have great difficulty trying "to recreate real people from [the] past without recourse to imagination." The assumption that she makes here, of course, is that such "recourse to imagination" is anathema to autobiography.

But many memoirists—prose and comic book alike—are not so sure. According to James Atlas, the key to a successful memoir is an imagination that shapes the material: "At its best, in the hands of a writer able to command the tools of the novelist—character, scene, plot—the memoir can achieve unmatchable depth and resonance" (26). And the fictive elements that inevitably form a part of the memoirist's work become "doubly obvious in the cartoon world of comics" (Hatfield 114). In fact, many comic book creators are highly attuned to this feature of their medium, and they highlight the idea that the comic book memoir is, at best, "approximate" truth. In the introduction to her book *One Hundred Demons*, for example, Lynda Barry wonders, "Is it autobiography if parts of it are not true? Is it fiction if parts of it are?" (7). Such inner debate leads her to coin a new term for what she does: "autobifictionalography" (5). This is as good a term as any for comic book memoir, which reminds us at every turn that retelling one's personal history is, in part, an act of invention. That is, the very nature of the medium—the fact that the images are drawn, the details arranged within panels, the panels arranged within a page—foregrounds that the comic book is an active reconstruction of the past. While this foregrounding occurs with varying degrees of subtlety, its existence makes comics the ideal medium in which to explore how "truth" is constructed, particularly in the memoir.

Prose writing can also call attention to the author's use of fictive devices. Though not a memoir per se, Tim O'Brien's *The Things They Carried* is very much about the nature of "constructed truth" in personal writing. In fact, one of the author's main points throughout the book is that "story-truth is truer sometimes than happening-truth" (O'Brien 203). As O'Brien makes clear throughout this inventive collection, the stories that we create from events can achieve a greater "emotional truth" than those adhering strictly to the facts. This sentiment is echoed by Laurie Stone in her introduction to *Close to the Bone: Memoirs of Hurt, Rage, and Desire* (1997) when she writes that "most memoirs fail as literature because their authors mistake their experiences for a story rather than search out the story in their experience. . . . What matters in the memoir, as in fiction, is the degree of insight and drama" (xvi). In this sense, she falls clearly on the side of critics like Sara Nelson, who contends that "a good memoir must share many of the traits of a novel" (5).

Several prose memoirists have highlighted the problematic nature of truth in their writing, one of the most sustained (and self-conscious) being Lauren Slater's *Lying* (2000). Slater challenges her readers' assumptions about truth and memoir with her opening chapter, which contains only two words: "I exaggerate" (3). Throughout the book, she calls attention to this characteristic of hers, as in this passage, where she undermines a potentially compelling narrative by deconstructing what makes it so potentially compelling. She writes,

> That was the night I started to steal. Maybe I'm wrong. Maybe I really started to steal a few days after that, or a few weeks before. Maybe it's just certain narrative demands, a need for neatness compelling me to say that was the night or and this led surely to this, my life a long link of daisies, a bolt of cloth unbroken, I wish it were. (69)

As the book progresses, we learn of her troubled relationship with her mother and the onset of her own epilepsy. We also learn, however, to suspect the various "truths" she tells us. After describing a scene in which she falls into a grave, she writes,

> This is a work of nonfiction. Everything in it is supposed to be true. In some instances names of people and places have been changed to protect their privacy, but the essential story should at least aim for accuracy, so the establishment says. Therefore, I confess. To the establishment. I didn't really fall into the grave. I was just using a metaphor to try to explain my mental state. (60)

Here, she sets up a theme that she returns to throughout the book— the act of lying as a way to create metaphors that bear "emotional" truths. She reveals to us that she might not really have epilepsy; instead, it may be Munchausen's Syndrome that was engendered by her mother's dysfunction and by her own insecurities.

But maybe even that is made up. As she tells us, "Perhaps I was, and still am, a pretender, a person who creates illnesses because she needs time, attention, touch, because she knows no other way of telling her life's tale" (88). Slater suggests that the power of metaphor is the only possible way to tell her truth. Her thematic intent comes through clearly in the book's most inventive chapter, "How to Market This Book," which is constructed as a letter from Slater to her editor at Random House about the very book we are reading. Among her points is that she wants "to ponder the blurry line between novels and memoirs" (160), self-consciously playing with the idea of truth, which she maintains "is not necessarily the same thing as fact" (160). Slater's book is a rare example of a memoir that both compels and confounds the reader by offering a very sophisticated and engaging examination of how autobiography is "a thing made out of a thing done" (Adams 10).

That memoirs are "made" is evident in recent high-profile, graphic-novel-length memoirs that show how comic book creators use the unique features of this medium to actively remake the past. Alison Bechdel's *Fun Home* (2006) is a moving portrait of growing up in a family where her father was a closeted homosexual who, quite possibly, committed suicide. One feature of the book that foregrounds its "made" nature is the way that Bechdel presents, through her visuals, various textual artifacts of her past. These artifacts include letters, books, diaries, newspapers, maps, and photographs, and they all become "translated" visually by Bechdel for insertion into her narrative (63, 78, 120). Even other images, like maps and photographs, are similarly delivered through Bechdel's drawing (126, 120). In all of these cases, it is clear that real documents are being "reinterpreted" by the artist's hand as if to reinforce the idea that we are always at a remove from the past— especially when reading a memoir, where the past we encounter is not even our own. *Fun Home* reminds us that presenting one's past is expressionistic and interpretive; it is not unfiltered.

A comic's narrative execution through panel composition and layout also plays a key role in understanding how such memoirs are partially constructed (as opposed to being pure reconstruction). The inventive role that visuals play in recreating the past is communicated on nearly every page of Craig Thompson's *Blankets* (2003), an extraordinary narrative of the author's growing up in a somewhat repressive household, his first experiences with love, and his doubts about his Christian faith. In one sequence, Craig is visiting his girlfriend, Raina. As she reads a bedtime story to her mentally handicapped sister, Craig retreats to Raina's room and reads—as is his habit—from his Bible. Over the course of the next several pages, Thompson takes us—via textual and visual narrative—into the Book of Luke, then to Raina's room, then to his child-

Figure 2.11. Copyright Craig Thompson.
Image appears courtesy of Top Shelf Productions.

hood when he was scolded for drawing a picture of a naked woman, and then back to Raina's room once again.

The segues between these different times and places are very fluid, and the visual renderings very impressionistic. As Craig returns to the "present" from the Bible story, both places are represented at once (see Figure 2.11). Here, Thompson depicts himself as staring at a woman from the story—an association that will play out over the next segment, where a portrait of Jesus reminds him of being scolded by his parents for drawing a naked woman (see Figure 2.12). On this particular page, Thompson provides small, telling details that convey his terror: his father's fingers locking the door, his mother's hand retrieving the taboo drawing from the garbage can, both of their faces obscured by shading and panel borders. Two pages later, Thompson uses unconventional layout arrangements to heighten emotion (see Figure 2.13). Here, the vertical panels all seem to be bearing down on the young Craig, who is hunched in on himself in the bottom right corner of the page—a position that, visually, conveys feelings of being threatened or constrained (Bang 56). Thompson later creates an impressive two-page spread that begins with a series of wordless panels depicting his guilt over drawing the picture and making Jesus "sad" (208). The last panel of this page—

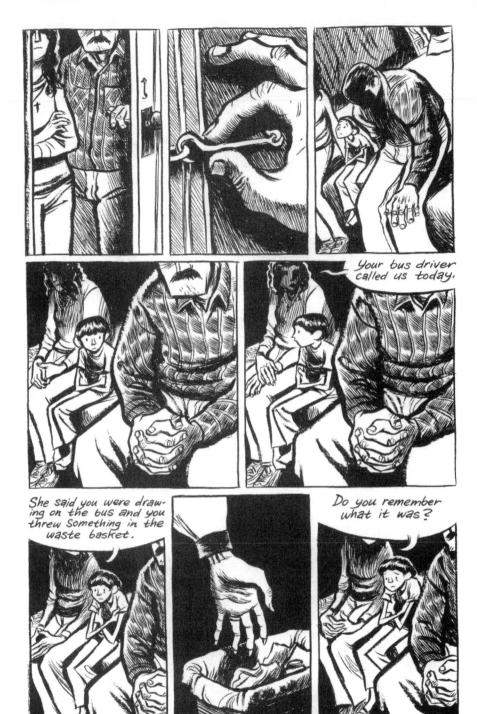

Figure 2.12. Copyright Craig Thompson.
Image appears courtesy of Top Shelf Productions.

Figure 2.13. Copyright Craig Thompson.
Image courtesy of Top Shelf Productions.

where Craig attempts to escape from the woman he has drawn (now headless)—then segues into a panel where that same drawing "morphs" into Raina, who has by now finished reading to her sister (209). This entire sequence, which runs thirteen pages, is a tour de force of comic book storytelling that makes one appreciate how wildly interpretive and impressionistic this medium can be. To read such a work is to understand at a fundamental level that the "truth" of memoir is something that cannot be tied simplistically to the facts; the power of Thompson's memoir lies primarily in its telling, which is subjectively arranged and presented.

As Thompson shows, comics are clearly artistic, and in them we see not the world but a representation of it. Such reminders can also be made through other visual elements. In her short autobiographical piece, "Oh, to Celebrate!" (2001), Miriam Katin juxtaposes her childhood in Hungary during the 1956 Russian invasion with her adulthood as she struggles to write about that past. In those panels depicting the present, Katin uses color; her past, by contrast, is rendered in black and white (144). We understand this contrast immediately, and it reminds us that the entire story is a constructed memory. Related to this method is Paul Hornschemeier's story, "Of This Much We Are Certain" (2003), in which the artist recounts an accident he had as a child. Yet rather than present this story in a straightforward manner, Hornschemeier is concerned with the difficulty of recapturing memory, so the story is split between panels that recreate the past and panels in which he depicts himself in the act of recreation. To complicate matters further, these latter panels are depicted as "in progress": the guide lines for both text and images are still present on the page (see Figure 2.14). Here, the reader is confronted with visual signs that the memoir is a reconstruction of the past and not that past itself.

By revealing to the reader the various ways of presenting one's past, memoirists call attention to the space between an event and its retelling. In her study of women's autobiography, Sidonie Smith argues that "autobiography is always, multiply, storytelling: memory leaves only a trace of an earlier experience that we adjust into story. . . . Even more fundamentally, the language we use to 'capture' memory and experience can never 'fix' the 'real' experience but only approximate it" (145). This concept becomes manifest in the comic book memoir because this medium allows memoirists to experiment with different autobiographical voices, and over a body of work, they can occupy a range of storytelling positions, from active commentators on their past to detached observers of it.

Such is the case with Joe Matt, whose three major autobiograph-

Figure 2.14. "Of This Much We Are Certain" copyright 2003, 2007
Paul Hornschemeier. Used with permission.

ical works—*Peepshow* (1991), *The Poor Bastard* (1997), and *Fair Weather* (2002)—reflect his interest in retelling his past with greater and greater distance. *Peepshow* takes a diary approach where each "day" is given its own single, multipanel page. Throughout these stories, Matt appears as a mediating figure, often setting up each story at its beginning. Throughout this book, Matt shows no compunction about his presence outside of the narrative proper; he spends one strip showing the different visual devices that he will employ (1991 16), and he spends another "outing" his work as a shameless rip-off of Robert Crumb's autobiographical stories (1991 17). All of these strategies lend themselves to a narrative that puts us inside of Matt's head but that nonetheless operates at a "meta" level that calls attention to its own construction. This situation changes slightly in Matt's second book, *The Poor Bastard*, which takes as its subjects his complicated relationships with various women and his addiction to pornography. This book contains no direct address, and in this sense, Matt's narrative operates more traditionally, where interiority is conveyed through thought bubbles and cutaway panels—usually of Matt's fantasy life, which involves the graphically sexual (1997 3). In his third book, *Fair Weather*, Matt goes further back in time, revisiting his childhood and presenting himself as an obsessive and disrespectful little terror, at one point threatening to burn down the house if his mother touches his comic books again (92). In terms of authorial presence, Matt is much more invisible in this book than in his first two; everything we know about young Joe is conveyed through scene and dialogue. The differences among these books reveal that memoirists make conscious decisions about how they tell their stories, and that the "truth" of the past is largely dependent on how that past is retold. Such dependence reminds us that narrating our past's truths is not objective; instead, uncovering those truths lies in the active, shaping hands of a storyteller.

This point that "truth" in memoir is largely subjective is made most clearly when memoirists provide different versions of the same event—a situation that ideally suits the comic book medium and its ability to manipulate words and images. Retelling the same story in different ways, in fact, is a favorite strategy of Harvey Pekar. The events in his story "Austere Youth" (1992), which appeared in his comic series *American Splendor*, are retold, in a slightly different fashion, in his graphic novel, *The Quitter* (2005). The original story, illustrated by Frank Stack, is fairly minimal in terms of overt authorial interjection. We learn that Harvey—here referred to as Herschel, his given name—has his hat stolen by some black youths. When his mother hears this, she makes him

Figure 2.15. Copyright Harvey Pekar. Used with permission.

tell his teacher—an act that Herschel knows will just get him in deeper trouble with his tormentors, and as he runs from a larger group of kids, he remembers his mother telling him, "the negro people have been treated terribly in this country. Worse than the Jews. The Jews and negroes should work together" (18). This memory, in essence, forms the only acknowledgment of racial tension in the story. Pekar's approach here is very sparse; he offers only occasional glimpses into Herschel's mind and provides no "voiceover" text box narration. Given this approach, Frank Stack's minimalist artwork is a perfect complement (see Figure 2.15). There are several wordless panels, and the characters' emotions—when the characters emote at all—are expressed mainly in the eyes; in addition, Stack often visualizes characters as either outlines or silhouettes, and readers are left to guess at their thoughts and feelings.

A sharp contrast in narrative strategy is evident Pekar's *The Quitter*, a graphic novel that details the violent world of his youth and attempts to reveal the origins of Pekar's pugnacious nature. Pekar chooses the same incident dramatized in "Austere Youth" to begin his graphic novel, but his framing and execution create a much different "truth" for this memory. In *The Quitter*, the subject of conflict is much more prevalent. Pekar begins with the immigration of his parents in order to set up the point that his parents—and especially his father—do not understand how American culture works, as evidenced by their handling of their son's being bullied. The issue of racial conflict is foregrounded as Pekar tells us:

> From the late 1930's to the mid 1940's my neighborhood was changing rapidly from white to black, and by 1946, I was about the only white kid my age living on my street. The black kids had a name for me, "White Cracker." It seemed that every day I came home from school, I had to fight through a bunch of them. I had no friends, and felt totally alienated. I started to think of myself as racially inferior. (np)

Unlike the original comic, where the racial conflict is limited to one of the bullies calling "Hey, white cracker" to Herschel (15), *The Quitter* presents the issue more directly. Also, Pekar ties the racial conflict in his neighborhood to the larger culture: he devotes an entire page to the issue and includes one panel that cuts away to depict a black man drinking from a water fountain marked "colored" (see Figure 2.16).

Dean Haspiel's visuals on this particular page provide a much different representation of these events than that in "Austere Youth" as well. Specifically, he uses background shading and precise linework

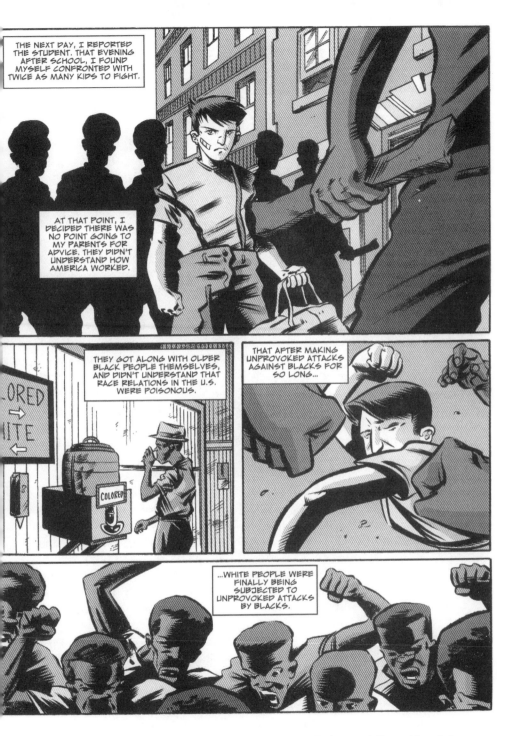

Figure 2.16. From *The Quitter*, copyright Harvey Pekar and Dean Haspiel. All rights reserved. Used with permission of DC Comics.

to create a more palpable sense of foreboding here, and he renders the fight scenes more realistically and dynamically, giving greater weight to the racial conflict. In addition, Pekar is visually represented as more defiant than in "Austere Youth." The large top panel on this page emphasizes the conflict and Pekar's determination to see it through—a portrayal that fits with the book's theme of tracing the author's penchant for conflict. The most striking difference between the two versions, however, is the presence of Pekar's narration, which drives the story by offering a running commentary on its influence over his identity. Whereas Pekar's first version of this story took on the shape and character of a somewhat hazily remembered event from his youth, this later version locates in this incident his view of other races, his own personality, and even his relationship with his parents: in "Austere Youth," there is no sense of the disappointment Pekar feels after following his mother's advice and getting pummeled for it; in *The Quitter*, however, his mother's failure marks a crucial turning point in his youth. He tells us, again in narration, that "I decided there was no point going to my parents for advice. They didn't understand how America worked." Taken together, these stories demonstrate how actively the past is shaped by the comic book memoirist, who can turn the same memory into quite different stories.

In Pekar's case, we get a sense of this circumstance by comparing two stories published thirteen years apart and in different books. Yet some memoirists who are conscious of their own "truth-making" will act as mediator right before our eyes. In her prose memoir, *Memories of a Catholic Girlhood*, Mary McCarthy takes such a role by writing two kinds of chapters—those that retell incidents from her past and appear in standard typeface and those that comment on the "truth" of the previous sections and are italicized. Part of the book's charm is that McCarthy does not hesitate to expose herself; she often begins the latter sections with statements like "There are several dubious points in this memoir" (47) or "This is an example of 'storytelling'; I arranged actual events so as to make 'a good story'" (164).

Providing such insight into the process of construction appears—though in slightly different form—in comics as well, as evidenced by Chester Brown's two stories, "Helder" (1989) and "Showing Helder" (1990). Taken together, these stories are less about the dramatic narrative of the former—Chester's run-ins with the belligerent boyfriend of a housemate—than about the complicated and compromised nature of autobiographical writing in general. In the first story, "Helder," Brown will often break the continuity of the narrative to deliver some information to the reader through direct address (see

Figure 2.17). One important effect of this device is to make the reader aware of at least two different "times" in which this story is operating: the past that Brown recounts and the present from which he is recounting. This device reminds us that the story as a whole is reconstructed and not a simple recitation of fact. Brown makes this point even more vivid in "Showing Helder," which is his account of the difficulties in putting together "Helder." The visual strategy that Brown uses here is to create panel-less pages, and this looser presentation emphasizes the structure—that is, the author's planned design—of the previous story. This emphasis is reinforced as we see, in "Showing Helder" how Brown has constructed the earlier story (see Figure 2.18). In "Showing Helder," Brown introduces us to the complicated negotiations that take place as he creates his autobiographical work. These negotiations involve artistic choices, such as the issue of direct address, but they also involve what might be called "ethical" choices, such as the presentation of other real people. Brown's friend Kris raises this very point to him, claiming, "I should have some say in the way I'm shown" (89). Through this objection, Brown reminds us that comic book memoir is an act of considerable construction. His focus on these incidents and on the resultant editing also makes us wonder what else might have been changed or excised entirely.

Brown's construction of the narrative in "Helder" is the main storyline of "Showing Helder," and as a result, his self-exposure emerges somewhat naturally. But this self-exposure can also be presented more jarringly. Robert Crumb has collaborated on several comics with his wife, Aline Kominsky-Crumb, all of which have been collected in *The Complete Dirty Laundry Comics* (1992). The conceit of these autobiographical strips is that the Crumbs—whose artistic styles are radically different—will draw themselves. Thus, the divergence in styles in each panel is a constant reminder that we are looking at constructed images and, by extension, constructed memories. The Crumbs push this device to interesting limits. In "Let's Have a Little Talk" (1974), the two present their idea and offer critiques on each other's style: Crumb writes, "Sure, your art's a little stiff, and your dialogue may be self-conscious, but so what?"; while Kominsky-Crumb comments, at the end of the page, "I'm cuter in real life" (7). Years later, in "Our Lovely Home" (1988), the Crumbs add text boxes to comment on both the process of comic book memoir and the art itself (109). Crumb writes, at one point, "It's a weird experience to deep drawing yourself over and over again," which delineates one of the main differences between representing the self in prose (by repeating the personal pronoun

Figure 2.17. Copyright 1990 Chester Brown. Used with permission.

Figure 2.18. Copyright 1990 Chester Brown. Used with permission.

"I") and in comic books (one must continually draw oneself). The comment also underscores the artifice of comic book representation, as do other comments on this particular page, such as Kominsky-Crumb's complaint in one particular panel that "Robert had the nerve to touch up this face." What the Crumbs' work does, in essence, is reinforce the ability of comics to represent one's life in an engaging and revelatory fashion and at the same time to convey that such representation can only ever be a construction.

Such a position—blatantly exposing the representational nature of the medium in order to comment on the "untruth" of comic book representation—is a favorite for memoirists who like to play with this malleable form. One such person is Chris Ware, an inventive and self-conscious comic book creator whose *Acme Novelty Library* is widely regarded as one of the most innovative explorations of the medium. Ware's dominant choice of narrative is fiction, but a rare foray into memoir, "I Guess" (1991), is a brilliant tale that lays bare the very core of comic narrative: the interplay of word and picture. He does this by telling two separate stories: one storyline is a series of memories from his childhood, and Ware uses all of the text in the comic to tell that story, including sound effects; the other story is about a masked superhero who foils the plan of a mad scientist and rescues the girl, and Ware uses all of the visuals to tell that story (see Figure 2.19). The effect is disconcerting and takes a few readings to appreciate, but the overall effect of Ware's story is to highlight the constructed nature of all comic narratives, which typically draw us in on the subtle interplay of word and image. In Ware's execution, however, this interplay continually announces itself, and it is impossible to read one narrative without slipping over into the other.

In addition to the many artistic elements of the comic book that creators have used to highlight the constructed truth of memoirs, we must consider the general attitudes that people have toward comics, for these attitudes also work, ironically, to strengthen the representational sophistication of comics themselves. Because many of us associate comics with talking animals or superheroes, we come to the medium with certain assumptions about the form. Specifically, we see comics as a metaphoric interpretation of reality and are therefore accepting—whether we are aware of it or not—of the subjective nature of "truth" in comics. This is why, when we read James Kochalka's collection of daily, four-panel diary entries, *American Elf* (2004), we are not outraged that the book violates the idea of "truth" as promised by the diary form because the author depicts himself and others as elves; we understand that such fanciful—and interpretive—representation is very much a part of comics' aesthetic.

Figure 2.19. Copyright Chris Ware.
Image appears courtesy of Fantagraphics Books, Inc.

This perspective is especially instructive in the case of Canadian comic book creator Seth (real name Gregory Gallant) and his memoir *It's a Good Life, If You Don't Weaken* (1996). This book chronicles with evocative linework and elegant prose his obsession with Jack "Kalo" Kalloway, an obscure gag cartoon artist whose work he discovers on one of his many random wanderings into used book stores. In the final chapter, Seth reprints the eleven Kalo cartoons that he has collected over the years, culled from various publications like *The Saturday Evening Post*, *The New Yorker*, and *Esquire*. But there is a problem. Jack Kalloway does not exist; the cartoonist is Seth's imaginative invention, a metaphor for the fruitless yet romantic pursuit of the past. What Seth does, in essence, is fabricate the events of his memoir in order to reveal emotional truths about himself and his sometimes counterproductive nostalgia. Ten years later, James Frey would be publicly excoriated for doing essentially the same thing. But what is the difference—aside from the fact that most people do not read comics? The difference is that readers already view comic books as "unreal," so any further distortion of reality becomes a mere extension of the form.

In light of Frey—and others like Forrest Carter and J. T. LeRoy, whose memoirs are even more blatantly invented[14]—it bears keeping in mind that "there's a difference between unavoidable distortions and willful deceptions. Some falsehoods come with the territory of the memoirist; others must be deliberately imported into it" (Grossman 60). Yet Frey remains a troubling case because many readers declared themselves "changed" by the story he told; they drew strength and inspiration from his tale. Even though crucial narrative events of *A Million Little Pieces* were fabricated, the fact remains that these fabrications accomplished good in the lives of some troubled individuals. Perhaps the ultimate point to be gleaned from Frey (and all the memoirists discussed in this chapter) is that the story of the life lived—which is different than the life itself—exerts a powerful hold over many readers. I believe that our attraction for the memoir arises out of more than a voyeuristic impulse; rather, we are drawn to others' lives out of the desire to connect with and learn from their stories, which have the ability to raise questions about the nature of art, our lives, and how the two intersect. That prose memoirs—respected literary entities—are able to accomplish all this is hardly surprising; that memoirs in comic book form—a largely disparaged medium—add depth to these accomplishments is, perhaps, where the true surprise lies.

Notes

1. At the time of the release of *A Million Little Pieces*, reviewers tended to fall into one of two camps—those who praised its "brutal honesty" (Murphy E1) and those who felt it "stylistically overcooked" (Turrentine R16). Some detractors also questioned—prophetically, as it turned out—the truth of the more dramatic parts of Frey's narrative, including the book's opening, when he wakes up unconscious and bleeding on an airplane with no recollection of boarding; his undergoing a double root canal surgery without any anesthetic; and his heroic rescue of a fellow patient from a crack house near a Minneapolis bus station (Rybak 1E).

2. Winfrey has arguably done more for reading in this country than any other individual. Since the inception of her book club in 1996, many previously unknown writers such as Jacquelyne Mitchard, Wally Lamb, and Ursula Hegi have enjoyed what is commonly referred to as the "Oprah Effect," whereby the chosen writer could count on an immediate increase in sales of as many as a million copies ("Oprah's Book Club"). When Oprah switched to more canonical authors like Faulkner, Tolstoy, and Hurston, sales for the chosen titles similarly skyrocketed. There is something refreshing about looking at a bestseller chart in 2004 and seeing *Anna Karenina* near the top of the list, and we have Oprah to thank for that.

3. In what may very well be the final chapter of this saga, Random House agreed in September of 2006 to refund $23.95 to anyone who purchased the hardback edition of *A Million Little Pieces* and can prove it by mailing in page 163–64 (Cruz 23).

4. As with so many terms, the particular name used for this kind of writing has undergone changes over time. The two most common terms are "autobiography" and "memoir," and they have been defined differently largely based on the community doing the defining. Back in 1976, academician Elizabeth Bruss authored a book entitled *Autobiographical Acts: The Changing Situation of a Literary Genre*, which is considered by some to be one of the earliest and most complete attempts to "establish a poetics of the genre [of autobiography]" (Eakin 1990 129). In her book, Bruss defines a "memoir" as those attempts by an autobiographer to reconfirm "his public character" (12). More recently, publishers and writers have attempted to distinguish between the "autobiography" and the "memoir" by maintaining that the former deals with the chronology of an entire life (an increasingly rare form of writing) while the latter deals more with a particular time within that life or a theme that runs throughout it. For my purposes here, there are no overriding political implications of using one term or the other. Because most of the prose works that I will deal with are contemporary, it seems to make more sense to discuss them as "memoirs." When discussing longer comics pieces, I will similarly refer to them as memoirs; however, because I also discuss shorter works—in both prose and comics—I will refer to them as "autobiographical" essays or comics because there is no non-awkward-sounding equivalent using "memoir." "Memoiristical"? "Memoiresque"? These don't quite work.

5. One of these issues has been generic definition. That is, how do we define autobiography? For certainly there is some fundamental difference between Snoop

Dogg's *The Doggfather: The Times, Trials, and Hardcore Truths of Snoop Dogg* (1999) and Tobias Wolff's *This Boy's Life* (1988); after all, I have several colleagues who teach the latter in their college-level composition and literature classes, and I only know of the former from spotting a remaindered copy on the "Entertainment" shelf of a local book liquidation store. But this observation is strictly personal, and the case may very well be that more people have read Snoop Dogg's book (written with Davin Seay) than Wolff's. Should popularity be the primary way to distinguish these two? What about the status of the books? Of the authors? How do we define "status"? Given the extremely limited scope of this particular comparison, it is clear how daunting these few questions—and the many more that I haven't posed—become when considering the many, many works that might fit the category of "autobiographical writing." Not surprisingly, then, several scholars have sought to address the generic characteristics and limits of this genre. Phillipe Lejeune's *On Autobiography* (1975) and Elizabeth Bruss's aforementioned study (see previous note) are two of the earliest—and they remain two of the most extensive—attempts to define this genre. Despite these and other efforts, however, the genre remains fluid and constantly renegotiated; such a circumstance is best—and, perhaps, finally—captured by Timothy Dow Adams, who contends that "the paradoxical ambiguity of autobiography—the impossibility of ever completely separating or refining either the word itself or the terms used in discussing it—is in a sense both its strength and its most defining characteristic" (4).

6. In addition to formal variation, the body of autobiographical writing is further complicated by the variety of authors who pen their memoirs. There are, for example, memoirs written by famous heads of state and political figures, entertainers and athletes, and writers at various stages of their careers—including those who do not become known as writers until they write their first memoir. This diverse array of memoirists extends at least as far back as A.D. 397, when Saint Augustine wrote his *Confessions*. The authors of comic book memoirs are somewhat less diverse than those writing prose memoirs (no head of state will, in all likelihood, author a comic book memoir). In addition, the history of autobiographical comics is somewhat shorter than their prose counterparts. Often cited as the true touchstone for most autobiographical comics, Justin Green's *Binky Brown Meets the Holy Virgin Mary* (1972) was actually predated by other examples of this kind of writing. Robert Crumb, for instance, was creating personal narratives in the 1960s. In addition, Wally Wood's "My World" (1953)—in which he describes different science fiction scenarios and characters only to reveal himself as their creator at the end—can also be read as autobiographical. Most surprisingly (due to its early date), French illustrator Gustave Doré wrote "A Fulfilling Career" in 1852. In this brief story, illustrations and ironic captions form a tongue-in-cheek remembrance of how his talent at drawing earned him the enmity of people in positions to do him ill.

7. See especially Carlos Baker, *Ernest Hemingway: A Life Story* (1969); Scott Donaldson, *By Force of Will: The Life and Art of Ernest Hemingway* (1977); Joseph M. Flora, *Hemingway's Nick Adams* (1982); John K. M. McCaffery (ed.), *Ernest Hemingway: The Man and His Work* (1950); Jeffrey Meyers, *Hemingway: Life into Art* (2000); and Louis Renza, "The Importance of Being Ernest" in Linda Wagner-Martin (ed.), *Ernest Hemingway: Seven Decades of Criticism* (1998).

8. One relevant trend in memoir that emerged in the 1990s and continues to draw attention from readers and critics alike is the "confessional" memoir. In these books, the memoirist attempts to create an intimate relationship with the reader by revealing his or her hidden pains and demons. Such revelations are often grounded in the details of some tragic past that typically involves illness, substance abuse, family and/or personal instability, or some combination thereof. The book often cited as initiating this subgenre is William Styron's *Darkness Visible* (1990), his memoir of his near-suicidal bout with depression. Since its publication, there has been a rapidly expanding market for memoirs narrating their writers' struggles with some kind of suffering or hardship. Some relevant titles include Susanna Kaysen's *Girl, Interrupted* (1993), which chronicles the two years she spent in a psychiatric ward with other teenage girls; Elizabeth Wurtzel's *Prozac Nation* (1994), a vivid account of being young, female, depressed, and out of control; Mary Karr's *The Liar's Club* (1995), which details her dirt-poor childhood in rural Texas; Frank McCourt's *Angela's Ashes* (1995), which recounts the author's squalorous childhood in Limerick, Ireland; Kay Redfield Jamison's *An Unquiet Mind* (1995), which addresses her struggles with bipolar disorder; Michael Ryan's *Secret Life* (1995), which delves into the specifics of his sex addition; Kathryn Harrison's aforementioned *The Kiss* (1996), about her sexual relationship with her father; Jim Knipfel's *Slackjaw* (1999), about his *retinitis pigmentosa*—or gradual blindness; and Augusten Burroughs's *Dry* (2003), about his struggles with alcoholism. As with any genre, the approaches are varied and the writing inconsistent, but what draws these and other works together is the autobiographical act of sharing one's pain. Part of the appeal of these memoirs is undoubtedly voyeuristic. But the best of these and other memoirs that fit this broad category are those in which the author engages the reader without exploiting their voyeuristic impulses.

9. In terms of autobiographical comics, Harvey Pekar's *American Splendor* (1976–present) is the most innovative and interesting body of work out there. While I reference it at various point throughout this chapter, the most insightful study of his work can be found in Joseph Witek, *Comic Books as History: The Narrative Art of Jack Jackson, Art Spiegelman, and Harvey Pekar* (1989).

10. Though it would be difficult to classify as a strictly "prose" memoir, one interesting departure is certainly Leslie Marmon Silko's *Storyteller* (1981), an extraordinary work in which the author presents her and her family's past through poems, short stories, and photographs. Even the shape of the book—a "landscape" design much wider than it is tall—sets it apart from other, more traditionally proportioned books. Of course, the point that I'm making in this chapter is that through the comics medium, memoirists can do certain things that cannot be accomplished in prose alone. Whether or not Silko achieves these same things is a subject for further discussion; that Silko's book operates well outside the realm of "strict prose" is not.

11. That we are "outside" the narrator is not always the case. Dan Clowes, in his five-page comic, "The Stroll" (1990), uses a "point of view" perspective so that we ostensibly see what he sees as he takes a walk around his neighborhood. Complementing this view are the text boxes, which contain his running inner monologue. As we look through Clowes's eyes, he makes an implicit comment about the nature of comics in general—they are always depicting the world as seen by the artist. This "camera's eye" view is an experiment that has been used

in film before, most notably in *The Lady in the Lake* (1947), where the viewer "is" Robert Montgomery and sees the story through his eyes; we only glimpse the actor when he walks by a mirror. Predictably, this device wears thin pretty quickly in the film and is little more than a gimmick.

12. Sometimes these differences are subtle, but at other times they are not. I remember once—and the key word here is "once"—displaying at a family dinner some of the bluster that I would routinely adopt, as faculty union president, during college committee meetings. My wife gave me a look and then voiced exactly what her look had wordlessly communicated: "Who are you?" Since then, I've become a little more shrewd about partitioning my "selves."

13. For a contrasting opinion of the relationship between "real life" and narrative, see David Carr's *Time, Narrative, and History* (1986). In this study, Carr argues against the notion that narrative imposes a form over experience. His argument is that both "historical and fictional narratives . . . [are] extensions and configurations of [reality's] primary features" (16). As I hope this chapter indicates, my own reading of both prose and comic book memoirs and the great variety and artistry displayed therein by their authors does not support Carr's views.

14. Forrest Carter's *The Education of Little Tree* (1976) purports to be the author's memory of his Cherokee childhood, but the author is not Cherokee. In fact, the author is Asa Earl Carter, a member of the KKK who is credited by some as having penned George Wallace's "Segregation forever!" speech (Steyn 50). J. T. LeRoy, who wrote *The Heart Is Deceitful above All Things* (1999), a memoir about growing up on the streets of San Francisco, is actually not a real person but a fictional construct invented by Laura Albert, who went so far as to hire a woman to play LeRoy on various talk show appearances (Steyn 50).

3.
REMAUSTERING THE PAST
Comic Books vs. Holocaust Memoir & Photography

As I discuss in the previous chapter, the issue of truth in representation is an important element of both prose and comic book memoirs, but it is dealt with by some memoirists in a playful and teasing way. In the case of one of memoir's more specialized subgenres—the Holocaust memoir—this notion of truth takes on a greater significance, at once more focused and sober.

More specifically, for those who survived Hitler's death camps and went on to write about their ordeals, two fears took hold upon their release and festered in the years that followed: that a prime motivation for surviving—to tell their stories—would be met with an audience either unwilling or unable to hear their tales, and that the stories that were told would be forgotten as the Holocaust receded into history. In the years since the liberation of the camps, both fears have become realized in one way or another, but the most immediate obstacle faced by Holocaust survivors was internal. That is, in the process of writing their stories, these individuals encountered the difficulty of translating their experiences into words. As Alvin Rosenfeld says about written Holocaust memoirs, "what really is involved here is the deep anguish and immense frustration of the writer who confronts a subject that belittles and threatens to overwhelm the resources of his language" (1980 14).

This anguish and frustration can be witnessed in the very specific case of Saul Friedländer, who writes in his memoir *When Memory Comes* (1978), "it took me a long, long time to find the way back to my own past. I could not banish the memory of events themselves, but if I tried to speak of them or pick up a pen to describe them, I immediately found myself in the grip of a strange paralysis" (102). Within this statement lies the central paradox of Holocaust memoirs, identified by Rosenfeld as the "contradiction between the impossibility but also the necessity of writing" (1980 8). On the one hand, the scope of the catastrophe is such that many survivors are driven to tell their stories; on the other hand, the very subject of the stories defies easy communication and representation. As these survivors soon discovered, the primary medium for communicating one's "truth"—prose narrative—is one that does not conform easily to the extreme nature of the Holocaust.

A medium that seems even less equipped to communicate this particular history would be the comic book. In fact, in terms of popular conceptions, it would be difficult to find two more mismatched subjects than the Holocaust and comic books, for the latter is commonly regarded as an immature diversion while the former, by contrast, has become frozen in most minds as a metaphor for ultimate evil, so sweeping are its horrors. Both perceptions are unfortunate, for neither the Holocaust nor comic books are served well by these generalizations. Despite the seeming incongruousness between comics and the Holocaust, however, Art Spiegelman boldly unites the two in his graphic novels *Maus I* (1986) and *Maus II* (1991).[1] Originally serialized in his underground comics anthology *Raw* from the late 1970s to the mid-1980s and then later released as two graphic novels, *Maus* tells in comic book format two parallel stories: Spiegelman's own troubled relationship with his father Vladek, a Holocaust survivor; and Vladek's life in both prewar Poland and later at Auschwitz. Adding to the disturbing notion of approaching the Holocaust in a comic book, Spiegelman employs an extended animal metaphor in which different nationalities are represented by various animals: the Jews are mice, the Germans are cats, the Poles are pigs, and so forth.

As I discussed in this book's opening chapter, *Maus* demonstrated to many non–comics fans that the medium could successfully grapple with serious issues, and the book was instrumental in helping to spark a rejuvenation of the comic book during the 1980s. What is more, the "literary" value of *Maus* is much more established than that of other comics; Spiegelman's books are often taught in college classrooms (including mine), and they have been the focus of several academic articles and even one collection of essays.[2] Both volumes were nominated for the National Book Critics Circle Award, and *Maus II* won an Eisner Award, a Harvey Award (both prestigious comics industry accolades), and the Pulitzer Prize. Such academic and critical recognition, coupled with the books' commercial success, firmly establishes these two volumes as being among the most important books on the Holocaust to be published in the twentieth century. Still, upon its initial appearance, Spiegelman's book and its approach to this subject matter invited a great deal of criticism. One irate group was the Polish-American Public Relations Committee, which published an opinion stating, in part, that "the comic book format is suited primarily to presenting stories to audiences of limited literacy in a simplistic form. As such, it cannot be considered an appropriate means for serious teaching of any academic subject" (Alvi 1).

Unfortunately, this position ignores the possibilities of the comic book in general and Spiegelman's accomplishments with *Maus* in particular. As I argue in Chapter Two, the medium of comics is particularly suited to engage the reader in ways unavailable through conventional prose. I continue this argument here, maintaining that the comic book displays its potential as a sophisticated literature by extending the elements of two important forms of Holocaust representations: written memoir and photography. Both of these forms seek to capture some truth about the Holocaust, and they do so with limited success—especially the latter. But by taking full advantage of the graphic language of the comic book, Spiegelman creates a powerful new narrative model that recognizes the complexities of retelling this history. More specifically, Spiegelman explores and extends two main features of these particular Holocaust representations: the act of "bearing witness" (and all that act implies) in the written memoir, and the narrative possibilities and limitations of the photographs that have come to largely define popular understanding of the Holocaust. In so doing, Spiegelman shows that rather than diminishing the Holocaust, the comic book medium is uniquely suited to bring about a deeper historical understanding of that particular history.

One of the defining features of Holocaust memoirs is the writers' desire to establish the documentary nature of what they witnessed. What is readily apparent to any reader of these memoirs is, to use the words of Terrence Des Pres, "a strong need to make the truth known" (30). This need is often expressed as a fear that no one would believe—or even listen to—the survivor's story. The opening pages of Elie Wiesel's *Night* (1958), for example, present the character of Moshe the Beadle, an odd figure from Wiesel's youth who assumed the role of informal religious instructor. Being a foreign Jew in Wiesel's town, Moshe is among the first to be deported. Miraculously, he escapes from capture, but not before witnessing acts of indiscriminate slaughter by the Nazis of Jewish men, women, and children. Yet after making his way back to Wiesel's town to warn his fellow Jews, he finds himself without an audience for his story. Wiesel writes, "[Moshe] no longer sang. He no longer talked to me of God or the cabbala, but only of what he had seen. People refused not only to believe his stories, but even to listen to them" (4).

In spite of this fear of not being heard, the need to bear witness is a powerful force among many survivors. A central feature of this need is the overt insistence on truth, and in many ways, Holocaust writing is a highly documentary literature in which both writer and reader share the need to confirm the "actual occurrence" of described events. James Young, in *Writing and Rewriting the Holocaust*, acknowledges that a number of Holocaust memoirs attempt to recreate a documentary mode. In his view, many of these memoirists believe that "for the survivor's witness to be credible, [the memoir] must seem natural and unconstructed" (1988 17). Though Young's ultimate argument is to undercut the "unconstructed" nature of these writings by examining how Holocaust writers also shape their material, what is most important to note here is the urgency that underlies these writers' need to establish documented fact.[3] In Holocaust memoirs, this need emerges when writers not only describe some atrocity but also when they highlight their position as eyewitness viewers. In *Night*, for example, Wiesel writes, "not far from us, flames were leaping up from a ditch, gigantic flames. They were burning something. A lorry drew up at the pit and delivered its load—little children. Babies! Yes, I saw it—saw it with my own eyes . . . those children in the flames" (30). Here, the event described so confounds belief that Wiesel must reestablish his own presence as a witness to what happened.

By combining words and pictures, the comic book allows Spiegelman to emphasize the direct act of testifying in ways unavailable through prose alone. In *Maus I*, for example, Vladek relates the time when he was captured as a Polish prisoner of war by the Germans. In a scene depicting one of the prison camps, Vladek is joined by two other Jewish prisoners. In side-by-side panels, one of the men describes the treatment of the Jewish prisoners (see Figure 3.1). He says, "the other prisoners get two meals a day. We Jews get only a crust of bread and a little soup." Here, Spiegelman finds a way to inform the reader about certain facts—in this case the different treatment accorded to the Jews in the P.O.W. camp. But what is interesting about this particular panel is the way that the speaker turns to face the reader from the first to the second panel, breaking the "fourth wall" in direct address. Through this visual, Spiegelman makes concrete the importance of the speaker–listener relationship in Holocaust memoir, where an intimacy between speaker and reader is more urgent than in perhaps any other genre of literature.

Spiegelman uses this technique elsewhere as well, most powerfully in *Maus II*, when Vladek eventually describes the gas chambers and chimneys (see Figure 3.2). As he does so, Spiegelman empha-

Figure 3.1. From *Maus I: A Survivor's Tale/My Father Bleeds History* by Art Spiegelman, copyright 1973, 1980, 1981, 1982, 1984, 1985, 1986 by Art Spiegelman. Used by permission of Pantheon Books, a division of Random House, Inc. In the United Kingdom, this image is used by permission of the Wylie Agency.

Figure 3.2. From *Maus II: A Survivor's Tale/And Here My Troubles Began* by Art Spiegelman, copyright 1986, 1989, 1990, 1991 by Art Spiegelman. Used by permission of Pantheon Books, a division of Random House, Inc. In the United Kingdom, this image is used by permission of the Wylie Agency.

sizes his words not only by depicting his father as facing the reader in the second panel, but also by reemphasizing Vladek's presence at the scene, not unlike the earlier excerpt from Wiesel's *Night*. In the central panel of this row, Spiegelman places a close, frontal view of Vladek, who, despite the minimalistically drawn eyes, stares directly at the reader as he says, "you heard about the gas but I'm telling not rumors, but only what really I saw. For this I was an eyewitness" (69). Spiegelman punctuates these words—and in particular the word "eyewitness"—with the chimney and a faint trace of smoke in the background. That Spiegelman chooses this particular point to emphasize the act of bearing witness is entirely consistent with memoirs written by Holocaust survivors. In such memoirs, writers sought to stress their presence during those moments of atrocity that lie the furthest beyond language. In *Maus*, Spiegelman recalls these moments by emphasizing the fact that the speaker (Vladek) witnessed the horrors of the gas chambers. Moreover, as with the previous example, Spiegelman is able to do more in representing the act of witnessing. Specifically, the visuals highlight the speaker–listener relationship by allowing us to "see" the eyewitness as he addresses us directly. Also, the linking in a single panel of the image of a chimney—a Holocaust icon of undeniable power—with the word "eyewitness" adds a directness that is possible only in a medium that so thoroughly integrates words and pictures.

Spiegelman also advances the theme of bearing witness by recasting that act in terms of the second generation—the children of Holocaust survivors. For first generation writers like Levi, Wiesel, and others, the urgency lies with the survivors; they are driven to tell their stories. As Spiegelman shows, this urgency becomes displaced in the second generation, where the children of survivors are driven to hear those stories, uncover their own connections with this past, and retell the history in their own unique manner. As stated above, a distinctive feature of first generation Holocaust memoir is that the survivor is often gripped by the paralyzing fear that there will be no audience for the stories. A powerful corollary consequence to this situation is the transformation of language: those who have survived the camps possess a vocabulary that the rest of us can only approximate and never truly understand. Levi writes that "[i]t is an irksome habit of ours to intervene when someone (our children!) speaks about cold, hunger, or fatigue. What do you know about it? You should have gone through what we did" (1989 89).

Levi here introduces a tension between the first and subsequent generations—the seemingly insurmountable gap of experience. Martin Bergmann and Milton Jucovy, in their book *Generations of the*

Holocaust, feel that this gap is a defining element of the relationship between the first and second generation. They write that "the child of a Holocaust survivor is exposed to the Holocaust as filtered through the experiences of the parents. The Holocaust thus becomes a significant [aspect] of the relationship of the parents and the family to the child" (28). One form this aspect takes is as a barrier, where the second generation has the need to access this past, but is impeded by the specific burdens that the Holocaust places on communicability. With this need, members of the second generation find themselves in the paradoxical role of being drastically affected by an event that they never directly experienced and cannot easily discuss.

It is this complex gap of experience between the first and second generation to which *Maus I* and *II* speak. More specifically, Spiegelman preserves the testimony of the first generation, but he frames this telling—sometimes literally—with a distinctively second generational perspective that seeks to understand the Holocaust and how it "serve[s] as a powerful organizing influence and reminder of one's identity as a child of [that event]" (Hass 31). As a member of the second generation who is driven to understand the Holocaust, Spiegelman has a fragmented sense of identity, and his quest to discover and represent what his parents went through is a means by which he can reassemble his sense of self. As I discussed in Chapter Two, the comic book medium—and in particular, its visual component—allows memoirists to represent this fragmentation of identity in unique, dramatic, and direct ways. Over the course of the two books, we are given no less than five versions of Art: as a young "mouse" in the prologue to *Maus I* (6); as an older "mouse" who interviews Vladek (1986 14); as a young boy in the photo that introduces "Prisoner on the Hell Planet" (1986 100); as a young man in that same section (100); and as the "man behind the mask" in the chapter "Time Flies" in *Maus II* (41). We assimilate these different images insofar as we recognize that they are versions of the same person. However, they are also radically dissimilar representations that visually communicate that identity is mercurial, multifaceted, and, sometimes, conflicted. Dori Laub suggests that "when one's history is abolished, one's identity ceases to exist as well" (82), referring in this case to Holocaust survivors. Yet his insight can be applied to the children of these survivors as well: as Spiegelman shows in *Maus I* and *II*, he is invested in uncovering and recovering this lost history of his parents in order to understand more fully his own identity as a child of the Holocaust.

But what does it mean to be a "child of the Holocaust"? This difficult question often consumes those in the second generation, many of whom understandably feel invested in this particular history. As Bergmann and Jucovy suggest, this investment is characterized by a need for resolution. They write that "resolving problems creatively to relive the Holocaust and undo its effect—in works of art, in political action, through education, and in one's own parenthood—enriches the lives of survivors' children and helps them to see themselves as part of the past, the present, and the future" (100). Spiegelman's own choice of addressing the Holocaust emerges through his collaboration with Vladek, when he dramatizes the transmission of the first generation's testimony to the second-generation listener. Yet throughout the two books, Spiegelman uses his words and pictures to demonstrate that his own need to hear the stories outweighs his father's need to tell them. At one point in *Maus II*, Spiegelman depicts where his interests lie (47). As Spiegelman listens to interview tapes with Vladek, he hears on the tape his anger and impatience with Vladek increase as the interview progresses. Over the course of these four panels, Spiegelman grows smaller and, in the final image, sighs in recognition of his obsessive need to hear about the Holocaust. His shrinking reduces him again to a child, emphasizing the connection between his need to hear and his status as a second-generation survivor; in effect, as his urgency to uncover the past becomes evident, so too does his generational relationship with that past. Here, too, we see how Spiegelman achieves a deeper meaning through the kind of visual acrobatics that are possible only in the comic book.

Spiegelman also uses visuals to define his relationship with Vladek and the Holocaust in ways that simultaneously unite and divide father and son. Spiegelman delivers a particularly pointed expression of this situation toward the end of *Maus I*, where Vladek tells Art of his and Anja's fate after escaping from the Ghetto. To lead into this story, Spiegelman uses a long panel where Art, on the far left, asks Vladek, on the far right, a question (see Figure 3.3). Spiegelman breaks this long panel in the "present" with a smaller frame—of Vladek and Anja—in the past. Visually, this frame serves the twin purposes of both linking and separating Art and Vladek, suggesting that the Holocaust serves a similar function. On the one hand, this history brings both father and son together; Spiegelman is talking to his father to find out about the past just as Vladek tells his stories because he wants to have Art around. On the other hand, this past also comes between the two, as evidenced by the tension in their relationship and the general anxiety Art feels about what his parents went through. At times, this anxiety explodes in startling ways, such as in the two moments when Art, incredibly, calls his par-

Figure 3.3. From *Maus I: A Survivor's Tale/My Father Bleeds History* by Art Spiegelman, copyright 1973, 1980, 1981, 1982, 1984, 1985, 1986 by Art Spiegelman. Used by permission of Pantheon Books, a division of Random House, Inc. In the United Kingdom, this image is used by permission of the Wylie Agency.

ents "murderers" (1986 103, 159). In light of what they have been through, these accusations seem grotesque. However, these moments also reveal the depth to which the Holocaust has scarred Spiegelman. He calls his mother a murderer for killing herself, and he calls Vladek a murderer for destroying his mother's journals—the journals being the only chance for Spiegelman to recover his mother's story. Both cases illustrate a frustrating lack of resolution for Spiegelman, both with the Holocaust and with his relationship with his parents.

Spiegelman uses this frustration to demonstrate his urgency to hear about the Holocaust, and in so doing he suggests a need that belongs to the post-Holocaust generation as a whole. In his illuminating analysis of *Maus*, Joseph Witek affirms that "Art has a psychological need to hear and render the truth" (114). He focuses his discussion on the insertion of Spiegelman's comic "Prisoner on the Hell Planet" into *Maus I*, maintaining that "the presence of this story . . . breaks the narrative flow of the Holocaust story and explains the emotional stake Art has in understanding his parents' lives" (98–100). This comic also provides a sharp visual counterpoint to the surrounding chapters that, in spite of employing an animal metaphor, are much more "realistic" than the highly expressionist woodcut style of "Prisoner on the Hell Planet." But what is most interesting about this short interlude is that Spiegelman asserts his status as a "child of the Holocaust" in every panel by depicting himself in the concentration camp uniform (102). Through such visual manipulation, Spiegelman layers additional meanings into his exploration of how his identity has been impacted by the Holocaust.

Specifically, this comic-within-a-comic makes us aware of the resentment and guilt Spiegelman feels toward his mother's suicide and his tension with his father. The comic also establishes that Spiegelman's need to hear these stories cannot be denied, and this urgency refocuses the testimony of his generation's literary—and literal—ancestors.[4] For just as Primo Levi and the first generation called upon their own experiences to emphasize the act of telling, so too does Spiegelman call upon his personal experience to emphasize the act of listening—an act that extends to all of us.

In addition to bridging the considerable gap between speaker and audience, Holocaust survivors who attempt to bear witness to that history's events are also confronted by the problem of memory. In an essay entitled "The Memory of the Offense" (1989), Levi explores what he calls the "marvelous but fallacious instrument" of memory (23). He argues that memory is our sole link to the past, but it is also an imperfect way to access that past, particularly when memories surface around personal trauma. He writes that "a person who has been wounded tends to block out the memory so as not to renew the pain" (24). In the case of many survivors, then, memory sometimes works against their intentions to retell their experiences. Levi is the rare survivor who is attuned to the limitations of memory—including his own. According to Levi, survivors may deliberately alter their memory, as in those cases when they "feel repugnance for things done or suffered" (1989 27); at other times, such alterations are not intentional but arise instead when survivors are unknowingly "influenced by information gained from later readings" (1989 19). Though the reasons behind memory's imperfections might vary, my point here is that personal narratives of this particular past are prone to spottiness.

In *Maus*, Spiegelman explores this theme in a way that expands upon Levi's prose by using comics' unique graphic language to illustrate (literally) this problem. At three separate points in *Maus*, Spiegelman uses a recurring graphic design to illustrate the tension between real occurrences and Vladek's memory of them. These instances all center on those parts of Vladek's testimony in which the exact happenings of certain events are not entirely known to him (1986 108; 1991 35, 50). In each of these excerpts, Spiegelman overlays Vladek's questionable memory with a visual "block"—a word balloon, a text box—that partially obscures the image. Thus, the reader is prevented from "witnessing" the event because Vladek's recall is questionable. The directness of this point is achievable only through the medium's combination of words and images. Typically in comics, these components work together to create a narrative; here, however, Spiegelman positions them against one another to illustrate how issues of memory are deeply imbedded in Holocaust writing.

As the previous points suggest, Holocaust writing is a very self-conscious literature in which the writer constantly doubts his or her abilities to adequately represent the events. That is, Holocaust memoirists tend to focus on the limits of language in representing their experiences. For example, in his essay "Torture" (1980), Jean Améry writes:

> It would be totally senseless to try and describe here the pain that was inflicted on me. Was it "like a red-hot iron in my shoulders," and was another "like a dull wooden stake that had been driven into the back of my head?" One comparison would only stand for the other, and in the end we would be hoaxed by turn on the hopeless merry-go-round of figurative speech. The pain was what it was. Beyond that there is nothing to say. Qualities of feeling are as incomparable as they are indescribable. They mark the limit of the capacity of language to communicate. (33)

Here, Améry's self-consciousness centers mainly on the inability of language to capture the essence of his ordeals. In this way, he is representative of the many Holocaust memoirists for whom the struggle to tell the story is as much a subject as the events of that story itself.

Spiegelman's own brand of self-consciousness is to undermine his attempts to recreate his father's Holocaust narrative.[5] Spiegelman questions his project most directly in those passages where he directly addresses the writing and drawing of *Maus*. Yet these moments do far more than simply play games with the reader; instead, Spiegelman uses them to raise important questions about the nature of his representation. The best example of this strategy comes toward the end of *Maus I*. Spiegelman is alone with Mala, his father's second wife and another Holocaust survivor, and he is explaining to her his concerns about his book. He says, "it's something that worries me about the book I'm doing about [Vladek] . . . in some ways he's just like the racist caricature of the miserly old Jew" (131). Later in this scene, Vladek appears and predicts that Art will one day be "famous like . . . Walt Disney" (133). In both cases, the conversation on one level calls attention to the process underlying the product in the reader's hands; on another level, however, Spiegelman uses this scene to open up a space in which we might question his representations. The first quotation allows us to see Vladek's representation as a stereotype, and the second calls to mind Mickey Mouse, which in turn highlights Spiegelman's own metaphor, which appears directly on the pages before us.

Highlighting artifice is a central component of Spiegelman's work and is also, as I discuss in Chapters One and Two, a defining feature of comics in general. Scott McCloud, in *Understanding Comics*, argues that comics uniquely explore the space between reality and representation because the visuals of any given comic operate primarily as icons. To illustrate this idea, McCloud reproduces, in the pages of his comic book, Magritte's famous painting *The Treachery of Images* (24–25). In the original painting, Magritte depicts a pipe with the caption, *"Ceci n'est pas une pipe"* ("This is not a pipe"). His point, of course, is that images are not the same as reality. In McCloud's version, we see that images become even more "removed" in the comic book because "a drawing is a translation" (Berger 93) and the narrative structure of comics repeats these translations.

In the specific case of *Maus*, Spiegelman constantly challenges his own project by raising questions about his animal metaphor. In so doing, Spiegelman shows an awareness that his books exist as representations and that looming behind his images is a larger, more imposing reality that can be approached only indirectly. At one point in *Maus I*, Vladek and Anja must hide out in a basement, where they encounter a rat (147). Spiegelman places a "realistic" drawing of this rat in a prominent position that, when seen in relation to his mouse characters, signals a breakdown in his metaphor (Spiegelman lecture). Later, when Art goes to see his psychiatrist, he calls attention to the numerous pets this man has and in an aside to the reader asks, "can I mention this or do I completely louse up my metaphor?" (1991 43). Spiegelman continues to highlight his artifice in the many scenes where characters wear animal masks that "draw attention to themselves as such, never inviting us to mistake memory of events for events themselves" (Young 1995 16). Spiegelman also foregrounds his metaphor at the beginning of *Maus II* when he and his wife discuss what kind of animal she should "be" (11–12).

Spiegelman exploits comics' innate self-reflexivity in order to explode his own metaphors, which he does not intend to be taken literally; in fact, his approach lays bare the dangers when such metaphors are taken literally. Perhaps the most important of these "breakdowns" of his metaphor comes through his positioning of family photographs amid the graphic illustrations in *Maus I* and *II*, a bold experimental move that derives its possibility and power from comics' graphic language. A total of four photographic images are used throughout these two books, all of which depict the "nuclear"

Spiegelman family. In *Maus I*, a photo of Anja and Art appears on the first page of "Prisoner on the Hell Planet" (100); in *Maus II*, there is a photo of Richieu on the dedication page (np); and there is a photo of Vladek toward the end of *Maus II* (134). All of these images—and especially the final one of Vladek—reconfirm the humanity of these characters by standing in sharp contrast to their illustrated representations as animals, and the photographs "bring into relief a tension that is always there, on every level of the text" (Hirsch 11). Vladek's picture reminds us, as we near the end, that these metaphors are only a device; the real power of the story lies not in the characters' outer symbolizations but in the humanity that lies beneath. Each of these moments is an example of Spiegelman's exploration of the comic book's unique potential to undermine the very possibility of "realistic" representation; his layered, mixed-media deconstruction of his own images reminds us that *Maus* is yet another construction of the Holocaust.[6]

But more than simply reminding us that *Maus* is a construction, Spiegelman also uses the unique features of the comic book to highlight—sometimes quite harshly—his own inadequacy as a narrator of this particular past. This self-doubt stems in no small part from the fact that Spiegelman has experienced the Holocaust only vicariously. His blunt self-examination comes through most pointedly in *Maus II*, at the beginning of the chapter entitled "Auschwitz (Time Flies)," where Spiegelman's self-criticism is at its most intense (41). He says, "At least fifteen foreign editions are coming out. I've gotten four serious offers to turn my book into a T.V. special or movie. (I don't wanna.) In May 1968 my mother killed herself. (She left no note.) Lately I've been feeling depressed" (41). Here, Spiegelman calls attention to the profit he has earned from this history, a situation that is visually represented by the depiction of himself sitting high atop a pile of corpses. The end line here, "Lately I've been feeling depressed," also betrays his exhaustion with the painful process and commercial implications of mining personal and public history. This moment reflects a similar emotion near the end of André Schwarz-Bart's Holocaust novel, *The Last of the Just*, when the narrator breaks into the narrative to pronounce, "I am so weary that my pen can no longer write" (370). In Rosenfeld's assessment of this moment, "this admission of the near-collapse of narrative power carries with it an honesty that is affecting and adds to rather than detracts from the veracity of the novel" (80). Schwarz-Bart's weariness here lies with the subject matter; for Spiegelman, his weariness is compounded by the possibility that he is profiting from such horror. Spiegelman does not spare himself; instead, he provides damning visuals in his frames—particularly the pile of corpses atop which he sits. Like Schwarz-Bart, Spiegelman affects a self-conscious level of honesty, but unlike Schwarz-Bart, he uses the comics medium to incriminate himself and his own position as narrator with a directness that would be impossible in prose alone.

Ultimately, Spiegelman questions not only his own project but also the idea of Holocaust representation in general. Theodor Adorno's contention that "writing poetry after Auschwitz is barbaric" implies that the Holocaust cannot be represented imaginatively because the aesthetics of such forms like poetry and fiction imply a possibility for pleasure—a feeling that should never be associated with mass murder. Spiegelman wrestles with this idea both in the above scenes and also in the conception of his project as a whole. He says at one point in *Maus II*, "I feel so inadequate trying to reconstruct a reality that was worse than my darkest dreams. And trying to do it as a comic strip! I guess I bit off more than I can chew. Maybe I ought to forget the whole thing. There's so much I'll never be able to understand or visualize. I mean, reality is too complex for comics . . . so much has to be left out or distorted" (II 16).

Spiegelman's blunt self-examination here adds a dimension to the books that calls attention to his metaphor and format. James Young argues for the value in this strategy when he writes, "by making the recovery of the story itself a visible part of *Maus*, Spiegelman can also hint darkly at the story not being recovered here, the ways that telling one story always leaves another untold, the ways common memory masks deep memory" (1998 682). Spiegelman makes that "recovery visible" through his chosen medium, which encourages readers to question the viability of any Holocaust representation. Holocaust scholar Lawrence Langer suggests that "the writer must record a reality that has become an expression of the impossible, [and] at the same time convinc[e] his audience that whatever distortions he employs do not negate but clarify reality and subject it to an illuminating metamorphosis" (1975 24). Spiegelman shows in *Maus* that comics are the ideal medium to achieve this feat. The inherent self-consciousness of the form is the means by which his "distortions" become a "truthful" representation of this history insofar as they communicate the inadequacy of any representational strategy.

All of these points serve to show how the comic book is capable of displaying unique complexity in its own version of one genre of Holocaust representation: the written memoir. But there is another genre of Holocaust representation that comics are particularly well-suited to redefine: photography. Theoretical explorations of photography are legion, and one of the most prolific critics of this form is John Berger. In *Another Way of Telling*, a collaborative work with photographer Jean Mohr, Berger begins his reflections by addressing the "problem" of photography. Part of this problem derives from Berger's belief that a good deal of a photograph's "meaning" is formed by the viewer, and such meanings become mutable given the spatial and psychic distance that might exist between the subject of the photo and the viewer. Berger writes, "the ambiguity of a photograph does not reside within the instant of the event photographed: there the photographic evidence is less ambiguous than any eye-witness account. . . . The ambiguity arises out of that discontinuity which gives rise to the second of the photograph's twin messages. (The abyss between the moment recorded and the moment of looking)" (88–89). This ambiguity is augmented by Berger's claim that "the truth [photographs] tell . . . is a limited one" (97); that is, they cannot tell a substantial part of the story behind that which they represent. Berger goes on to argue that certain photographs achieve a higher level of expressiveness by "turning . . . discontinuity to advantage" (128), whereby a viewer's piecing together the incomplete truth of a photograph becomes a marvelously expressive exercise. But such is not often the case with Holocaust photographs, where the "abyss" between the moment recorded and the moment of looking is so vast that silence tends to fill the void.

A point of clarification is necessary. "Holocaust photography" is a broad term, so for my purposes here, I focus on two types of photographs, which I wish to position more or less against one another: family photographs taken before the camps (such as those found in the Holocaust Memorial Museum in Washington, DC), and photos of atrocities taken within the camps. In her analysis of Holocaust photographs and *Maus*, Marianne Hirsch argues that Holocaust photographs illustrate what she calls "post-memory," which "is distinguished from memory by generational distance and from history by deep personal connections" (8). "Post-memory," in Hirsch's view, is "mediated by the processes of narration and imagination" (9) and is therefore partially constructed by the person who views a photograph. She maintains that photos taken of families before the camps, as well as photos of atrocities, provoke a sense of disbelief in the viewer that "brings home . . . the enormity of Holocaust destruction" (7). She goes on to argue that in both types of pictures "the viewer fills in what the picture leaves out: The horror of looking is not necessarily in the image but in the story we provide to fill in what is left out of the image" (7). Like Berger, Hirsch sees Holocaust photos as containing a potential expressiveness that becomes realized by their viewer's reflections. Hirsch's argument is persuasive, particularly as it pertains to family photos of the Holocaust.

One example supporting Hirsch's claims is Jeffrey Wolin's *Written in Memory: Portraits of the Holocaust* (1997). For this album, Wolin photographed and interviewed a number of Holocaust survivors, and what is most striking about this project is the way he presents his material. Each survivor is featured on a two-page layout: on the left side is a small pre-war photograph of the person, and on the right side is a full-page contemporary portrait of that same person. Filling the background of each large photograph is a short narrative of that survivor's experience, in his or her own words. By combining text and images, and by eliminating photographed atrocity completely, Wolin's photographs become an evocative, expressive entry into Holocaust history and confirm many of Hirsch's contentions about photography.

But where Hirsch's argument runs into a problem is in photographs of atrocity. With such images, there is little room for the stories of the victims to emerge, so graphic is the content. One example of this circumstance is the book *Auschwitz: A History in Photographs* (1993), a work that attempts to represent the camp that has become synonymous with the Holocaust. Although it begins with a short narrative, *Auschwitz* consists mainly of archival photographs that were taken by members of the Gestapo, resistance organizations, and liberating armies. The range of photographs is similarly wide and includes photos of maps, buildings, objects (glasses, hair, shoes), Nazi officials, family portraits, and, of course, various atrocities. In terms of number, this last group by no means dominates the book's other photos. The impact of these photos, however, is quite another matter. Depictions of emaciated bodies—both living and dead—ravaged by hunger, typhus, overwork, grisly medical experiments, and the myriad tortures inflicted upon them exist on a plane separate from the other photos and so command and repulse our attention that the subtle play of narrative and imagination argued for by Hirsch seems impossible here.

Photographs like these—when they overshadow other representations—pose a threat to our historical understanding of the Holocaust. In her book *On Photography* Susan Sontag discusses the proliferation of images in contemporary American culture, at one point observing that "photographed images do not seem to be statements about the world so much as pieces of it, miniatures of reality that anyone can make or acquire" (4). Her focus here is twofold. First, she argues that photography is a medium unlike any other because of its convenience and availability. Second, she argues that "images consume reality" (179) insofar as photographs carry a much greater weight than words in contemporary culture and often come to replace the subject photographed. In its worst incarnation, this phenomenon "turn[s] living beings into things, things into living beings" (98). Moving from these observations to the erosion of historical memory is a relatively short step. If photography does have the capacity to overwhelm and objectify the subject photographed, as Sontag believes, then images of atrocity create a distance between viewer and subject. Of course, such distance is necessary in Holocaust studies, for the gap of experience between those who suffered this history and those who study it is immense and needs to be respected. Yet the distance inherent in photography is different insofar as it forces us, however subtly, to see people as objects.

Undoubtedly, such photographs are a vital part of this history as they form part of its documentation. As Ilan Avisar writes, "since many of the Nazi atrocities were literally unbelievable, the photographic image has become an indispensable evidence of this awful past" (1988 4). What is more, as Mary Price argues in her contribution to photographic theory, *The Photograph: A Strange, Confined Place*, pictures of Holocaust atrocities need not shut off action; to emphasize this point, she cites how the proliferation of photographed atrocities of the Vietnam War and Ethiopian famine resulted in some positive political action (17–18).

In Price's argument, however, an important distinction needs to be recognized. Her examples focus on events in which the atrocities were more or less still taking place, thus allowing for some response to be made. In the case of Holocaust atrocities, the only action open to us is inquiry into the history during which these atrocities took place. And while Avisar's contention that photographic documentation is important, it is also true that this evidence, if overused, has the potential to overwhelm historical inquiry. James Young identifies this very possibility:

> Unfortunately, the unassimilable images of the wretched dead and survivors have become for many in America not only the sum of European Jewish civilization but also the sum of knowledge about the Holocaust and its survivors. Too often the point of departure for the "popular study" of the Holocaust begins and ends with these images alone, the unmitigated horror at the end of Jewish history in continental Europe, not the conditions of history, politics, culture, and mind—or the rich history of European Jewry—that preceded it. (1988 163)

Sontag, too, has voiced such concern, arguing that graphic images have a numbing effect, and not only because we become used to atrocities; in addition, we are repeatedly forced to become used to more and more graphic representations. As she writes, "photographs shock insofar as they show something novel. Unfortunately, the ante keeps getting raised—partly through the very proliferation of such images of horror" (19). Thus, photographs of the atrocities of the Holocaust are paradoxical; they are vital pieces of history that at the same time have the power to silence historical inquiry. This silence stems from the ability of photographs to distort the reality of human persecution. When we view a frozen moment of atrocity, the essential humanity of the people becomes lost, for the photographs dwell almost entirely on the physical, and we see only victims and corpses. In the end, we turn away from these images— and, by extension, from the history of which they form a part— because such images "so rivet a viewer's attention that the conditions and events that caused so many people to be murdered can be overlooked" (Barlow 1424).

Nevertheless, images depicting the physical persecution of the Jewish people are important to Holocaust history, for we must never forget—and here my cliché may be an example of the very reduction against which I am writing—"man's inhumanity to man." Spiegelman's most remarkable achievement with *Maus* is his use of comics' graphic language to transcend the limitations of Holocaust photography. As he demonstrates, the comic book in general and the animal metaphor in particular both reflect the importance of these images and revise them in ways that help recapture their vital role in historical understanding of the Holocaust. His revision suggests that images might be used creatively to emphasize the humanity and the stories of the victims rather than overwhelm these features, as realistic representations—especially of atrocity—are wont to do.

Such an emphasis becomes possible through the very nature of narrative in comics. When atrocity becomes a central subject, as it does in any survivor's tale, distance is needed. In many stories told by first generation Holocaust memoirists, this distance is provided through language: words depicting atrocities are far less silencing than their photographic counterparts because they do not provide a visual shock. What is more, the atrocities described in testimonies and autobiographies retain an element of humanity through the autobiographer's voice. With words, the reader controls the pace and emphasis of the reading; with pictures, the viewer is more or less assaulted by the image. Regarding the silencing impact of photographs, Sontag writes, "only that which narrates can make us understand" (23), and, as Spiegelman well knows, comics are an ideal medium for transforming images into narrative. More specifically, by mediating his images with the survivor's voice, Spiegelman controls our visual reaction to the realities of the Holocaust.

One example in particular is worth mentioning. In his essay "The Gray Zone," Primo Levi describes the importance of food in Auschwitz: "Even apart from the hard labor, the beatings, the cold, and the illnesses, the food ration was decisively insufficient for even the most frugal prisoner; the physiological reserves of the organism were consumed in two or three months, and death by hunger, or by diseases induced by hunger, was the prisoner's normal destiny, avoidable only with additional food" (40–41). As discussed earlier, the victims' suffering in the face of such conditions has been gradually replaced by graphic depictions of emaciated bodies, and the graphic realism of these photographs, in turn, repulses and silences the viewer, thus preventing any further connection with those depicted.

In *Maus II*, Spiegelman retells the conditions of which Levi speaks by incorporating drawn images that do not overwhelm but emphasize the story being told (see Figure 3.4). The central panels of this page depict the food line, but what navigates the reader through these images is Vladek's narration. Also, Spiegelman uses the visual dimension of comics to remind us continually that what we are seeing is a representation: the food line is framed by the drawings of father speaking to son, and the silhouette technique of these drawings stands out from the rest of the page, calling attention to the stylization of this particular sequence. In the final panel, Spiegelman complements Vladek's words "if you ate how they gave you, it was just enough to die more slowly" (49) with an image of a few prisoners dying in the background. Because comics are illustrated and therefore do not usually make claims to realistic representation (an even tougher claim to make when the characters are animals), Spiegelman is able to incorporate into his story the images of atrocity, but not at the expense of the story itself. The corpses are there, but they are clearly stand-ins for the reality that lies behind them because "cartoons . . . evoke rather than record the human form" (Doherty 74). Thus, the understatement of the corpses on this particular page, the fact that these corpses are illustrated, and Spiegelman's animal metaphor in general all ensure that his images of atrocity neither overwhelm the viewer nor provide the complete vision, as photographs might.

Throughout *Maus*, Spiegelman uses images of emaciated corpses to raise questions about the Holocaust rather than to silence discussion. The most powerful example of this strategy comes on a

Figure 3.4. From *Maus II: A Survivor's Tale/And Here My Troubles Began* by Art Spiegelman, copyright 1986, 1989, 1990, 1991 by Art Spiegelman. Used by permission of Pantheon Books, a division of Random House, Inc. In the United Kingdom, this image is used by permission of the Wylie Agency.

page discussed earlier, where Spiegelman struggles to complete his work after the death of his father (1991 41). The opening panels begin with Art making a series of increasingly startling juxtapositions: Vladek's death and a time when he was alive, Vladek's job in the camps and Art's "job" of writing about it, and a child's birth and a mass killing. These panels lead to the largest panel on the page, in which Spiegelman depicts himself atop a pile of corpses. What is important to note here is that the corpses are not presented as the "complete" image. Instead, they help emphasize the gulf between past and present, inviting the reader to reflect—as Spiegelman does—on how the two fail to be easily reconciled, if they are at all. Spiegelman also uses this panel to criticize the use of photography as a representational medium for this past. At the right edge of this panel, one of the press photographers shouts "alright Mr. Spiegelman . . . we're ready to shoot! . . . " (41). Here, the word "shoot"—a common photographic term—becomes startlingly reso- nant, reflecting Sontag's contention that "there is an aggression implicit in every use of the camera" (7). With the word balloon posi- tioned next to the bodies and below a guard tower framed by a win- dow, the statement creates an image of camera as weapon and sug- gests that a covert violence exists in the casual use of film to repre- sent graphic images.

Spiegelman's revision of realistic images is a move that Caryn James suggests is necessitated by the historical distance of the Holocaust. She writes that "for many artists, the passage of time has diminished the effectiveness of realism. . . . The farther the war recedes into the past, the more imagination is needed to wrench it into the present" (1, 14). While she effectively supports this state- ment with many examples of contemporary "reimaginings" and while she is perceptive in focusing on the images of the Holocaust, her comments must nonetheless be qualified, for given the direction she advocates, the reality of the Holocaust will eventually become dom- inated by imagination. A better guide for those who seek to recreate this particular past comes from Holocaust film scholar Ivan Alisar, who writes, "any truly creative and responsible treatment of the Holocaust cannot ignore the demanding moral aspects of the sub- ject, which call for a consideration of the enormity of the event and the limits of its representation, together with the imperative to remember, the necessary caution involved in what to remember, and the humility required when approaching how to remember" (1997 56). Spiegelman's work embodies these qualities, and he uses the conventions of the comic book both sensitively and self-consciously in order to preserve historical memory.

Spiegelman wrenches the stories from the past in ways that are attributable to the graphic language of the comic book, but many have balked at his decision to represent the Jews as mice and the Nazis as cats. However, this strategy is Spiegelman's boldest revision of Holocaust representations, for it brings a sense of newness to the story and "sidestep[s] the 'already-told' quality of the Holocaust" (Witek 103). Yet this "newness" is not simply novelty for novelty's sake; instead, Spiegelman's use of animals to represent people, his drawing style, and his arrangement of these images help establish, paradoxically, the humanity of his characters. That is, to draw a realistic representation of Auschwitz would attempt to bring popular reductive images to a medium in which "realism" is highly relative.[7] Comics' stock in trade is not, I would argue, "realism" but impressionism. Knowing this, Spiegelman employs a brilliant minimalist style, which is a prime example of what Scott McCloud terms "amplification through simplification," whereby the comic book artist "strip[s] down an image to its central 'meaning,' [and] amplif[ies] that meaning in a way that realistic art can't" (30). Spiegelman's realization of this idea is evident in the self-revision he performed on *Maus*, which originated as a three-page comic entitled "Maus" (1972).

In order to appreciate the visual differences between the two comics, we need look only at a single example (see figure 3.5). In the original comic, Spiegelman's style is much more detailed and provides many visual clues to the characters' expressions and feelings. Not only are the characters' eyes completely depicted with pupils and whites, but we can even see the individual hairs on their bodies. The result is that the panels become "crowded" with visual details that render the characters' emotions unambiguous. In *Maus*, by contrast, Spiegelman provides minimal facial details, and we are not overwhelmed by the image. As Witek points out, "even though the *Maus* panel is much less detailed, the experience of reading it is more dynamic and controlled than in the rather static 'Maus' version" (106). Also, the characters in "Maus" are more obviously mice, whereas in *Maus*, the openness of expression, achieved through the minimalist style, allows the reader to project more human qualities onto the characters. Spiegelman's approach in *Maus* is both radical and necessary given the extreme nature of the Holocaust; he so alters our conceptions of this history's representations that we are able to see those who endured that time period as people rather than as simply victims or corpses.

With each passing year the Holocaust recedes further into the past. With this recession, those events that seemed so unbelievable to those who experienced them will become even harder to call forth

Figure 3.5a. Copyright 1977 by Art Spiegelman, permission of the Wylie Agency.

Figure 3.5b. From *Maus I: A Survivor's Tale/My Father Bleeds History* by Art Spiegelman, copyright 1973, 1980, 1981, 1982, 1984, 1985, 1986 by Art Spiegelman. Used by permission of Pantheon Books, a division of Random House, Inc. In the United Kingdom, used by permission of the Wylie Agency.

and understand. Lawrence Langer captures the inevitability of this situation when he writes,

> When the dreadful history behind those puzzling words ["All of us walk around naked," from Borowski's *This Way for the Gas, Ladies and Gentlemen*] has fled from mental view, how will readers react to the news that in a place called Auschwitz (footnote), garments are being deloused (another footnote) with Cyclon B (yet another footnote), which kills lice in clothing—and humans in gas chambers (will that one day require a footnote, too)? (1995 235)

This situation is not helped by the fact that every year new distortions emerge, both intentional and not, either by groups using the Holocaust as a metaphor of persecution or by groups and individuals denying that it ever took place. And every year there emerges more and more writing about the Holocaust, and writing on writing about the Holocaust, and so forth. For better or worse, this chapter hardly stands as an exception to this circumstance. What this situation indicates is that the original desires of the survivors—to speak and to be heard—have been complicated by a sea of texts and images that vie for our attention as we find that our need to understand the Holocaust becomes more and more difficult to satisfy. In the face of these truths, Alvin Rosenfeld argues that "the lines that separate fact from fiction need to be scrupulously observed, therefore, lest the tendency to reject the Holocaust, already strong, be encouraged by reducing it altogether to the realm of the fictive" (161). In *Maus*, Spiegelman calls attention to this line, which exists not only between fact and fiction but also between reality and representation, and he does so by using a medium—the comic book—that is uniquely suited to raise these very questions. By demonstrating that they can be a powerful model for historical understanding of the Holocaust, Spiegelman makes a persuasive case for the literary value of comics. For in the end, he shows that comics' graphic language and its particular brand of self-consciousness are able to retain a firm and responsible connection to the voices of those who survived and the memories of those who did not.

Notes

1. In actuality, Spiegelman was not the first comic book artist to address the Holocaust. In March of 1955, a new comic book appeared on the newsstands. Its title was *Impact*, and it would be the first of several new titles launched by publisher Entertaining Comics (EC) in the wake of the anticomics hysteria that reached its pinnacle a year earlier with Senate subcommittee hearings and the creation of the Comics Code. Though at the time hopes remained high that *Impact* and the other books would revive the struggling company, whose main comics were gutted by the Comics Code, these books proved to be, commercially, the dying gasp of a once-great company. Artistically, however, these books are highly regarded by comics scholars. One artist and story in particular stand out: Bernie Krigstein's "Master Race," which appeared in *Impact* #1. This eight-page story tells the story of a man named Carl Reissman, who is plagued by his memories of Nazi Germany and the Holocaust. While riding on the subway, he recognizes a man from that time—a persecutor, the reader assumes—and the story plunges him into a nightmarish series of memories intercut with his running from this dark clad figure. In classic EC fashion, the story ends with a twist as we discover that Reissman was not a persecuted Jew but a Nazi commandant, and the mysterious figure chasing him was one of the survivors. The story is too complex to fully explicate in this space, but it does bear mentioning because of its mature and prophetic presentation of important themes and images of the Holocaust before they were a part of popular conception of that event. Of particular note are the idea of the "banality of evil" and the images of persecuted prisoners.

2. See Deborah Geis, *Considering Maus: Approaches to Art Spiegelman's "Survivor's Tale" of the Holocaust* (2003).

3. For somewhat different reasons, this need to present one's account in a consciously "unvarnished" way is shared by writers of other autobiographical genres, most notably the slave narratives. The quintessential example of this genre is Frederick Douglass's *Narrative of the Life of a Slave*, and in this work Douglass goes to great pains to establish that his descriptions of potentially incendiary incidents are being recollected in a measured, rational way. Douglass establishes a model for the slave narrator, where he takes great care in presenting his story and himself; in the case of slave narratives both story and narrator were delivered in the most restrained manner possible, for such restraint would illustrate objective and factual truth, on the one hand, and quell the fears of the narrator's largely white audience, on the other. As James Olney writes, "what is being recounted in the narratives is nearly always the realities of the institution of slavery, almost never the intellectual, emotional, moral growth of the narrator" (154). While the suppression of such growth is certainly not the case in Holocaust memoir, it is interesting to note the correspondence between the two genres in terms of establishing a documentary mode in the face of recreating atrocity.

4. Many of these urgencies and strategies are reflected in two other significant works about the second generation written by a child of Holocaust survivors: Helen Epstein's *Children of the Holocaust* (1979) and *Where She Came From: A Daughter's Search for Her Mother's History* (1992). The former title is a book

that is part memoir, part study of survivors and their children. Upon cursory examination, this book bears little resemblance to *Maus I* and *II* (as few books do), but on closer inspection it becomes clear that Epstein embarks on a quest that mirrors Spiegelman's. Psychologically, Epstein and Spiegelman are very similar; when she says that "I wondered what I could do in my life that would even register on the grand, heroic plain of the past" (1979 169), her sentiments find an echo in Spiegelman's own admission, to his therapist Pavel, that "no matter what I accomplish, it doesn't seem like much compared to surviving Auschwitz" (1991 44). Also like Spiegelman, she "bears witness" by delivering historical facts, such as when she overviews the plight of postwar survivors (1979 94–97), and by allowing those she interviews to tell their stories freely and without interruption. At the same time, we are given to understand that, like Spiegelman's books, Epstein's are also highly personal. She tells us, in Chapter One of *Children of the Holocaust*, that the book began with her recognition of a figurative "iron box" where she stored her connections with the Holocaust, a history that she, like Spiegelman, lived through her parents: "the box became a vault, collecting in darkness, always collecting, pictures, words, my parents' glances, becoming loaded with weight. It sank deeper as I grew older, so packed with undigested things that finally it became impossible to ignore" (13). Like Spiegelman, Epstein cannot separate her feelings toward the investigation of the past from that past itself. In fact, for the second generation, the two are inexorably intertwined. This realization is made most succinctly when, after talking with Rochelle, the daughter of a survivor and a woman with whom Epstein identifies heavily, she writes, "I typed with tears blurring my view of the paper on which I was transcribing her words, and I began to remember things I had never allowed myself to remember before" (1979 45). The latter title is even more closely related to Spiegelman's work insofar as it is a chronicle of Epstein's attempt to reconstruct the stories of her mother, grandmother, and great-grand-mother. In a particularly unguarded moment, Epstein reveals her investment in these stories, which finds echoes in Spiegelman's own work. She writes, about her obsession with recreating these narratives, "I sensed that for me, for my mother, and maybe for those other women in my family that I knew so little about, it had to do with warding off suicide" (1992 14).

5.   It is worth pointing out that Spiegelman has a rich history of deconstructing the medium of comics. Not only did he found *Raw* magazine—the periodical in which *Maus* was first serialized and which collected work by other comic book "deconstructionists" like Chris Ware, Richard McGuire, and Robert Sikoryak—but he also released a landmark collection of his own work, entitled *Breakdowns* (1977). In addition to containing the original, three-page "Maus" and "Prisoner on the Hell Planet"—both discussed earlier—*Breakdowns* also showcases a good deal of Spiegelman's earlier work that exposes the workings of the comic book. In "The Malpractice Suite," for example, the narrative operates on several levels. The text is repetitive, imitating the banalities of soap opera dialogue. Likewise, parts of the images Spiegelman creates—those contained in the smaller frames of each panel—copy a tradition of romantic comic book art from the 1950s to the 1970s. The originality of the piece lies outside of these smaller frames, where Spiegelman concocts bizarre, surrealistic scenes that surround the typical images. In this short, two-page comic, Spiegelman explores the territory that lies beyond the comic's borders in order to call attention to those borders themselves, even the ones that contain his strange images. In

terms of purpose, "The Malpractice Suite" lies closer to a metafictionalist like John Barth, who tends to see the deconstruction of language as an end in itself, than to a writer like E. L. Doctorow, who calls attention to his own fictionalizing in order to make statements more grounded in the world he represents. At best, "The Malpractice Suite" is playful and only raises some incidental questions about its artistic format.

6. In 1994 Spiegelman released another version of his *Maus* series: *The Complete Maus* on CD-ROM. Contained on this disc is a wide assortment of ancillary materials relating to both the Holocaust generally and *Maus* specifically, including a section that chronicles the making of a single page from *Maus*, excerpts from an interview with Spiegelman, related writing and comics by Spiegelman, various maps, a family tree, and transcripts of the interviews with Vladek. In adding this last feature, Spiegelman invites interested parties to recognize the extent to which he has reshaped Vladek's testimony, providing it with a more streamlined and imaginatively rendered narrative. At one point in *Maus I*, for example, Vladek retells of his time in the Polish Army, when he was captured by the Germans. In the transcripts, a portion of this episode reads as follows:

> And then—he took us to go back to left, to the left side. Water. And he said, we ha—we have to pick up here all German who are wounded, and to bring them over here. So the action started. But I, I knew around how it looks, and I knew where I was laying on the other side. And I knew where I was shooting, to the—to the tree, and the tree fell down, so I—I told them, "Oh, I think that here, I have noticed somebody laying" (I didn't notice yet). But when we were going there, closer, we have seen somebody is laying. So one of the-one-dis [inaudible] approached to him: "He is not alive anymore." And everybody had you see such a chain with his name, his name was Jan. And he said "Ausgeblutet," it means, he ran—his blood ran out, that he is dead. So we took him also, on the car. And still other ones, and—and I knew that I killed him. But I said "At least, I did something." (1994 The Reels: Part I)

As translated by Spiegelman, this episode has a much more dramatic and smoother presentation (50). The page begins with a large panel that quickly establishes the situation: the prisoners are to collect the wounded and dead Germans. However, much of the action described by Vladek—action that takes up the bulk of the transcript excerpt—is either excised or handled visually in the four standard-sized square panels. The most interesting change comes at the end of this brief narrative. Like the transcript, the page ends with Vladek's unsentimental reaction to the killing. Unlike the transcript, however, the page emphasizes the final part of the story with a long panel, the effect of which is to stretch out a timed sequence and call attention to that moment (Eisner 30). On the CD-ROM, Spiegelman makes clear his reshaping of the testimony by choosing and dramatizing key emotions and episodes from Vladek's words; in effect, he calls attention to the constructed nature of *Maus I* and *II*. Such revelations are made even more apparent in the central part of the CD-ROM—the reproduction of the complete text of *Maus I* and *II*—where viewers can move from page to page on the computer screen. The most interesting feature is that, on each page of the book, one or more panels are highlighted; when viewers click on these panels, they are allowed to see the background of the panel: early drafts, Vladek's spoken narration, research materials used, Spiegelman's recorded comments, film clips of Poland today, and the like. What this does, even more so than the book version of *Maus I* and *II*, is to demonstrate to the reader the constructed nature of these works. As viewers dissect the contents of *Maus* with the computer mouse (a coincidental pun that Spiegelman would appreciate), the representational features that Spiegelman employs cannot be ignored; the realities of the Holocaust loom larger than any recreation.

7. Two recent graphic novels about the Holocaust are good examples of this danger. On the one hand is Pascal Croci's *Auschwitz* (2002), which takes readers inside the infamous death camp. Given the fact that the book is illustrated, there is a certain level of unreality to its representational strategy. Nevertheless, Croci aims for a much more realistic visuals than does Spiegelman, and the effects weaken his vision. What is particularly noteworthy are the images of atrocity, handled so effectively in an understated manner by Spiegelman. In Croci's book, images of atrocity dominate the narrative, and this domination is a function not only of the relatively realistic illustration style but also of Croci's use of full-page panels to depict the corpses. A more effective approach is reflected by Joe Kubert's *Yossel: April 19, 1943* (2003). This graphic novel is written from the point of view of the titular character, a young boy in Warsaw during the time of the Warsaw Ghetto uprising. The format employs diary entries in text boxes surrounded by Yossel's sketches of what he sees. The illustrations are intentionally crude as they are meant to be seen as drawn hastily by someone in dire circumstances. This crudeness, however, functions in a similar fashion to Spiegelman's animal metaphor: it reminds us that the past is being mediated, that representations of the past are ever and always mediated for us. And in this way, *Yossel* achieves a level of self-knowing and sophistication that *Auschwitz* does not.

4.
THE "NEW JOURNALISM" REVISITED
Comic Books vs. Reportage

On September 25, 1965, *The New Yorker* ran a story that began, "The village of Holcomb stands on the high wheat plains of western Kansas, a lonesome area that other Kansans call 'out there'" (3). Despite the relative quietude depicted in this sentence, it would be difficult to overestimate the volatile impact that these words (and the piece as a whole) had on journalism philosophy and practice at the time and in the years that followed. The story was Truman Capote's *In Cold Blood*, which appeared in four weekly installments in *The New Yorker* during the fall of 1965 and then in book form the following year. Defining what its creator dubbed a new genre of literature— the "nonfiction novel"—*In Cold Blood* depicted the events surrounding four brutal murders and their aftermath in a small Kansas town. What set Capote's work apart from other then-contemporary works of journalism were carefully constructed scenes, engrossing characters, and structured suspense: in short, features more typically associated with page-turning novels. To encounter such elements in a work of reportage was, in the eyes of many readers, reviewers, and fellow writers of the time, nothing short of remarkable.

That same year, Tom Wolfe's *The Kandy-Kolored Tangerine-Flake Streamline Baby* also appeared and received similar reactions. Wolfe had been gaining attention for his work in the *New York Herald Tribune* and *Esquire*, and *Kandy-Kolored* collected the best examples of his journalistic pieces on contemporary culture. On the surface, Capote's and Wolfe's styles of writing could not be more dissimilar. *In Cold Blood* reads like a novel insofar as Capote becomes a largely invisible narrator who foreshadows tragedy and reveals the thoughts of a wide range of characters, some of whom he never met. By contrast, Wolfe's highly impressionistic and hyperkinetic narrative style establishes his presence as a conspicuous observer—and sometime participant—in virtually every scene he reports, whether he is shadowing a gambling junkie on a seventy-two-hour bender through the Las Vegas strip or milling about bouffant-hairdoed teens doing the "hully gully" at a customized auto show in Burbank, California. Despite these stylistic differences, however, what both writers shared was the desire to narrate real-life events and present people in ways designed to tell a truth that lay beyond the facts; like the best memoirs discussed in Chapter Two, the most important "truths" at stake were largely emotional. Taken together, Wolfe's and Capote's works signaled the arrival of a new brand of reportage that came to be known, sometimes contentiously, as the "New Journalism"—a poorly defined, catch-all term that nonetheless referred to "a fundamental shift in our understanding of what constitutes serious writing" (Webber 14). What this "shift" largely amounted to was a body of writing "that combine[d] fictional techniques with the detailed observations of journalism" (Hollowell 10).

In the process of "fictionalizing" the facts, the New Journalists called attention to the mediation that takes place in any journalistic enterprise; that is, far from being unfiltered, works of New Journalism forced readers to consider the idea that truth is never completely objective and that the facts alone do not necessarily reveal a given event in the most meaningful way. This position had strong political undercurrents, for the model of journalism that it attacked was often aligned with deepseated power structures: tradition-based corporate news organizations, the government, industry. Predictably, this radical position and the writers who embraced it generated much controversy. But a funny thing happened as the tumult of the late 1960s and early 1970s gave way to the increased conservatism and economic expansion of the 1980s and beyond: the once-radical philosophical features of New Journalism gradually became commonplace, proving that familiarity does not always breed contempt. In fact, in the case of New Journalistic devices, familiarity has bred an acceptance that has dampened their more radical implications. Walk into any Barnes and Noble today and you will find bookshelves overflowing with examples of what would at one time have been called New Journalism, but are now referred to as the more reader-friendly "creative" or "literary" nonfiction.[1] Like works of New Journalism, these books are highly personal and stylized accounts of real-life events and people; unlike works of New Journalism, many bear an "Oprah's Book Club" logo and contain "readers' guides" at the end of the text proper. Aside from savvy marketing, the main difference between these contemporary works of literary nonfiction and earlier works of New Journalism is their reception: the elements that once surprised readers and raised questions about how truth is communicated are now either ignored or used to sell more books.

Perhaps the general acceptance of radical elements is inevitable when those very elements become both exhausted and familiar. Exhaustion results when the limits of a medium—in this case, prose journalism—are reached, and writers can no longer "break the rules" in a fresh manner; familiarity results when a once-radical genre or style is absorbed into the mainstream and its "radical" elements proliferate and lose their power to surprise. Such has been the case with New Journalism. However, over the last fifteen years or so, another medium for journalism has emerged to reinvigorate the issues raised by the New Journalists: the comic book. In ever-increasing numbers, various comic book creators have produced reportage demonstrating the ability of this medium to expand and enrich the literature of journalism in general and of New Journalism in particular.

Comics journalists have taken full advantage of the graphic language of the medium to reanimate the most salient feature of New Journalism: the foregrounding of the individual perspective as an organizing consciousness. In addition, comics journalists achieve layers of meaning inaccessible to prose journalism alone because of comics' graphic language that blends words and images. What is more, like the New Journalists, comics journalists embrace a pointed anti-"official" and anticorporate attitude. However, unlike the absorption of New Journalism into the mainstream and the resulting dilution of its radical message, comics journalism retains, paradoxically, a powerful marginal status that will make it difficult for these works to ever be fully "co-opted." When one talks about the literature of journalism, works of comics journalism should be included, for they deliver stories and raise important issues of representation and truth in ways unavailable to strictly prose journalism, "New" or otherwise.

At the outset, New Journalism attracted both its champions and detractors. In addition to Capote and Wolfe, some other prominent writers attached to this movement were Gay Talese, Norman Mailer, Hunter S. Thompson, Joan Didion, Pete Hamill, George Plimpton, Gloria Steinem, and Michael Herr. While these writers' styles, subject matter, and critical reception differ, all were subjected, to varying degrees, to the two main criticisms of New Journalism: that it wasn't "new"[2] and that it could lead to reporting that was irrelevant at best and irresponsible at worst. Claims of irresponsibility arose mainly from the New Journalists' redefinition of "truth." More specifically, New Journalists suggested both implicitly and explicitly that objective truth was an illusion. Instead, these writers argued, the best reportage was actively constructed by the journalist's impressions, attitudes, and art.[3] Tom Wolfe, the unofficial spokesperson for this movement, called New Journalism "the use by people writing non-fiction of techniques which heretofore had been thought of as confined to the novel or to the short story" (quoted in Robinson 67).

As discussed in Chapter Two, this idea of the blurred line between factual and fictional representational strategies connects with a similar debate initiated by Hayden White about historians, and his views are relevant here as well. In his several studies of historiography, White examines how the role of the historian changed over time and that there is a long tradition of the historian using fictive devices as a means of retelling the past. White states that the writing of history was "prior to the French Revolution . . . regarded as a literary art . . . [for] the imagination no less than the reason had to be engaged in any adequate representation of the truth; and this meant that the techniques of fiction-making were . . . necessary to the composition of a historical discourse " (123). White's contention here is that the majority of historians in pre–French Revolution Europe retold the past through largely fictive means, for it was primarily through these means, they believed, that true historical understanding could emerge. Similarly, the New Journalists self-consciously employed elements of fiction-writing to retell actual events and created, in Wolfe's words, "a subjective reality that people had always gone to the novel for" (quoted in Robinson 67).

This idea that the facts alone provide a limited understanding of any event certainly came to widespread critical attention with Capote, who "fictionalizes" the facts to tell what he sees as a more significant truth. Thus, in the first part of *In Cold Blood*, "The Last to See Them Alive," Capote alternates sections between members of the doomed family (the Clutters) going about their daily business, and the itinerant killers (Perry Smith and Dick Hickock) as they make their way toward Holcomb, Kansas. The effect is riveting and meaningful due to Capote's suspenseful—and thoroughly engineered—crosscutting. For example, Capote ends one section with a scene in which Mr. Clutter greets five pheasant hunters on his property: "Then, touching the brim of his cap, he headed for home and the day's work, unaware that it would be his last" (13). Capote then begins the next with a description of Perry Smith, Mr. Clutter's future killer: "Like Mr. Clutter, the young man breakfasting in a café called the Little Jewel never drank coffee" (14). At work here are at least two literary devices: the foreshadowing at the end of the first section, and the link between Clutter and Smith at the beginning of the second section—a link that eventually takes on metaphorical weight as

Capote introduces a key theme about "two Americas," one privileged and hardworking, the other desperate and angry, that informs the entire book. Clearly, this structure does not magically "arise" from the facts; rather, it is built by Capote's artistic and thematic vision—both products of his imagination.

The difference between a purely fact-based truth and a more imaginatively rendered one is illustrated nicely by comparing two pieces about the Vietnam War: Peter Arnett's "Hill 875" (an AP wire report from November 22, 1967) and a section of Michael Herr's *Dispatches* (1977). Arnett's piece, though not without a certain flair, is an example of traditional war reportage in which he begins with an overview of the battle, provides numbers of casualties, recaps the main incidents in the battle, and then speaks with the participants themselves. This last feature is most telling in that it fails to reveal the soldiers in any meaningful way. Arnett writes, "D Company, hearing the roar of battle below it, returned to the crest of the hill and established a 50-yard perimeter 'because we figure we were surrounded by a regiment,' one officer said" (268). Here, the officer's quote is designed not to reveal the emotion of the battle but to convey information that could just as easily be delivered by Arnett himself. Even when commenting on the vagaries of war, the dialogue is flat and hollow, as evidenced by Arnett's quote of a young soldier commenting on the friendly fire death of thirty US paratroopers: "'A foul play of war,' said one survivor bitterly" (268).

The limitations of this approach are perhaps imperceptible if such stories are the only ones available. And in fact, Arnett's work is representative of the majority of print reportage from the Vietnam War. However, we are also fortunate to have the writing of Michael Herr, whose *Dispatches* not only presents a vastly different approach to war reporting but also criticizes the version of the war fed by the military to the official press corps, who in turn delivered that version in colorless prose. In Herr's famous estimation, "conventional journalism could no more reveal [the Vietnam] war than conventional firepower could win it" (218), and an example of his "unconventional" journalism comes in his own piece about Hill 875 that ignores all references to casualty numbers and instead focuses on the soldiers. *Dispatches* as a whole is often maddeningly—yet effectively—free of closure, and nowhere is this more apparent than in his chapter "Illumination Rounds," a series of twenty brief vignettes about the war. In the vignette on Hill 875, Herr presents a scene in which the survivors of the battle are greeted at the Dak To landing strip by inappropriately cheerful Red Cross girls. Herr writes,

the men from the 173rd just kept walking without answering, staring straight ahead, their eyes rimmed with red from fatigue, their
faces pinched and aged with all that had happened during the
night. One of them dropped out of line and said something to a
loud, fat girl who wore a Peanuts sweatshirt under her fatigue
blouse and she started to cry. The rest just walked past the girls
and the large, olive-drab coffee urns. They had no idea of where
they were. (169)

Though Herr is much more invisible in this piece than Arnett is in his,
he makes his presence clear by shaping the story into a dramatic
scene. Even more telling is the scene's message: Herr suggests that
the real story of war cannot be found in what we commonly regard
as important facts (dates, places, numbers of casualties); in fact, he
suggests that the real story of war cannot be communicated easily—
if at all—through language.

Traditional journalism like Peter Arnett's has long operated under
the assumption that real events could be reported objectively, that
the facts could unproblematically "speak for themselves," but the
New Journalists questioned the very possibility of objective truth. So
what accounted for the ideological shift among journalists in the mid-
1960s? In part, what led many away from traditional reportage was
the rapidly eroding authority of "official" versions of history, the
Vietnam War being but one example. This decade also bore witness
to the civil rights movement, various race and political riots, and several assassinations—all events in which conflicting points were of
view were played out in a developing mass media. More and more
during this time, journalism was seen as a field upon which power
was exercised, often in the name of "objectivity"; information—the
journalist's stock and trade—was regarded as a tool of control, and
therefore subject to abuse. As Jack Newfield argues, sometimes this
abuse comes when the journalist grips too tightly the idea of objectivity as his or her ultimate goal. He writes, "The point is not to equate
objectivity with truth. It was objective to quote Joe McCarthy during
the 1950s; it was the truth to report that most of what he had to say
was unfounded slander. . . . Truth is not the square root of two bal-
anced quotes. . . . Certain facts are not morally neutral" (64).

Rather than "hiding" behind objective—and seemingly authorless—prose, the New Journalists embraced their role of selecting,
transforming, and interpreting reality (Hellmann 4). Embracing this
role meant that these writers often flaunted their subjectivity, writing
about an event or people in terms of their perceptions. In the words
of journalist Janet Malcolm, "every work of nonfiction draws on art"

(154),[4] and the New Journalists, in the estimation of many (especially themselves), were just more honest about their role as artist. Accordingly, many of these writers appear in their works as "self-conscious and highly obtrusive narrators" (Hellmann 13). Thus, reading works of New Journalism was—and is—a layered experience as readers learn something about a particular event, but are also forced to consider how all works of journalism, regardless of presentation, are to some degree constructed by a "shaping consciousness" (Hellmann 15).

The ways in which this "shaping consciousness" is presented in New Journalism are as numerous as journalists, and the choices made by some writers often generated controversy. Consider, for example, this passage from Hunter S. Thompson's *Fear and Loathing: On the Campaign Trail '72*: "Wisconsin is the site of the next Democratic primary. Six serious candidates in this one—racing around the state in chartered jets, spending Ten Grand a day for the privilege of laying a series of terrible bummers on the natives. Dull speeches for breakfast, duller speeches for lunch, then bullshit with gravy for dinner" (125). What emerges in this passage is the distinctive and idiosyncratic voice of Thompson, who establishes his presence; that is, there is no mistaking that we are receiving a filtered perspective of the experience—and not the simple facts—of the Wisconsin Primary.[5] It is hardly surprising that this very feature was castigated by some critics who contended that these writers "sacrifice knowledge for a parading of personality" (Gold 284). In some cases this criticism is accurate, but it is also easy to disparage self-conscious writing in a field that had been too conservatively defined and practiced. It is also easy to miss one of the main points of the New Journalists: that all "truth" is mediated, and we ignore this fact at the expense of our critical faculties.

Like the New Journalists who no doubt inspired them, comics journalists foreground their role as reporter in the stories they cover. That comics journalists do this visually as well as textually makes comics journalism an even more powerful statement about mediation than was New Journalism, whose practitioners called attention to themselves strictly in terms of language. Obviously, language is a powerful tool to this end: it is impossible to read Norman Mailer, Tom Wolfe, or Hunter S. Thompson without recognizing that someone with a distinct personality and worldview is telling the story. Comics journalism builds on this use of language to foreground the author, but given the nature of the medium, it adds a visual component that always reminds the reader of the story's "shaping consciousness."

This reminder comes across in several ways. First, the visuals

Figure 4.1. Copyright Peter Bagge.
Image appears courtesy of Fantagraphics Books, Inc.

can be seen only as interpretive for the simple reason that they are drawn products of an author's hand. For example, in "The Second Coming of Alan Keyes" (2001), a story about the 2000 Republican primary race, comics journalist Peter Bagge employs his trademark hyperbolic artistic style that effectively reminds readers of the interpretive satire taking place in his coverage. One representative panel features a newswoman reporting that "the two candidates are duking it out" in the foreground, while in the background Bush and McCain fight, comic strip style (in a cloud of dust where #s and @s abound) and Keyes complains, "What about me?!" (see Figure 4.1). Bagge's style is classic satire in that he exaggerates emotions and physical attributes. One effect of such exaggeration is to communicate that the "truth" here is purely Bagge's; no one would mistake this image for anything other than a personal, stylized interpretation.

Similarly, Sue Coe's *Dead Meat* (1995), a graphic investigation into the meat industry, derives its power through her suggestive and highly interpretive illustrations. Though not technically a comic book, *Dead Meat* is a hybrid that nonetheless relies intensively on the combination of words (Coe's brief essays about the various dairies, chicken farms, and slaughterhouses that she visits) and images (Coe's sketchbook artwork depicting what she sees). The book opens with a personal memory in which Coe recounts growing up near a slaughterhouse and seeing, as a young child, three slaughterhouse workers give chase to an escaped pig. It is at this point Coe writes, "Maybe this was the first time I saw all was not well with the world" (40).

This reflection sets the tone for the book, in which Coe provides impressionistic drawings of the meat industry. Her written observations are shocking and her images even more so, for they boldly suggest the "humanity" of the animals and the inhumanity of their wardens. In one image entitled "Debeaking," Coe depicts the process by which the beaks of chickens are seared off to prevent them from pecking one another (see Figure 4.2). Coe provides us with two close-ups of debeaked chickens who, in her rendering, possess humanlike eyes that stare at the viewer. Meanwhile, in the center of the picture, is a heavily shaded "debeaker." His face is obscured—a detail that makes him less of a person to the viewer—and he very nearly blends into the inanimate objects of the background, unlike all of the chickens in the picture, which are bright white. As with Bagge's art, this image can only be seen as an artistic interpretation, thus reminding us visually that while *Dead Meat* is a powerful document, it is nonetheless mediated. In terms of their connection to New Journalism, Bagge and Coe are the visual equivalents of a Wolfe or Thompson in that their visions are seen most effectively as personal interpretations and not as objective representations. These two—who are emblematic of comics journalists in general—provide artistic renderings that stand in sharp contrast to photographs or traditional reportage, both of which are often presented (and read) as authorless.

Visuals in comics journalism also foreground the presence of the author when that author appears as a character in the story. These moments serve to remind readers "of the new journalist's shaping presence" (Hellmann 16), where the story is not simply about the "facts" but about how those facts were gathered, perceived, and presented. Kim Deitch, in "Ready to Die" (1999), presents the story of Ronald Fitzgerald, an accused murderer on Virginia's death row. Deitch covers the background of the crime, certainly, but he is more interested in the days leading up to Fitzgerald's execution. Over the story's six pages, Deitch depicts himself several times, but nowhere so tellingly as when he interviews the family of one of Fitzgerald's victims. In this panel, Deitch places himself on his knees in front of the parents, his arm holding a tape recorder in the faces of the parents, who are leaning back (149). Deitch places himself at the visual center of the panel, describing the moment as "the most uncomfortable" in his research. What is interesting about this self-depiction is the aggressiveness of Deitch's outstretched arm and the imposition suggested by the backward angle of the parents. Through these details, Deitch wants readers to apprehend his—and perhaps all reporters'—obtrusive presence in the stories they cover and write.

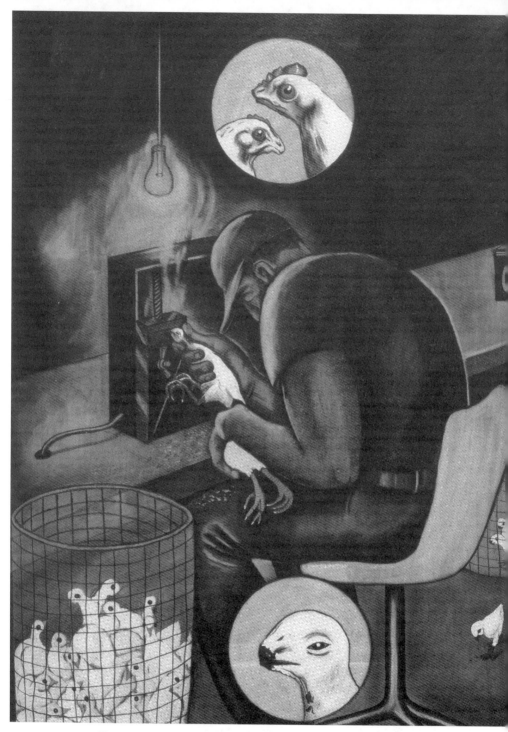

Figure 4.2. Sue Coe, *Debeaking*. Copyright 1990 Sue Coe.
Image appears courtesy of Galerie St. Etienne, New York.

Joe Sacco, whose works of comics journalism have garnered a great deal of critical praise, is also a master of foregrounding his own presence. His first major work, *Palestine*, was originally published as nine separate comic books in the early 1990s, collected into two graphic novel collections in 1994 and 1996, and then collected into a single volume in 2001. The book is a chronicle of several months that Sacco spent wandering through Palestine and Israel in 1991 and 1992, and most of the stories he retells are those of the Palestinians with whom he spends time and shares meals. Sacco's second major book, *Safe Area Gora□de* (2001), retells the Bosnian War through the eyes of the titular city's residents. As Sacco himself has said about his work, "It's very clear I'm subjective. I'm not trying to pretend I'm objective. . . . I didn't want to be objective and stay out of these stories because otherwise these stories would not be told" (quoted in Kauffman B7).

Throughout both books, Sacco foregrounds his role as reporter not simply through his presence but also through his artistic style. That is, Sacco draws himself in a much more cartoonish and exaggerated manner than the others around him, and this strategy causes him to stand out as someone who doesn't quite "fit" into this landscape or with its native inhabitants. Early on in *Gora□de*, for example, Sacco is describing his relationship with Edin, a native whom Sacco relies on as tour guide and translator. As Sacco waits—somewhat impatiently—to talk with a family, he depicts himself in much less realistic detail than the others in the panel. What is more, he gives himself the cartoonish "anger lines" usually employed in the far broader realm of the comic strip (see Figure 4.3). This style carries over from his earlier work, *Palestine*, where the first page of each chapter features a scene from the story where Sacco depicts himself in bold relief against a faded background. Both strategies visually emphasize Sacco's presence as an "intruding" agent in the lives of these people and serve to remind readers that he is filtering the events through his own unique perspective.[6]

Aside from their visual or linguistic style, comics journalists also foreground their presence through a comic's larger narrative style. In *Palestine*, Sacco employs different—sometimes radically so—styles for each of the book's different sections. In one section, for example, Sacco presents the narrative in the layout of a columned newspaper story with drawings instead of photographs (46), while in another he recreates the torture of a Palestinian, Ghassan, in sharp, claustrophobically paneled pages that contrast with the loose style of paneling elsewhere in the book (110). Both of these variations, as well as the others throughout Sacco's work, remind the reader that all of the

Figure 4.3. Copyright Joe Sacco.
Image appears courtesy of Fantagraphics Books, Inc.

stories employ narrative choices made by an author.

Another comics journalist, David Collier, also uses the overall structure of his work to remind readers of his shaping hand. Collier has created several works of comics journalism, but none as interesting as two stories about David Milgaard, a man who was wrongly convicted of a murder in Saskatchewan in 1969: "Saskatchewan '69" and "Milgaard and Me" (both 2001). The former story is a recreation of the events surrounding the murder, investigation, trial, and aftermath of the case in which Collier presents facts that clearly exonerate Milgaard; the latter story chronicles Collier's own frustrations in Sasketchewan and, obliquely, his discovery of the controversial murder case. What is unique about this pair of stories is that Collier presents them side by side so that all of the pages of "Saskatchewan '69" are on the left side of the book and all of the pages for "Milgaard and Me" are on the right side. As Collier helpfully informs us in his foreword, the stories can be read "concurrently or at the same time." However one chooses to read them, the point is clear: one cannot—and perhaps should not—separate the story from the teller. Both Collier and Sacco (as well as a host of other comics journalists) remind us that no news—whether it covers the Palestinian-Israeli conflict or a murder investigation and trial—arrives to us unfiltered; the news is composed of stories, and stories always have authors.

Comics journalists also use comics' graphic language to create layers of meaning that are unavailable in prose alone. The most obvious manner in which this deeper communication takes place is the visual detail. In fact, a small visual detail can often add a great deal of power to an author's point. In Ted Rall's *To Afghanistan and Back* (2002), for example, the author chronicles his travels to the Asian country just after the US bombing campaign commenced following the World Trade Center attacks of September 11, 2001. His book is a hybrid work in which he fuses prose memoir, the comic strip, and extended comic narrative. At the end of his comic narrative, Rall remembers another journalist's warning that covering Afghanistan was not a "game" (37). Reflecting on this remark, Rall concludes that the man was wrong, and he delivers this realization in a one-page panel where a simple detail shades his comment, "It was just a game," with ominous meaning (see Figure 4.4). The composition within the panel is angular and skewed; the visual lines of the walls, window, plants, and baseboard all lead down to the bottom right corner where Rall sits. The crucial detail is seen outside the window, as a barely discernable plane is flying to the left of two tall buildings. Taken out of context, this image could denote any cityscape that might contain an airplane and tall buildings. However, given Rall's larger narrative, this image immediately recalls the World Trade Center attacks. What is more, given the image of Rall in the lower corner—clean, civilian-attired, relaxed—this image suggests a chronological shift back to the event that propels Rall to travel to Afghanistan in the first place. The tragedy evoked in this simple image also acts as a counterpoint to the text. In the minds of the leaders who design foreign policy and order bombings that will never affect them directly, Rall suggests, it is a game, but for many others, it is a game with deadly consequences.

Joe Sacco also employs telling visual details that show how comics journalism can be more layered than prose journalism. In his comic "The War Crimes Trials" (1998), for example, he recounts the tribunal for war crimes committed during the Balkan wars. In two parallel panels, Sacco suggests the disconnect in time and space between the acts of atrocity and the later legal examination of these acts. Sacco gives us two tall panels that are meant to be "mirrors" of one another (see Figure 4.5). The panels bear a compositional symmetry, yet the details differ markedly. The first panel depicts Sacco's "present" (in the Netherlands during the tribunal), and the second depicts his "past" (in Bosnia writing about the war a few years earlier). The visual juxtapositions are alarming: the background building in the present promises comfort in the form of Heineken beer and a quaint hotel, while the background building in the past is a bombed-out shell; the vision of youth in the present is a healthy, trendily dressed young woman, while the vision of youth in the past is a young boy with a look of distress on his face; finally, the right side of

Figure 4.4. From *To Afghanistan and Back*, copyright 2002 Ted Rall, published by NBM, New York. Used with permission.

Figure 4.5. Copyright Joe Sacco. Originally appeared in *Details* magazine. Used with permission.

the panel depicting the present contains a girl enjoying an afternoon ride on her bicycle, while the same side on the facing panel contains a man carrying wood, an ax, and the weight of someone who has no time for the leisure of a bike ride. One can read these panels as a simple segue from present to past, but the pointed parallel and contrast in the details call attention to the gulf that exists between the two settings and suggests that they cannot be easily reconciled— even with legal proceedings, which do nothing to prevent the causes of the crimes that they attempt to punish. Sacco emphasizes this point in one of the final panels of the story where the words "Pronouncing the word genocide after the fact is a lot safer than stopping it" appears above a picture of a bulldozer burying several bodies (265). The words and image here work together to echo Sacco's earlier suggestion of our collective hypocrisy; that is, the safety of distance, be it measured in miles or years, does not absolve us from the responsibility of preventing injustice.

Sacco is not the sole practitioner of such visual subtlety. Sue Coe also uses telling visual details to emphasize her points. In two pieces she did for *The New Yorker*—"Sweatshop, 1994" (1994) and "Liverpool's Children" (1993)—Coe uses visual details to emphasize a particular mood or idea. "Sweatshop, 1994" is a story that emerged from Coe's "ride along" with three Department of Labor investigators on their rounds in New York's garment district (230). Early in the story, she quotes one of the investigators, Andy Chan, as saying, "The youngest garment worker I have seen was a ten-year-old floor worker in Chinatown" (230). Three pages later, in a depiction of a shop in which "the workers had not been paid in five weeks" (232), Coe draws a young Asian girl, half-hidden behind some dresses (233). Her image recalls Chan's earlier comment and, coupled with the unpaid workers, underscores the human rights violations that take place in the apparel industry.

Coe provides an even more chilling visual detail in "Liverpool's Children," a story in which she uses the killing of two-year-old James Bulger by two older boys as the impetus to examine life in Liverpool, one of England's poorest areas and the site of the killing. The overall visual strategy of the piece is arresting: Coe begins with a structured panel-by-panel depiction of Bulger's killing and the aftermath, but then the story adopts a more diffuse "sketchbook" style, filled with Coe's random comments and images of Liverpool, as if the devastation of the opening event makes a smooth narrative impossible. Even more jarring is the story's end, where the final page's central image of a sleeping child echoes the image of Bulger from the first page: head down, eyes obscured, brown matted hair, gray pallor (102, 107).

These visual echoes force the reader to consider that the environment in which children murder other children is due in part to unfeeling, anonymous governmental policy. This indictment of the government is evident elsewhere in the final panel by the dehumanized and dehumanizing half faces of government workers who peer callously at the unemployed individuals before them (107). Coe's work demonstrates how a comic's visual details create meanings that cannot be achieved by prose alone.

Manipulating the larger visual structure in a piece of comics journalism is another technique that reveals the possibilities of this medium. Art Speigelman's "A Jew in Rostock" (1992) is a short piece about the author's visit to the then newly unified Germany. At the time of his visit, tension between Romanian gypsies seeking asylum and the native Germans was escalating, and although Spiegelman is careful to delineate differences between Germany in the 1930s and in the 1990s, he nevertheless cites increased instances of neo-Nazi activity in the area (120–21). The comic consists of two sixteen-panel pages in which the backdrop throughout a majority of the panels is a building that was occupied by gypsy asylum-seekers and firebombed by neo-Nazis (120). Spiegelman uses this narrative and visual backdrop to build toward his final panel: an image of a brick wall, on which is spray painted a large swastika and, beneath it, the smaller words "Nazi Raus" ("Nazis get out"). This image appears above the panel's text, in which Spiegelman acknowledges that the situation is perhaps not "really serious . . . but it always rains where it's wet" (121). The conflict implied by the graffiti contradicts the idea that the antagonism among people in Rostock is a mere nuisance and not indicative of more dangerous feelings.

Spiegelman also uses other visual details to emphasize the progression from a seemingly "acceptable" situation to one that is truly dangerous. To pull this off, he takes advantage of how we read comics "dually"—one panel at a time in succession but also as an entire page—in order to gradually reveal small details that together form a large single image. For example, the four panels in the top left quadrant of the first page reveal a pleasant living space, complete with plants sunning on the porch balconies (120). The four panels in the bottom right corner of the second page tell a much different story in terms of details: those panels feature broken windows and the aforementioned graffiti (121). These panels are part of the same backdrop, however, and the image as a whole shows a harsh dichotomy between those who live "up above" in the building (the native residents) and those "down below" at street level (the gypsies). In terms of narrative progression, Spiegelman moves us through a situation that superficially might not appear serious, but that upon closer inspection contains deeper fissures. Certainly this meaning could be conveyed through prose, but not nearly as effectively as Spiegelman does here with his overall architecture of the page and his telling visual details.

All in all, what Speigelman delivers in "A Jew in Rostock" is a story that could not be told as effectively in another medium.[7] This point is also made by Carol Lay in "Pinups & Playmates" (1999), a piece that she did for Salon.com about the 1998 Los Angeles Glamourcon. Throughout the story's four pages, Lay examines and subtly criticizes America's visual culture generally and its fetishization of the female body specifically. The importance of visuals in her story is made apparent from the very opening, which features a long panel bordered on the left side by an image of the author hiding behind a placard bearing a "cheesecake" shot of a model and on the right side by a buxom blonde sporting a "Playboy" tee shirt (see Figure 4.6). The panel gives us, in essence, the dichotomy that Lay criticizes: the hyperidealized female body (represented by the blonde on the right) and the vast majority of "ordinary" women who are overshadowed by these images (represented by Lay on the left).

The dependence of Lay's message on her images continues throughout the piece. When Lay writes, "The rows of playmates put me off because they all looked alike" (see Figure 4.7), she underscores this comment with an image of four identical women—an effect that can be achieved only through illustration. Later in the story, Lay writes, "When I stepped into the ladies' room that evening, I was shocked to see that I wasn't blonde, slender, and beautiful" (3). Here, the image of Lay looking at herself in the mirror powerfully complements her words and theme. Not only do we see an "ordinary" woman, but we see that woman examining how she looks. This image, in effect, represents the often harmful process of physical self-scrutiny to which many women in this country subject themselves. To "see" this happening, as opposed to merely reading about it, adds a powerful dimension to Lay's story and her overall point.

In addition to exploiting the visual component of their medium, many comics journalists also embrace antiestablishment attitudes that can be traced back to the New Journalists. As a means to determine the motivation of the New Journalists, former Columbia journalism professor L. W. Robinson asked the question "What does one do when he finds out the world does not correspond to the world as described by authority?" (66). His question cuts to the heart of a key feature of this writing: its rejection of "official" narratives of real

Figure 4.6. Copyright 1999 Carol Lay. Used with permission.

Figure 4.7. Copyright
1999 Carol Lay.
Used with permission.

events because of those narratives' allegiance to government, corporations, or both. A good deal of New Journalism addresses this
skepticism indirectly, insofar as the writers address not "official"
views of events but instead work "to reveal the story hidden beneath
the surface facts" (Hollowell 23). Norman Mailer's *Miami and the
Siege of Chicago* (1968), for example, covers the same events as
conventional journalists: unruly young protesters causing violent
trouble at political events. Yet Mailer's approach is not to reconfirm
what has been reported in the mainstream media, but to deliver
another angle. His objective is revealed before the reader ever gets
to the narrative proper: the book's subtitle is "An *Informal History* of
the Republican and Democratic Conventions of 1968" (emphasis
mine). That Mailer succeeds in subverting the mainstream news is
suggested by critic Jay Jensen, who writes, "[Mailer] does give a picture of the conventions, both in Miami and Chicago, that one would
not find ordinarily in a newspaper or even a magazine, much less
radio or TV" (23). Similarly, Jack Newfield praises New Journalists
like "Studs Terkel, Robert Coles and Paul Cowan who are trying to
record history from the bottom, through the eyes of the average,
unfamous people, rather than through presidents" (61–62). Unlike
the mainstream media, New Journalism tells the stories of those
occupying society's margins.

In addition, many New Journalists disdain the "official" story by
being "openly critical of the powerful interests that control the dis-
semination of the news" (Hollowell 22). One of the most obvious
examples of such criticism is Herr's *Dispatches*. A good part of
Herr's criticism is captured in his richly metaphoric language, and
one passage, in which Herr describes the press briefings delivered
by the military to the news correspondents, is particularly evocative:
"Rounding Le Loi there was a large group of correspondents coming
back from the briefing, standard diurnal informational freak-o-rama,
Five O'Clock Follies, Jive at Five, war stories; at the corner they
broke formation and went to their offices to file, we watched them,
the wasted clocking the wasted" (36–37). Here, the subtle connection between the military and the press (the reporters "break formation") is given fuller space in the long chapter entitled "Colleagues."
In this chapter, Herr examines what it means to be a journalist by
contrasting the work being done by him and other likeminded
reporters with the work being done by more "traditional" war correspondents. Herr suggests that any "truth" delivered by the mainstream press was severely compromised because these individuals
"worked in the news media, for organizations that were ultimately
reverential toward the institutions involved: the Office of the

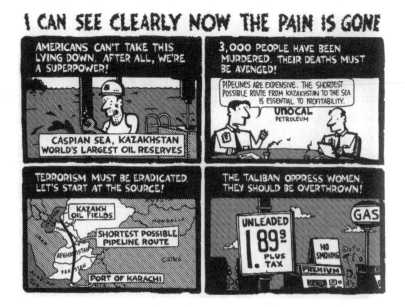

Figure 4.8. From *To Afghanistan and Back*, copyright 2002 Ted Rall, published by NBM, New York. Used with permission.

President, the Military, America at war, and, most of all, the empty technology that characterized Vietnam" (214).

In our current era, when corporate conglomerates like General Electric, Viacom, Rupert Murdoch's News Corp, and AOL/Time-Warner own an evergrowing number of media outlets, the need for diversity in the mainstream news is even greater than when Herr was reporting. What gives Herr's criticism its sharp edge is that he goes further to identify why the work being done by traditional correspondents is dangerous, why a truth that goes beyond the "official" version does matter:

> The press . . . never found a way to report meaningfully about death, which of course was really what it was all about. The most repulsive, transparent gropes for sanctity in the midst of the killing received serious treatment in the papers and on the air. The jargon of Progress got blown into your head like bullets, and by the time you waded through all the Washington stories and all the Saigon stories, all the Other War stories and the corruption stories and the stories about brisk new gains in ARVN effectiveness, the suffering was somehow unimpressive. (215)

Herr suggests here that the "official" vision of things is an inhuman one; such a vision sacrifices the humanity of those who suffer for a version of events that simply justifies military policy.

Herr and Mailer are but two examples of how the work of the New Journalists was radical in both style and content. Comics journalism continues in this same vein, attacking governmental and corporate views of political events. Throughout *To Afghanistan and Back*, for example, Rall makes clear his belief that economic gains underlie America's flexing of its military might. Early in the book he includes the piece "I Can See Clearly Now the Pain Is Gone," a four-panel strip in which he exploits comics' unique blending of word and image to illustrate the conflict between the "official" and "secret" stories (see Figure 4.8). In each panel, the text on the top represents the popular rhetoric surrounding the American bombing of Afghanistan. These text boxes deliver platitudes like "3,000 people have been murdered. Their deaths must be avenged!" and "The Taliban oppress women. They should be overthrown!" What deflates these proclamations is the visual narrative, which suggests that invading Afghanistan is motivated by the desire on the part of American petroleum interests to move oil from the Caspian Sea to the Port of Karachi in the most direct (i.e., profitable) manner possible.

In another four-panel strip, Rall evokes Herr more directly as he satirizes the emptiness of the mainstream news (28). The first three panels of this strip depict an anchorman who delivers absolutely no information about the war, saying things like, "Today in the war, some stuff happened. They're not saying what, but whatever it was may or may not have been a big deal." Rall's point is that one could watch any of the major media outlets and still not have any idea about what is going on. Or more precisely, one would know only what the government or media corporations want people to know. The import of this situation is contained in Rall's final panel, where one man voices an uninformed objection to the war ("Bush's war is stupid") only to be criticized by his friend, who replies, "How can you be against something you don't know anything about?" The implication is that if most people digest only what is served up by the mainstream press—which is what tends to happen, given that alternative news media in general and comics in particular are seen as disreputable—then the rhetoric of opposition is severely limited and therefore contained. Yet working against such containment are Rall's strips, which qualify as personal, idiosyncratic visions of a journalist who has researched and experienced the events at hand.

Another comics journalist whose work echoes the anticorporate stance of the New Journalists is Sue Coe, whose power lies primarily in her bleakly visceral, impressionistic drawings. In her 1983 collaboration with Holly Metz, *How to Commit Suicide in South Africa*, she takes on apartheid and the struggles of oppressed blacks in South Africa. The book, whose title refers ironically to the frequency with which black South Africans die in custody, ends with a chapter entitled "Free World," where Coe and Metz put the blame for apartheid's endurance and human rights violations squarely on the shoulders of American corporate interests, going so far as to list companies with investments and/or loan interests in South Africa (40). The book ends with a visual suggestion of the racist link that exists between South Africa and the US, and that at its root lies money. The closing visual image is of a heavily shaded urban street corner, and in the lower right corner of this scene, Coe writes, "Harlem U$A Soweto $A" (42). More recently, in *Dead Meat*, Sue Coe never fails to connect inhumanity to corporate interests—especially large meat industry corporations like Farmer John's (86) and McDonald's (64). Both depictions are decidedly anticorporate: the former image draws striking visual parallels between the Farmer John's stockyard and a concentration camp (barbed wire, smoking chimney) while the latter depicts the McDonald's logo on an imposing branding iron being held ominously by an unseen hand.

But perhaps the comics journalist who has most effectively carried on the New Journalists' torch of undermining the "official" story is Joe Sacco, whose books *Palestine* and *Safe Area Gora☐de* report those conflicts through the eyes of the Muslims in those locations—the people whose stories are "underrepresented in the mainstream American press and television" (Hajdu 2). Sacco's exploration of the danger with an "official" version is most pointed in "Getting the Story," from Chapter Five of *Palestine*. In this section, Sacco gets wind of an incident in Hebron the day before, during which a conflict with Jewish settlers led to the shooting of four Palestinians. Intrigued, Sacco pursues the story and interviews several people who witnessed the incident. After several false starts and diversions—valuable pages in which Sacco reminds us that behind every polished published story lies a lot more material that journalists and their editors discard—he finally finds his eyewitness to the previous day's shooting. The man tells Sacco what happened in Hebron:

> [The Jewish settlers] attacked homes and caused damage. They threw stones at the windows . . . women and children began screaming, calling for help. People came and began throwing stones at them, and the settlers began shooting in all directions. One of [the four Palestinians] injured was trying to close his shop. He was trying to get his things inside. The people wounded were passing by, not the ones throwing stones. (132)

Sacco illustrates the man's account in the top half of the page; on the bottom half, Sacco posts a clipping that appeared in "the Israeli English-language daily" and gives what he describes as "a different slant" (see Figure 4.9). The story's lead reads, "A group of Jewish families, members of the Kach-affiliated Committee for Safety on the Roads, were patrolling in the Harat a-Sheikh section of Hebron, when they were attacked by several hundred Arabs. They said they were pelted with rocks and bottles from rooftops and alleys." Sacco juxtaposes his graphic narrative and this mainstream press narrative in order to suggest that the "truth" of any matter is subject to a variety of factors.

However, Sacco clearly undercuts the "official" view by visually depicting the Palestinian version, complete with details that include a stone-throwing Israeli with a homicidal look on his face and an unseen Israeli gunman shooting an unarmed Palestinian. In addition, a key panel contains the man who witnessed the event. He says, "The soldiers came to protect the settlers." Tellingly, Sacco depicts the man in a close-up, his eyes locked with the reader's. The man's words—but more important, the image of him looking the reader in the eye—effectively undermine the version of events as they are impassively rendered in the *Jerusalem Post* at the bottom of the page.

Taken as a whole, the anti-"official" and anticorporate attitudes that define so much of comics journalism are the legacy of New Journalism—perhaps its most important legacy, for these attitudes pose a central yet often unasked question about truth: "Who creates it and why?" But there is a danger in attracting attention on the margins. Specifically, a marginal yet increasingly popular movement runs the risk of being co-opted by the mainstream, and when that happens, the movement's power is diluted. In the case of prose New Journalism, such an absorption and "naturalization" of radical elements is exactly what happened: contemporary works of literary nonfiction retain stylistic traces of New Journalism, yet the vast majority of reviews either ignores completely or openly praises features that at one time generated fierce debate over their implications concerning truth and how it is communicated.

One such case is evident in Jon Krakauer's *Into the Wild*, a book in which he investigates the death of Chris McCandless, a young man who cut himself off from his family and material comforts in order to wander the country alone. In *The New York Times*, a book reviewer writes, "In Mr. Krakauer's eloquent handling, this [story] is not merely sad. Because the story involves overbearing pride, a reversal of fortune, and a final moment of recognition, it has elements of classic tragedy. By the end, Mr. Krakauer has taken the tale of a kook who went into the woods, and made of it a heart-rending drama of human yearning" (Lehmann-Haupt 1996 C17). Here, the

Figure 4.9. Copyright Joe Sacco.
Image courtesy of Fantagraphics Books, Inc.

reviewer does not hesitate to praise Krakauer's ability to "transform" the facts into a more meaningful vision. Thirty years earlier, such a transformation on the part of a journalist created a firestorm of debate on the nature of truth and objectivity.[8]

More examples of praise abound for journalists who present truth subjectively. One example is the critical response enjoyed by John Berendt's *Midnight in the Garden of Good and Evil* (1994), a book in which he examines the eccentric denizens of Savannah, Georgia. A reviewer for *Booklist* specifically congratulates the experiential nature of Berendt's "truth." She writes of the book that "its plot centers on murder, but Berendt takes his sweet time getting around to that fact, allowing the reader to be as surprised as he must have been watching the events unfold" (Schoolman 414). Here, the very fact that the journalist delivers the story through his own eyes and not "objectively" is lauded. This attitude also informs reviews of Susan Orlean's *The Orchid Thief* (1998), an investigation into exotic flower poaching in Florida. One reviewer writes, "If her narrative has a flaw, it lies in its occasional tendency to report certain events and conversations too deadpan, as if it were self evident why Ms. Orlean found them whatever way she found them. This makes for a few tedious stretches. But most of the time she lets the reader know exactly what she was feeling" (Lehmann-Haupt 1999 E8). Amazingly, the reviewer sees the book's strength as lying in the journalist's impressions of the events she witnesses and describes. While this may very well be the book's strength, what is important to note here is how thoroughly the once-radical features of New Journalism have been adopted into the mainstream. Such books are no longer seen as raising controversial issues about how truth is communicated; instead, these journalists' blending of imagination and fact is a pathway to something far more market-friendly: titles that are "solidly rewarding read[s]" (Schoolman 414).

In his collection of interviews entitled *The New New Journalism* (2005),[9] Robert Boyton declares that the current crop of writers authoring literary nonfiction represents an "evolution" of the New Journalists (xi). His argument is that these writers' "most significant innovations have involved experiments with reporting" (xiii), and he cites examples like Ted Conover, who became a guard in order to report on prisons in *Newjack* (2000) and Adrian Nicole LeBlanc, who spent ten years reporting on a group of residents in a rundown Bronx neighborhood in *Random Family* (2003). He might have also added Barbara Ehrenreich, who took a series of minimum-wage jobs in order to see if it was possible to eke out a reasonable existence in America (her conclusion: it isn't) and reported her story in *Nickel and*

Dimed (2001). With this point of Boyton's I have no problem; I am fully in agreement that the work being done today under the banner of literary nonfiction is among the best that writing has to offer, and that a good deal of it is political and speaks for the disenfranchised—the above titles being but three examples. In fact, my choice of journalism as this chapter's focus is indicative of my belief that such writing constitutes an important form of literature.

But I disagree with Boyton's contention that "the days in which nonfiction writers test the limits of language and form have largely passed" (xii) and that "debates over 'journalism' and 'literature'—between 'subjective' and 'objective' reporting—weigh less heavily on this generation" (xxx). In these days, when corporate conglomerates own the mainstream media, when technological innovations like photograph editing software and computer generated images reign, when "creative" writers and reporters continue to mix the real with the invented, "parsing the philosophical line between fact and fiction" (xii) is not simply a passé diversion. It is more crucial than ever. And the point that I wish to make in discussing the "new new journalists" working today is that their readers, by and large, do not recognize those elements of their work that ask us to question "objective" truth.

New Journalism was a radical idea in its time, and while its aim of examining "truth" may have faded over the years with the rise in mainstream popularity of literary nonfiction, such a fate seems unlikely for comics because of their "disreputable" status. Joe Sacco has commented that he likes to give people copies of his comics to read because there is something subversive about them; the recipients do not expect much from the comics, but they are soon caught offguard by their content and power (Sacco lecture). Similarly, a key reason that Sue Coe was given such unlimited access to various companies' operations in her research for *Dead Meat* was that she did not carry a camera; her pencil and sketchpad were considered "harmless" ("Commitment to the Struggle"). Both Sacco's comments and Coe's experiences accurately capture the widespread perception of the medium: most people classify comics as "kids' stuff," and despite attempts on several fronts—including this book—to change such attitudes,[10] comics will most likely maintain their "outsider" status.

While many of us comic book boosters lament this situation, it is also possible to see a power in such marginality. Like the unruly children that most people imagine are the medium's sole readership, comic books refuse to be easily disciplined. That is, so long as comics in general and comics journalism in particular are left on the margins of literature, they may continue to surprise readers and level powerful criticisms against corporate interests, including the mainstream media. More important, they may provoke us to think about the constructed nature of truth in all forms of journalism. The fact that most people will always see a contradiction between a "juvenile" medium and "adult" content is enough to ensure that comics journalists will be free to be as radical as they wish. In "A Jew in Rostock," Art Spiegelman includes a quote from German cartoonist Wilhelm Busch that certainly summarizes the position—and possibility—of comics journalism: "Once your reputation's shot, you can get away with quite a lot."

Notes

1. The debate over the taxonomy of journalism has been a lively one, as evidenced by this passage from Barbara Lounsberry's *The Art of Fact*:

> What label might be applied to these writers' enterprises? Terms like the French *reportage*, "journalit," or the "new" or "high" journalism seem too narrow, given the reach of much work beyond reporting or journalism. Other names, like Dwight Macdonald's "parajournalism," are merely pejorative. Phrases highlighting the "hybrid" nature of the form, its application of narrative techniques often associated with fiction to nonfictional subject matter, seem somewhat better. However, Truman Capote's "nonfiction novel" or Norman Mailer's "true life novel," tip the scales towards the fictive side of the equation. "Faction," Alex Haley's term, avoids this problem, but it has not caught on. (xii)

   More recently, John Hartsock has argued that the multitude of names used to denote this particular literature is, in part, indicative of a larger narrative concerning how and why this genre is named by the various literary communities that seek to discuss it (433). Hartsock may make what he will of my study and the literary "faction" it represents; for purposes of ease and clarity in my discussion and because it is important for my argument that I delineate between at least two distinct periods in this literature, I will refer to the initial, radical presence of this writing as "New Journalism," and to the later, New Journalism–influenced works as "literary nonfiction." At the same time, I will acknowledge the basic truth of Hartsock's work, which is that naming is never innocent but always hints at some larger purpose or relationship.

2. The most cogent and exhaustive examination of this idea comes from Michael J. Arlen, who outlines in his "Notes on the New Journalism" the literary and journalistic tradition that has displayed the so-called "new" features of new journalism long before the 1960s. In particular, he acknowledges that there has "been a vein of personal journalism in English and American writing for a very long time" (245). The writers and works most often cited are Daniel Defoe for *Journal of the Plague Year* (1722), George Orwell for *Homage to Catalonia* (1938), and Mark Twain for his newspaper and magazine journalism from 1851 to 1871. *Journal of the Plague Year* comes up because of the elaborate "hoax" that Defoe plays upon his readers: he delivers a journal that purports firsthand observation and experience of events (the Plague in Europe) when in fact the writer was only five years old during that time; thus, Defoe employs fictive devices to recreate actual events, much like Capote in *In Cold Blood*. Somewhat similarly, Orwell employs devices such as characterization and scene construction—two strategies heralded later by New Journalists and those who praised their work—in *Homage to Catalonia*, which blurs the distinction between the various genres of memoir, history, and journalism. Finally, Twain's journalistic writing often undermined the illusion that reportage must maintain a strictly "objective" and "distant" perspective—a key "breakthrough" later claimed by the New Journalists. Twain whittled away at this illusion through his wry, humorous interjections, perhaps best captured in his story "No Earthquake," which ran in the San Francisco *Daily Morning Call* on August 23, 1864. The story describes the anticlimactic disappointment felt by San Franciscans when a predicted earth-

quake failed to arrive. Twain writes that the city's denizens "suffer when they have to go without it . . . we know of nothing that will answer as a substitute for one of those convulsions—to an unmarried man" (1).

3. Clearly, the attitude that journalistic "truth" is constructed is subject to abuse. In fact, there have been many examples of what happens when journalists take liberties with truth in their work, Jayson Blair's fabrications of scenes and interviews in *The New York Times* being a recent example (Kurtz A1).

4. The book in which Malcolm makes this assertion, *The Journalist and the Murderer* (1990), is in fact a highly critical analysis of the unhealthy relationship between the journalist and his or her subject. She investigates the conflicting narratives that characterize any journalistic endeavor by examining a lawsuit in which convicted murderer Jeffrey MacDonald sued author Joe McGinniss for libel. She writes, about the position of any person whose story is told by a journalist, "On reading the article or book in question, he has to face the fact that the journalist—who seemed so friendly and sympathetic, so keen to understand him fully, so remarkably attuned to his vision of things—never had the slightest intention of collaborating with him on his story but always intended to write a story of his own" (3). Clearly, Malcolm's cynicism about this relationship is readily apparent, but what is most arresting about her assessment is the assumption that there is no single "truth" waiting to be uncovered about a given event; rather, meaning is achieved (or muddied, as is more often the case) by the multitude of stories surrounding that event. Thus, the product of the journalist is not "the" story but "his" (or "her") story.

5. Thompson is a writer whose work spans the gamut from the best to the worst of New Journalism. He is also a writer who injects so much of his personality and personal life into his writing that he has become a celebrity. In the comic book world, Thompson's iconographic status has been cemented in Warren Ellis's brilliant series *Transmetropolitan* (1997–2002), which focuses on a journalist named Spider Jerusalem who, through both physical resemblance and demeanor, is a clear homage to Thompson.

6. In addition to his artistic style, Sacco's text is every bit as stylized as classic New Journalists. In several instances in *Palestine* and his other works, Sacco's writing style is reminiscent of Michael Herr's *Dispatches*: a hip, simile- and metaphor-rich riff on events and observations. Herr writes, for example, about life after the Vietnam War: "Home: twenty-eight years old, feeling like Rip Van Winkle, with a heart like one of those little paper pills they make in China, you drop them into water and they open out to form a tiger or a flower or a pagoda. Mine opened out into war and loss" (250). In "Christmas with Karadzic" (1997), Sacco writes, "Admittedly, the picture of Bosnia's rebel Serbs didn't look too good in those days . . . it looked like fucking hell, if you want to know the truth, like that thing locked away in Dorian Gray's attic, degenerating through successive layers of ugliness with each new outrage . . . but, anyway, we hadn't come to help Dragan pull off an 11th-hour makeover" (5). John Hollowell, in *Fact and Fiction: The New Journalism and the Nonfiction Novel*, argues that "the voice of the new journalist is frankly subjective; it bears the stamp of his personality" (22). Herr and Sacco are ample proof of Hollowell's assertion, for both writers' language reveals their own characters and reminds readers of the impressionistic nature of journalism in general.

7. Spiegelman makes this exact same point—that the comics medium is uniquely suited to tell certain stories—in his "WORDS, Worth a Thousand," a profile of the New York Public Library's Picture Collection and the man who runs it, senior librarian Arthur Williams. Spiegelman intersperses real photographs among his comic book panels throughout the story to achieve a powerful "layering" effect that visually demonstrates the richness of the collection. Because so much in this particular story depends on the visuals, a purely prose piece of journalism would not be able to capture the essence of the topic here. Even the piece's title—a reference to pictures—underscores the value of the visual.

8. There are several ties to New Journalism in this particular book, which not incidentally happens to be excellent. In addition to the "literary transformation" Krakauer achieves, he also calls attention to himself as the subjective "shaping consciousness" of the narrative. Though *Into the Wild* is ostensibly focused on McCandless, Krakauer includes analogous examples of young bravado, including two chapters in which the author recounts his own reckless adventures as a directionless twenty-three-year-old who went on a dangerous solo climb in Alaska and almost died. Throughout this section, Krakauer draws several parallels between himself and McCandless, including their age, literary interests, penchant for dangerous activities, isolation from others, and estrangement from their fathers (134–35). What this lengthy interlude achieves (aside from convincing readers of the utter insanity of mountain climbing) is to establish Krakauer's close emotional ties to McCandless and his story. With these chapters, then, Krakauer completely destroys any possibility of being viewed as an "objective" journalist, a point he emphasizes at the outset, when he writes in his "Author's Note" that he "won't claim to be an impartial biographer"—or journalist, we may assume. Given his past, Krakauer is emotionally invested in making meaning out of McCandless's story, a point completely ignored by the vast majority of the book's reviewers.

9. When I first wrote this chapter in the fall of 2003, its original title was "The New New Journalism." I congratulated myself on the cleverness of this title and tucked everything away to move on to other chapters. So imagine my chagrin not two years later when I came across Boyton's newly published book and its familiar title. Ah, well . . .

10. Despite this attention, however, comics continue to suffer from bad PR. In most cases, this problem stems from the fact that "serious" comics continue to be overshadowed by those in the superhero genre, which is actually a much more interesting genre than the film versions of those titles might suggest. However, the success of these films attracts all the attention and perpetuates the fallacy that all comic books are mindless entertainment. The problem also stems from the so-called "supporters" of comics, who often damn the medium with faint praise. One recent article in the *New York Review of Books* captures this situation nicely. The writer, David Hajdu, delivers positive reviews of the graphic novels *Safe Area Gora□de*, *Palestine*, and *Ghost World* (1997), but in the process he makes several misstatements about narrative conventions in current comic books, and he begins with a proclamation—"Comic books, the rock 'n' roll of literature, have always been a rigorously disreputable form of junk art for adolescents of body or mind" (1)—that not only does he let go unchallenged but to which he largely subscribes.

5.
GUERILLA WARFARE
AND SNEAK ATTACKS
Comic Books vs. War Films

The idea that I raise at the end of Chapter Four—that comics are able to "get away with something" because of how they are regarded—takes on even greater weight in this chapter, where I position comics against what is perhaps the most popular of the "literatures" that I discuss in this book: film. That film is a superior medium to comics is largely perceived to be self-evident, for as any film critic worth his or her DVD Collector's Edition of *The Godfather* knows, the easiest way to insult a movie is to refer to its characters, plot, visual style, tone, or some combination thereof as "comic book." Such comparisons communicate to the reader that the film in question is mindless and juvenile, and as such it clearly fails to live up to the rich potential that cinema has to offer. The implication about the two media, of course, is that comic books cannot hope to equal—or even feasibly duplicate—the maturity and artistry of film. This implication also carries with it the assumption that readers will share this view of comic books, that no further explanation of either the film being reviewed or the entire medium of comics is needed; both are easily dismissed. Unfortunately, this is probably a safe assumption to make. Yet the truth of the matter is that comic books are by no means an inferior medium to film; in fact, they have proven themselves to be every bit as sophisticated an artistic form.[1]

An extended comparative study of film and comic books could never hope to be exhaustive because of the sheer magnitude of both media. The number of American films released between 1917 and 1979 alone is over 35,000 (Ray 9), and in the first sixty years of the comic book, over 300 publishers produced more than 10,000 titles (Benton 11). While there has been valuable discussion comparing the two media—R. C. Harvey's *The Art of the Comic Book: An Aesthetic History* (1996) and David Kunzle's *The History of the*

Comic Strip: The Nineteenth Century (1990) are two examples of books that dedicate space to discussing film and comics in relation to one another—these studies have been almost entirely formalistic in nature, comparing and contrasting how comics and film communicate visually. What also demands attention are the two industries themselves and the extent to which their operations and politics inform the thematic and formal differences in their products. A rich area for such a study is American war films and war comics produced during the World War II years and in the decade that followed. During these decades, striking parallels and divergences between the two media become clear. More specifically, during the 1940s and 1950s, the makers of war films and comic books were influenced by the political climate and constricted in how they represented their subject. However, certain war comics escaped their constrictions much more effectively than did war films of the same period, thus demonstrating the political and artistic sophistication of which comic books are capable.

These achievements were indicative of the medium as a whole in a fairly limited fashion, but they were most pronounced in two specific comic books published by Entertaining Comics (EC): *Two-Fisted Tales* (1950–55) and *Frontline Combat* (1951–54). What these titles demonstrate is that comic books can deliver a powerful, unpopular—and therefore necessary—political message. During the 1950s, the nature of the comic book industry and, paradoxically, the generally low regard in which it was (and continues to be) held allowed the EC books to subvert the dominant ideology of Cold War conservatism through their stories' political messages and their artists' exploitation of the medium's graphic language. The driving force behind this subversion was Harvey Kurtzman—writer and editor of these two books—who used various narrative and visual strategies that not only helped define the rapidly maturing medium but also presented war in a fuller, more complicated fashion than films of the time. Like war films, the popularity of war comics has waxed and waned over the years in accordance with the cultural zeitgeist, but the legacy of Kurtzman's work on the EC war titles endures.

As anyone well versed in clichés knows, the first casualty of war is truth. Put less glibly, wartime brings with it a certain conservatism that extends primarily to a culture's mass media. In the case of film and comic books during the war years of the 1940s, this conservatism was expressed primarily in the politics of the works created by the two industries and in the financial risks that those industries took—or did not take. One of the key features of war films of the early war years was their drive to justify US involvement. The first of these films was Warner Brothers' *Sergeant York* (1941), a true story about Alvin York (Gary Cooper), a simple, honest man who deliberated heavily over his decision to enter World War I and ended up becoming its most decorated hero. Released two months before Pearl Harbor, the film provided an isolationist nation with a lesson in interventionism through the character of York, and this film went on to become the number one grossing film of 1941. Clearly, this film resonated with a great number of people in America, and the success of *Sergeant York* was not lost on others in the movie industry, who then became less cautious of politically oriented films and took an "aggressively interventionist" stand (Koppes and Black 39).

The most famous and enduring of these interventionist pictures is undoubtedly *Casablanca* (1942), the number three grossing movie of 1942 and one that has become firmly embedded in America's film pantheon.[2] While a plot summation of this famous film is no doubt superfluous, it is nevertheless important to understand its interventionist subtext: Rick Blaine (Humphrey Bogart), an American living in wartime Morocco who "sticks his neck out for no one," eventually takes sides against the Nazis by sacrificing both his professional refuge (his café) and personal happiness (Ilsa Lund, played by Ingrid Bergman). Both *Casablanca* and *Sergeant York* were part "of a cycle of American films made between 1941 and 1945 with a definite propagandistic intent" (Ray 113).

During the war years, the public craved Hollywood products. As Robert Sklar points out in his book *Movie-Made America*, "in some locations, where factories operated around the clock, theaters never closed and were crowded even in predawn hours by workers getting off late-night shifts" (250). And consistently, the films that drew audiences were those about the military and the war: *Sergeant York*, *Dive Bomber* (1941), *Mrs. Miniver* (1942), *Casablanca*, *This Is the Army* (1943), *Since You Went Away* (1944), and *30 Seconds over Tokyo* (1944) all placed in the top five moneymakers of their years of release (Sackett 5). These movies capitalized on the public's interest in and attitudes toward the war, but being so dependent on the marketplace meant that filmmakers had to be very sensitive to these attitudes, one of which was a fear that the safety and sanctity of the home were threatened. Thus, MGM delivered *Mrs. Miniver*, one of the studio's most profitable movies during the war years, and one that works hard to reaffirm the strength of family and home. This film focuses on the lives of the Minivers, a British family living in London during the war. The title character, Kay Miniver (Greer Garson), must contend not only with the constant aerial assaults by German bombers, but also with the possible loss of her husband and son, both of whom undertake dangerous missions for the war cause. The struggles continue when one particularly destructive air raid nearly destroys the Miniver home, but the family refuses to give up. Then, toward the end, the film hints toward the imminent death of Mrs. Miniver's son, Vin (Richard Ney), but instead delivers the death of his wife Carol (Teresa Wright), thus preserving the central family unit.

Also addressing anxiety about the home is *Since You Went Away* (1944), a film that both recognizes the war's strains on the homefront and seeks to alleviate those pressures. This film follows Anne Hilton (Claudette Colbert) and her daughters, Jane (Jennifer Jones) and Brig (Shirley Temple), as they try to cope with the absence of their father, gone to war. The movie attempts to ease homefront suffering by proclaiming the strength of the family unit— evidenced from the very start by written narration that declares the film to be the "story of the unconquerable fortress: the American Home—1943"—and then proceeding to depict the home as exactly that. One example of this strategy is reflected in the friendship between Anne and Tony Willett (Joseph Cotton); that their desire for one another never proceeds beyond mild flirtation reinforces not only the sanctity of marriage, but also the idea that even the hardships of wartime separation are not so powerful as to spawn infidelity. Most obviously, however, is the film's ending: on Christmas Eve, Anne gets a call that her husband is safe and on his way home, and the family unit is once more—or about to be— restored. That these ideas found purchase in the American consciousness of the time is confirmed by the film's box office performance: it was the number three moneymaker of its year.[3]

Like Hollywood, the comic book industry viewed the war in the 1940s, in part, through the lens of profitability. Because war comics "have been marginal to a field dominated by other genres" (Witek 1996 37), their own evolution had been slow, and their early years were clearly influenced by the market forces created by one particular genre: the superhero comic. As I discussed in Chapter One, the appearance of Superman in *Action Comics* #1 had a profound impact on the economics of the medium. Within two years of his appearance, Superman was accounting for a circulation of over 1.2 million copies and a gross of nearly one million dollars in 1940 alone (Goulart 78). Following this lead, comic book publishers began to churn out a variety of superhero titles, and in 1940 comic books featuring new superheroes surpassed the newspaper strip reprint books on the newsstand (Benton 27), thus solidifying the position of superheroes as the dominant genre—a market reality that continues to this day.

The success of these particular books meant that in the early 1940s the development of other genres—most notably, war comics—was heavily influenced by the profits enjoyed by the superhero titles. As a result, World War II, as depicted in the comic books of the time, fit comfortably within the conventions established by the superhero comic. As Roger Sabin writes,

> During the war years patriotic superheroes were sent off to fight for their country, and the conflict was polarized into one between supermen and supervillains: Tojo, Hitler and Mussolini stood no chance. These comics were unashamed morale-boosters, and retailed in unprecedented numbers: by 1943 it is estimated they were selling nearly 15 million copies a month, thereby totally dominating the industry. (146)

In general, comic book publishers played it safe by delivering what the public apparently wanted—superheroes—and by staying close to home. One of the era's most famous heroes, Timely's (later Marvel's) Captain America, did his fighting not on the battlefields of Europe or the Pacific but in the good old USA, defending the homefront against spies and infiltrators.

In terms of comics that focused exclusively on war stories, there were few during the 1940s (Benton 185). Those that did exist usually featured strong central characters whose adventures continued from issue to issue. Some of the most popular of these characters came from DC Comics and appeared in the pages of All-American Comics: Blackhawk, Captain Rip Carter and the Boy Commandos, and Hop Harrigan (Uslan 5). By facing some seemingly insurmountable obstacle, overcoming it, and moving on to the next battle, these characters and the comic books in which they appeared bore more than a passing resemblance to their superhero cousins; they were missing only superpowers and snappy wardrobes. In sum, comic book publishers during the early 1940s "were loath to mess with success" (Uslan 5), and their dependence on the demands of the marketplace influenced—and limited—their presentation of the war.

While both industries bowed to the pressure of the marketplace and approached the war cautiously, it would be a mistake to equate their situations completely. For one thing, "the cinema as a whole, and, even more emphatically, any individual movie, is massively overdetermined" (Ray 6). Ray uses this term to refer to the vast number of influences that are exerted in the development, production, and release of any given film. Because film is "a technologically dependent, capital-intensive, commercial, collaborative medium regulated by the government and financially linked to mass audiences, the movies find themselves immersed in at least the histories of technology . . . economics . . . competing commercial forms . . . filmmakers . . . other media . . . politics . . . and the audience" (Ray 6). By contrast, comic books are far less dependent on technology and capital than film, so comic book publishers were much freer than filmmakers to experiment in terms of style or content. In addition, comic books require less time for production and are less collaborative in nature than film, allowing comic book creators to respond more quickly to current events and to convey a personal vision in their work—a situation that was apparent in the war comics of the 1940s and 1950s. In his narrative history of the comic book, *Men of Tomorrow: Geeks, Gangsters, and the Birth of the Comic Book*, author Gerard Jones acknowledges this very circumstance. He writes that in the 1940s comics "remained the most free and most idiosyncratic of mass media. Movies and radio shows were group products, pulp fiction was shaped by each magazine's editorial philosophy, but the best comics flew off cartoonists' drawing boards with little time for editorial interference" (75).

Politically speaking, film is regarded as a highly influential medium, and this realization took hold during the war years. Thomas Doherty writes,

> Not until Hollywood enlisted as an active agent in the Second World War did the ephemeral popular art dedicated to "mere entertainment" suddenly and seriously matter. . . . Recalibrated as a weapon of war, the mass medium that magically deployed sound and moving image, that wedded technological wonder to creative artistry, garnered the respect due the possession of potent firepower. (5)

Thus, one important influence on film production during the 1940s was the government, which formed a partnership of sorts with the studios at the time.[4] The most significant outside agent was the Office of War Information (OWI); during the war years, in fact, the OWI "wielded as much influence over movie content . . . as the PCA [Production Code Administration]" (Schatz 297), and this content dealt expressly with the representation of war. Following America's declaration of war, "the OWI requested that Hollywood concentrate on six subjects: the enemy, the Allies, the armed forces, the production front, the home front, and the issues" (Schatz 297), and during the war years, the OWI screened the scripts of every film under consideration by the studios (Davis 132).

While the name of this agency suggested that it would inform Americans about the war, the reality was quite different. As World

War II historian Richard Polenberg writes, "although OWI steered away from blatant appeals, its aim resembled that of the propagandist: to inspire right-thinking and acceptable forms of behavior" (52). While the word "propaganda" may seem harsh, it was nonetheless invoked by OWI head Elmer Davis himself, who said that "the easiest way to inject a propaganda idea into most people's minds is to let it go in through the medium of an entertainment picture when they do not realize that they are being propagandized" (quoted in Koppes and Black 64). This influence was not entirely unwanted; after all, various studios received support from the military in making these films, and acknowledged as much in opening credits (Basinger 112, 115). Such cooperation often resulted in the "whitewashing" of the war in ways that served the military: "straitjacketed by government censorship and Production Code prudery, directors averted their eyes, and screenwriters bit their tongues. The War Department, the Office of War Information (OWI), and Hollywood's studio heads colluded in keeping the awful devastations of combat from the homefront screen—sometimes by outright fabrication, usually by expedient omission" (Doherty 2–3).

This "collusion" led to the standardization of how the war was represented on screen. In addition to justifying the war in *Casablanca* and a slew of combat films during this time (Kane 145), these films were also consistent—and constricted—in how they represented the horrors of the battlefield. Due partially to the automatic censorship of violence and due partially to the public's tastes, cinematic death remained for the most part quick and bloodless—a sharp contrast to the realities of the battlefield. Thus, during these years, the public was treated to sanitized deaths in several popular films, the most notable being the popular combat films *Bataan* (1943), *Battleground* (1949), *Sands of Iwo Jima* (1949), and *Battle Cry* (1955). As a general principle in these films, American deaths are rare, and those Americans "who did die expired with thoughts of home, immortal longings and a smile on their lips; there wasn't a trace of blood" ("War Is Certainly Hell to Film" 69).[5] This distortion of wartime reality appeared in most of the period's films and had the intent of creating, if not a completely positive image of the war, then one which would not foster divisive protest or concern. Economics and politics—the two strongest factors influencing the representation of war in these movies—dictated that morale must be maintained until the war was over, and maintaining morale meant shielding the public from certain truths. In the end, this "tendency to avoid the ideological aspect of the war, to sugarcoat unpleasant realities, and to package wartime attempt to link Chinese and Americans not only as military allies, but also as people possessing the same democratic spirit. Considering the later demonization of the Chinese in American popular culture during and after the Cold War, the hypocrisy of this position hardly needs mentioning.

One of the key reasons that comic books escaped the same close scrutiny and pressure experienced in the film industry was that they—to borrow a military cliché—flew under the radar. Dismissed predominantly as "children's entertainment," comic books were never taken as a forum for political argument, unlike film. Being held in such regard, however, allowed—and continues to allow—comic books to be much more politically subversive than film.[6] Unfortunately, many cultural critics—even those who support comic books—continue to see the medium as largely reactive. For example, Andrew Smith—or "Captain Comics," as he's known to his *Memphis Commercial Appeal* readers—writes that "comic books are an entertainment medium and don't guide public opinion so much as reflect it" (F6). He goes on to qualify his comments somewhat, targeting mainstream comics more so than independent titles, but even this qualification fails to recognize the political achievements made by mainstream comic books during the 1940s (in a somewhat limited fashion) and the 1950s (in a more significant manner). For example, Martin Goodman, the founder of what eventually became Marvel Comics, published comic books "which declared war more than a year before the United States government did" (Daniels 1991 36). These comics, like *Marvel Comics* #4 and *Marvel Comics* #17, depicted superheroes like the Sub-Mariner and the Human Torch, respectively, taking on the Nazis.

The most blatant call for intervention in the war, however, appeared in *Captain America* #1, which appeared in March of 1941—a full four months before *Sergeant York* premiered and almost ten months before America entered the war. Depicted on this comic book's cover is an image of Captain America delivering a knockout blow to Adolf Hitler (see Figure 5.1). In an isolationist climate, this cover was very brazen, implying as it did that Hitler was a threat who needed to be stopped by America. Today, taking on Hitler might not seem so daring, but it was at the time because he was a leader about whom public opinion had not yet reached consensus. Thus, this image is a much bolder statement than *Sergeant York*, which is a more diffuse argument about intervention, and it rivals—for political chutzpah—films like *Confessions of a Nazi Spy* (1939) and Charlie Chaplin's *The Great Dictator* (1940). In the case of the former film, the target was not so much Hitler as a group of Nazi

Figure 5.1. Image appears courtesy of Marvel Comics, Inc.

issues as though they were soap and soft drinks could only mean a further dilution of public understanding" (Koppes and Black 135).

Censors, public opinion, and political pressures also shaped the representation of American allies so as to create support for those countries. The ally that benefited the most from this representation was Great Britain, whose demand on American military and financial strength was substantial, and not completely supported by all Americans (Schindler 26–27). One important film in this regard was the aforementioned *Mrs. Miniver*, a film that Franklin Roosevelt claimed "had appreciably lessened the problems attendant upon increased aid for Britain" (Schindler 49). Another pro-Britain film was *The White Cliffs of Dover* (1944), a film centered on American Susan Ashwood (Irene Dunne) and her adoption of England as her home. Her marriage to Sir John Ashwood (Alan Marshall) becomes a metaphor for the union of America and Britain, reinforced by the scene when their baby son enters the film for the first time at the same moment that American troops arrive to help Britain during World War I. This scene is repeated at the film's end, as their now-grown son John II (Peter Lawford) dies while American troops arrive during World War II. Thus, the alliance between America and Britain in World War II is represented as something natural: on a grand scale, these two nations formed a successful union during World War I; on a more intimate scale, "representatives" of these nations—the heroic and sympathetic Ashwoods—formed their own success-ful union of family and home.

Yet another ally whose representation came under close scrutiny was China. The OWI took a particular interest in seeing that this country did not become the target of the same racist depictions lev-eled against Japan. The government felt it vital that Americans per-ceive China "to be on the road to modernity and democracy. [And] public and private propaganda mills . . . were summoned to create 'the new China'" (Koppes and Black 236). One film to obey this directive was *30 Seconds Over Tokyo* (1944). In this movie, which chronicles James Doolittle's air raid of Tokyo in 1942, pilot Ted Lawson (Van Johnson) crash lands in China after successfully bombing Japan. Under constant threat of capture, Lawson and his men are taken in by the Chinese and nursed back to health. Throughout this part of the film, the Chinese villagers make numer-ous sacrifices for the Americans, even transporting them many miles to safety on their backs. Toward the end of the film, as a healthy Lawson leaves for America, he tells his Chinese friend Chung, "You're our kind of people." This statement, in light of the political pressures to represent China favorably, becomes an obvious spies infiltrating the US; in the case of the latter film, Chaplin's intent is satirical, captured best when Hitler doppelganger, Adenoid Hynkel, bounces a large balloon in the shape of a globe around his state room, a dance that is "a symbolic extension of meglomania" (Sarris 41). Though Chaplin delivers an impassioned plea for peace at the end of this film, his belief that "Hitler must be laughed at" (quoted in Koppes and Black 31) seems tragically naïve given the realities of what Hitler was to become. *Captain America* #1, by contrast, offers a far more direct and aggressive solution to Hitler during a time when "isolationism remained widespread" (Daniels 1991 36).[7]

As I discussed in the previous chapter, comics are not expected to deliver significant social or political criticism and therefore possess what I call a "powerful marginality" insofar as they are freer to express subversive or unpopular political ideas. The comic book issues described above are but a few examples of such statements. Another significant achievement would come in the following decade in the pages of the newspaper. Specifically, Walt Kelly's landmark strip *Pogo*, which followed the adventures of a group of anthropomorphic animals living in the Okeefenokee swamp, broke new ground through Kelly's satire of Joe McCarthy and others involved in the communist witch hunts of the 1950s. In the spring of 1953, Kelly introduced the character of Simple J. Malarkey, a badger who comes to the swamp and takes over the Bird Watcher's Club; over the course of the next several weeks, Kelly used Malarkey's nefarious activities in the swamp to expose McCarthy's red baiting. On May 16, 1953, for example, Kelly makes clear how "bird watching" is a metaphor for the witch hunts, which are clearly a sham (27). In this particular strip, two dogs approach Malarkey and he asks them, "What kind of a bird is you?" When they deny being birds, Malarkey says that with some tar and feathers "we can make the child into any bird we chooses . . . all nice and neat" (27). Kelly's work on *Pogo* was subversive in at least two important respects. First, at the time these strips ran—spring and summer of 1953—McCarthy was still a popular figure in many American minds (Harvey 1998 vii). And second, *Pogo* ran in many newspapers, including several owned by the Hearst Corporation, which had a very conservative slant. By contrast, film did not address McCarthyism until at least 1962, when *The Manchurian Candidate* featured as one of the villains Senator John Iselin (James Gregory), who in the movie claims to have a list of known communists and capitalizes politically on the fear that his statement generates.

Still ahead of the curve, comic books would address the Vietnam War in July of 1962 in Dell's *Jungle War Stories*—long before that war was represented in film (Benton 187). Even more recently, there have been several comic books that almost immediately addressed the attacks on the World Trade Centers, including Marvel Comics' *Heroes* (2001), *Amazing Spider-Man* #36 (2001), *A Moment of Silence* (2002), and Alternative Comics' *9-11: Emergency Relief* (2002). Also, while Art Spiegelman's *In the Shadow of No Towers* did not appear in book form in the US until 2004, these broadsheet-style comic pages depicting the tragedy and his responses to it began to appear in England, France, and Germany in early 2002. There have also been several comics that have used the attacks as a backdrop, including Vertigo Comics' *Human Target* #2 and #3 (2003) and Ted Rall's *To Afghanistan and Back* (2003)—a book that I discuss at length in the previous chapter. By contrast, the first mainstream films to address the attacks did not appear until 2006: Paul Greengrass's *United 93* and Oliver Stone's *World Trade Center*.[8] The point of all of these examples is that comics, because of their "marginal" status, are freer—politically—to address hot-button issues.

But the clearest example of this "powerful marginality" lies in the great number of comics that emerged during the 1950s addressing the Korean War. To appreciate this achievement, however, it is important to place it within the context of the cultural shift that swept America during the 1950s. America had emerged victorious from World War II with an economy that was healthy from the wartime production and that would not be taxed by rebuilding itself, unlike the war-ravaged countries of Europe and Asia. The strong economy, coupled with proven military might, put the US in a seemingly secure position. However, this security was threatened in the minds of many Americans with the emergence of the U.S.S.R. and China as powerful countries dedicated to a way of life—communism—that was opposed to those two bedrock values of American society, democracy and capitalism. Politically, "the neo-liberalism of Roosevelt was replaced by the increasingly reactionary governments of Truman and Eisenhower" (Sabin 147), and hate mongers like Joseph McCarthy controlled the discourse of patriotism. Also, a perceived rise in juvenile delinquency—a situation that had particular significance for comic book creators—and the fact that "the rest of the world, alien and unsettling, seemed to press closer now than many Americans wanted" helped characterize the 1950s in America as "a mean time" (Halberstam 9).

As the American comic book and film industries moved into this tumultuous decade, both experienced substantial changes. At the beginning of this decade, comic books were on the cusp of a shake-up, which came in the form of Senate hearings on juvenile delinquency. These hearings culminated in the creation of the Comics Code that I discuss in Chapter One. For film, the shakeup came in the form of the 1948 Paramount decree. Up until this point, the Hollywood studio system was a classic example of vertical integration, whereby studios owned all of the production, distribution, and exhibition networks. This system allowed studio heads to exert great control over their studio's "vision," certainly, but because these studios also owned theater and distribution chains, there existed a guaranteed outlet for product. The Paramount decree, an antitrust decision, forced studios to divest themselves of theater ownership, resulting in a loss of such guarantees. This change, coupled with the rise of television, the increase in foreign film production, and the aforementioned cultural dislocation felt after the war years resulted in an increasingly fragmented audience.

All projects became riskier, so studios began to avoid controversial subjects like war as topics for features. Worsening this situation was McCarthyism, which had spread to Hollywood in the form of rabid anti-communists and the blacklisting of the "Hollywood Ten." The end result was a far greater conservatism in terms of ideas; by examining the films of this era, it becomes clear that "the fear of being labeled 'un-American' encouraged the production of bland, politically neutral movies (Ray 131). Film historian Robert Sklar praises the historical "iconoclasm" of film, but he goes on to cite this attribute as the main casualty of "The anti-Communist crusade" in the 1950s (267). Robert Bresler seconds this opinion, offering that the conservatism of the era "had a chilling effect on the daring and creativity of moviemaking" (66).

Thus, what emerged during this decade was a very confused Hollywood, and the films reflected this trait. New genres, like the film noir, developed and more established genres took on a "new, harder edge, antisentimental and antiheroic" (Spiller 4), as if the anxieties of the time became sublimated in the tone of this era's films. Notably, however, war films were rare, and successful war films even more so. During the 1950s, in fact, only one combat film—*Battle Cry* (1955)—broke the top five annual moneymakers, and the other war films to share this honor—*From Here to Eternity* (1953), *Mister Roberts* (1955), and *Bridge on the River Kwai* (1957)—were not traditional American war films. The first two films are more properly categorized as romance and comedy, respectively, and the third film was adapted by a Frenchman (Pierre Boulle) from his own novel, directed by a Brit (David Lean), and filmed on location in Sri Lanka—hardly an "American" endeavor. Tellingly, none of these films addresses the Korean War. As David Halberstam argues in his book,

NOT MANY DAYS AGO HORDES OF LITTLE MEN IN QUILTED UNIFORMS ALSO SCREAMED AND HOWLED AS THEY CAME CHARGING FROM ACROSS THE BORDER WITH BUGLES, CYMBALS AND GUNS!

Figure 5.3.Image appears courtesy of Marvel Comics, Inc.

Figure 5.2. Image appears courtesy of Marvel Comics, Inc.

Figure 5.4. Copyright 1943 William H. Wise & Company.

The Fifties (1993), "in contrast to World War Two and Vietnam, [the Korean War] did not inspire a rich body of novels, plays, or even movies" (73). Certainly there were Korean War movies released during this decade—most notably The Steel Helmet (1951), One Minute to Zero (1952), and The Bridges at Toko-Ri (1955)—but by and large they were ignored by the public at the time.[9]

Such was not the case with war comic books, whose popularity increased during the 1950s. In sharp contrast to Hollywood, comic book publishers actually benefited from the Korean War as readers' interest led to a flurry of new titles (Benton 49). However, while comic books' outsider status imbued them with the potential to subvert the Cold War mentality that dominated public discourse about the Korean War, most comic books of the time challenged very little. In general, such 1950s titles like War Comics, Battle, and Our Army at War were subversive mainly in the fact that they existed at all during a time when Korea was not being addressed in other creative media; taken together, the vast majority of war comic books in the 1950s, whether they were about Korea or World War II, did little but reinforce the predominant stereotypes and clichés of the time regarding warfare and enemies of the US. For example, in "Bataan!"—a story that appeared in Battle #32 (1954)—the third person narrative voice continually refers to the enemy forces as "The Japs." James Dower cites this term as one containing potent racism during World War II, because unlike the word "Nazis," "Japs" does not differentiate between the enemy soldiers and the citizens of Japan: "The implications of perceiving the enemy as 'Nazis' on the one hand and 'Japs' on the other were enormous, for this left space for the recognition of the 'good German,' but scant comparable place for 'good Japanese'" (78–79). That this slur emerges from the comic's narration and not in dialogue between characters serves to legitimize the term. As a dubious complement to such language, many of these comics are filled with various demeaning images of the Japanese soldiers: bucktoothed (see Figure 5.2), savage (see Figure 5.3), or as an animal of some sort, as in the cover of 1943's The United States Marines #3 (see Figure 5.4).

One story that goes to unusual lengths to dehumanize the enemy comes in the story "The Face of the Enemy," from War Comics #8 (1952). The story begins with the ominous opening, "Is the enemy human? Is the enemy just another guy like you or me . . . but dressed in a different uniform? It took corporal Walton 12 horrifying hours to find out the truth about . . . the enemy!" (1). Set during the Korean War, the story focuses on said corporal Walton, who early in the story has the temerity to suggest that just because their job is

Figure 5.5. Image appears courtesy of Marvel Comics, Inc.

"killin' the enemy . . . don't mean the enemy ain't human!" (1). After Walton's crew is ambushed and he is the only survivor, he is captured by an enemy soldier and, expecting the worst, is surprised to find that his captor has bandaged his wounds and is treating him humanely. Of course, all the visual clues suggest that there is a sinister purpose behind his actions: his face is severely drawn with angled eyebrows and a leering mouth that would suggest, if not for the accompanying text, malice (see Figure 5.5). The truth slowly dawns on Walton, who realizes that he is being kept alive only to lure other American soldiers into the open. The comic ends with Walton's proclamation to "never trust the enemy" (6).

Although the majority of war comics of the 1950s—like their film counterparts—failed to challenge Cold War conservatism, the comic books *Two-Fisted Tales* and *Frontline Combat*, both published by EC, demonstrated that comic books could be politically and artistically sophisticated—even more so than film. The company that would eventually change its name to "Entertaining Comics" began as "Educational Comics," and it was founded by Max Gaines, who was an instrumental figure in the early years of the developing comic book, playing a key role in the launching of *Famous Funnies* in 1934. When Max was killed in a boating accident in 1947, EC passed into the hands of his son William, who then introduced a line of horror, crime, science fiction/fantasy, and war titles that breathed new life into these genres; in fact, the EC comics are generally considered to be "the most revolutionary group of comic books ever produced" (Daniels 1971 62). William Gaines attracted a number of talented writers and artists who flourished under his leadership. By paying them when they turned in their work, allowing them to ink their own pages, and encouraging them to develop their own style rather than conforming to a "house style," Gaines ensured that the artists would be motivated and that the EC titles would be distinctive (Harvey 1996 129).

One of the two editors working under Gaines was Harvey Kurtzman (the other was Al Feldstein), who had been knocking around in the business for a few years, his most notable feature up to this point being *Hey, Look!*, a series of one-page features that were used as "filler pages" in other comics (Harvey 1996 127). Gaines took him on at EC, and Kurtzman eventually wrote and edited the company's action-adventure title, *Two-Fisted Tales*, which later evolved into a comic book focused on war stories. Due to that title's popularity, a second war book, *Frontline Combat*, was developed, written, and edited by Kurtzman, who was a veteran of World War II. Both comics focused on war stories throughout history, but the Korean war stories vastly outnumbered the others (Witek 1989 40). Although Kurtzman only occasionally illustrated his work, he provided the scripts, page layouts, and panel compositions for every story that appeared in the two series. Unlike EC's horror titles, which were under the editorship of Al Feldstein, the war books took much longer to produce, due mainly to Kurtzman's painstaking research, which is now legendary.[10] In specific terms, the EC war comics stand in pointed ideological and artistic contrast to war films of the same period in the representation of four main subjects: military victory, the enemy, killing and death in war, and foreign civilians impacted by war. In each case, the EC stories express views that challenged the dominant discourse of 1950s America—a challenge that certainly was not being made in American war films of the time.

One major difference between war films and the EC war comic books lay in their conflicting attitudes toward US military victory. Almost without exception, war films reveled in the celebration of American military might. Kurtzman, on the other hand, did not frame his stories in terms of American victory; such a presentation would have undoubtedly come off as jingoistic, a position that Kurtzman vehemently rejected. A case in point is the battle of Iwo Jima. In the film *Sands of Iwo Jima*, the opening is given over to a dedication to the Marines and their cooperation in the filming of the movie. This dedication sets the tone for the film, contextualizing this battle in terms of the history of the Marines and their sacrifice in this particular battle and war. In contrast to this presentation stands *Frontline Combat #7* (1952), the title's designated "Iwo Jima" issue. This issue contains four interrelated and roughly chronological episodes in the battle for Iwo Jima, and the issue's first story, "Iwo Jima," frames the battle in a very different way than does *Sands of Iwo Jima*. The story begins with an introduction of two pilots who must perform an emergency landing on the island and then quickly segues to several pages that depict the geological history of Iwo Jima. By devoting so much space to the formation of this island, Kurtzman places the battle in a much larger context than the film. For Kurtzman, this battle is not about the glory of the Marines; rather, it is just another skirmish in a much larger history that makes the dealings of humans pale by comparison.

And even though Iwo Jima was an American military victory, Kurtzman underplays this fact. For example, in that same issue's story "The Landing," Kurtzman reimagines one of the most enduring images to come out of World War II: the raising of the flag on Mount Surabachi. Not surprisingly, this image is showcased near the end of *Sands of Iwo Jima*, and it comes wrapped in the strains of the "Marine Corps Hymn." In "The Landing," however, this moment is downplayed to an almost ludicrous extent. During a lull in a firefight, one of the soldiers calls to his sergeant that the flag is going up (see Figure 5.6). In the panel, this image that has come to represent American military determination is a mere speck.

Another point that very clearly demarcates differences between the war films of this era and the EC war comics is the depiction of the enemy; more specifically, unlike the films of the time, which dehumanize the enemy—and especially the Asian enemy—the EC war stories about World War II and Korea go to great lengths to prod readers to understand and empathize with this enemy.[11] In "Silent Service," from *Two-Fisted Tales #32* [#15],[12] for example, the story begins in the interior of a Japanese destroyer, one of two escorts for an aircraft carrier. On the first page, the narration calls attention to three framed portraits of Emperor Hirohito on the wall, posing the question to the reader, "Why three??" (1). The next few pages take us into an American submarine which has targeted the convoy. The sub is able to sink one of the escorts and, in a climactic and tensely paced series of panels, avoids depth charges from the other. The coda, however, in which the mystery of the portraits is solved in bittersweet fashion, belongs to the Japanese. As the surviving escort returns to pick up sailors from the destroyed ship, the following narration appears over three textless images: "There's just enough time to salvage one last memento . . . there's just enough time to salvage

Figure 5.6.
Copyright William M. Gaines, Agent, Inc. Used with permission.

Figure 5.7. Copyright William M. Gaines, Agent, Inc.
Used with permission.

one last remembrance . . . one last beloved symbol from the bridge of their sinking ship" (see Figure 5.7). The comic's final image is a long panel in which we see the portraits and a Japanese officer with downcast eyes. The text reads, in part, "back in the Japanese captain's stateroom hang four pictures . . . four obituaries of the Imperial Navy of Japan!" (8). Rather than demonizing this enemy, these panels show that the Japanese are humans who suffer loss and mourn their dead just like anybody else. Such a sympathetic portrait of the enemy was never conveyed in films of the time.

To get a sense of how the enemy was depicted in films of the time, we can turn once again to *Sands of Iwo Jima*, a film that was released long after the war was over but that still retains much of the racism that characterized the Pacific theater. For example, throughout this movie, the main characters—a group of Marines—refer to the Japanese as "Nips," "Japs," and—in a racial epithet that never quite caught on—"little lemon-colored characters." In terms of their physical presence, the Japanese soldiers remain largely unseen, except in a few notable scenes, and even then they remain faceless. At one point, two Marines are surprised in a foxhole by a group of Japanese, and the attacking soldiers' faces are obscured as they mercilessly stab the Marines and then slink away. Demonizing this enemy was a legacy of the war itself, when "many Marines went into battle with the legend 'Rodent Exterminator' stenciled on their helmets" (Dower 92), and the sentiment that the Japanese—soldier and civilian alike—were vermin was not confined simply to the battlefield but extended to the American homefront as well (Dower 92). *Sands of Iwo Jima*, by uncritically presenting this racism, tacitly endorses it.

A more studied and pointed examination of this racism comes in the story "Korea," from *Two-Fisted Tales* #29 [#12] (1952). In this story, a group of American soldiers is pinned down by sniper fire, barely escapes, and then is able to fire back at their Korean assailants, killing all but one of them. Of the two Americans, one continually repeats that the snipers "killed his buddy" and refers to them as "gooks." In fact, this soldier repeats this term several times over the course of any given page. Unlike the casual use of "Nips" in *Sands of Iwo Jima*—a racist sentiment that is not challenged within the film—"Korea" does not endorse this soldier's point of view; in fact, the narrative repudiates it. The surviving Korean soldier surrenders to the two men, and it is only because of the intervention of the other American soldier that he is not killed. This soldier carries the wounded Korean to a jeep and delivers him to a field hospital. In the final two panels, he muses, "When you see your buddies being killed, it becomes so easy to kill a man! . . . It becomes the easiest thing in the world! And yet, in the middle of all this killing, how many of us will remember that each and every human being . . . each and every life on this earth is important . . . ?" (8). By presenting the other soldier as bloodthirsty and by giving this more thoughtful soldier the last word, the narrative rejects the hatred conveyed by "gook" and instead puts forth an antiwar message. Given the Cold War mentality of the 1950s, such a message was subversive in the extreme. That it appears in the pages of a comic book is a testament to the political daring of which that medium is capable.

Also serving to contrast with the portrayal of the Japanese soldiers in *Sands of Iwo Jima* is the story "The Caves," the third chapter in *Frontline Combat*'s "Iwo Jima" issue. "The Caves" stands out from the other three stories in this particular issue because it takes the reader inside the cavernous mazes that provided refuge for many Japanese soldiers during the waning hours of the battle. From its outset the story takes a radical position. On the splash page, we see Japanese soldiers retreating deeper into the caves as a result of the Marines' use of flamethrowers (see Figure 5.8). The faces of the majority of soldiers are frightened, and in the page's final panel, one soldier is engulfed in flames, his face frozen in pain. Here, the Americans are now the unseen threat while the Japanese are the focal characters with whom our sympathies lie. The story continues in this remarkable fashion by delivering the thoughts of one Japanese soldier who does not desire to "take ten Americans with him" in a suicide retaliation. The soldier thinks, "I want to live! I have no desire for death!" After almost being shot and then lacking the nerve to kill himself with a grenade, the unnamed soldier is left alone in the cave and decides that he cannot return home a survivor; he will be labeled a coward and a disgrace. With no options left, he runs out of the caves and toward a group of American soldiers, who quickly cut him down. In the final panel, one of the Americans remarks that "They commit suicide every time!" to which a fellow soldier says, "I wonder why?" (7). Because the reader has gained some insight into the Japanese soldier and understands that his decision to commit suicide arose from several complications, we are not aligned with the Americans, from whom understanding is withheld. Instead, the reader identifies and sympathizes more with the Japanese soldier.

In fact, the EC war stories consistently imagined the enemy in far more complicated terms than the films of the time, subverting the ideology of paranoia and "otherness" that dominated 1950s American pop culture. In "Enemy Assault," from *Frontline Combat* #1, for example, two soldiers—one American and one North Korean—come upon

Figure 5.8. Copyright William M. Gaines, Agent, Inc.
Used with permission.

Figure 5.9. Copyright William M. Gaines, Agent, Inc.
Used with permission.

Figure 5.10. Copyright William M. Gaines, Agent, Inc.
Used with permission.

Figure 5.11. Copyright William M. Gaines, Agent, Inc.
Used with permission.

each other in a trench. Both are armed, but neither pulls the trigger, deciding to "wait and see who comes along first" (5). The two strike up a conversation, and in a bold page from the story, we are given nearly nine full panels of the enemy solder facing the reader directly as he tells the American soldier about the time he spent in New York City (see Figure 5.9). What Kurtzman achieves with this single page is to humanize the enemy in a way absent from films of the time—or from most contemporary war films, for that matter—where the enemy's face is rarely even shown. Although the soldiers must eventually take sides (resulting in the American killing the North Korean), this resolution does not eradicate the sympathy for the enemy that Kurtzman has created.

Arguably, an even bolder story is "Buzz Bomb," from *Two-Fisted Tales* #25 [#8] (1952). The title of this story refers to a jet-propelled bomb designed and used by the Germans in World War II. The bomb's operation is particularly well suited to generate tension in the medium of comics: its motor emits a buzzing growl that conks out shortly before it falls and detonates, so strewn across various panels throughout this story are text sound effects that link the static images. The story's most impressive move, however, is to make the protagonists a group of German paratroopers caught behind enemy lines. In an O. Henry–esque twist of fate that was the bread and butter of the EC line, these soldiers become targeted by the buzz bomb from their own country's arsenal. On the second page of the story, we see a series of four panels depicting American troops as victims of the buzz bomb (see Figure 5.10), and these images are echoed three pages later in a series of four wordless panels with the German paratroopers (see Figure 5.11). This visual echo links the Americans and Germans by shared experiences, suggesting that they have more in common than we might think. This layout design, coupled with Kurtzman's decision to use German protagonists and generate tension on their behalf, results in reader sympathy for the enemy.[13]

Besides their two-dimensional and often propagandistic depiction of the enemy, war films of this time were very limited in terms of how to represent the killing that took place. As discussed earlier, these limits were carefully set during the war years by the OWI. Yet "toned down" violence extended into the postwar era as well, and its contrast with comic book representations—particularly in the EC war comics—marks the latter medium as one more willing to confront the brutal realities of war. One clear point of comparison is in the representation of hand-to-hand combat in the film *Battleground* and the comic "Corpse on the Imjin" from *Two-Fisted Tales* #25 [#8] (1952). In *Battleground*, there is a scene where the protagonists, a group of

American soldiers, are attacked by Germans and must engage in hand-to-hand combat. Visually, these fights take place off camera and involve the now-cliché shot of the victim's legs kicking violently, then more softly, then not at all. The filmmakers censor from viewers' eyes what is undoubtedly a grim and disturbing struggle and, in effect, sanitize the realities of war.

By contrast, "Corpse on the Imjin" wants the reader to take a long look at one soldier killing another. The story is set during the Korean War and opens with the image of a corpse floating down the river. An unnamed American soldier sitting on the bank of this river sights the corpse and begins to think about the various ways one could die in war. Of the possibilities that he considers, hand-to-hand combat seems to him the most remote; advances in weaponry all but guarantee that he'll "never get closer'n a mile to the enemy" (2). As (bad) luck would have it, an enemy soldier springs from behind the bushes, and three of this story's seven pages are taken up by the brutal struggle between these two men. The story is remarkable in several respects, not the least of which being its presentation of a fight that fully exploits the graphic language of comics in order to eradicate all pretense of romance or glory from killing. Kurtzman knows that comics communicate best through a skillful blending of words and images, and he uses this strategy to humanize the enemy, a technique that makes the killing much more shocking. The narration describes the Korean soldier as "wet and scared and hungry" and the visual depicts him as more desperate than sinister (see Figure 5.12). Sympathy is repeated at the end of the comic, as this same soldier's dead body floats down the river. Accompanying these images are the words, " . . . he is now not rich or poor, right or wrong, bad or good! Don't hate him! Have pity . . . " (6). Certainly, a plea for pity regarding the enemy—a communist, no less—would be unthinkable in a medium such as film during the 1950s.

Another dimension of comics' graphic language is pacing, and Kurtzman brilliantly manipulates this device when he delivers a gruesome series of images in which we see the American soldier drowning his attacker (see Figure 5.13). With these panels, Kurtzman stretches out the killing to an uncomfortable degree. This is no quick, offscreen death; rather, the reader must examine the agony of a killing in some detail. The transitions between panels here are "moment-to-moment" in which a small amount of time elapses between the images depicted (McCloud 70), and such transitions have the effect of stretching out an incident for dramatic purposes. The second row of panels continues to transition from moment to moment, but Kurtzman also moves us closer to the

HE IS WET AND SCARED AND HUNGRY, AND HIS EYES GO FROM YOUR GRATION CAN TO YOUR RIFLE! THE WIND HIDES ALL SOUND *AS HE SPRINGS!*

Figure 5.12.

E KICKS TO STAY UP, BUT U ARE HEAVIER AND U *PRESS HIM UNDER!*

IT REMINDS YOU OF SOMETHING...AND YOU *PRESS HIM UNDER!*

LIKE DUNKING, WHEN YOU WENT SWIMMING! YOU *PRESS HIM UNDER!*

YES...YES...LIKE DUNKING AT THE SWIMMING HOLE... YOU DUNK...*DUNK...DUNK...*

IS HANDS HAVE STOPPED LAWING AT THE AIR...HIS FEET AVE STOPPED THRASHING...

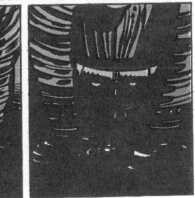

...BLOOD AND BUBBLES ARE COM-ING TO THE SURFACE AND THE MAN YOU ARE HOLDING RELAXES!

IT SEEMS LIKE HOURS HAVE GONE BY! THE BUBBLES ARE BARELY TRICKLING UP AND ALL IS STILL!

Figure 5.13. Copyright William M. Gaines, Agent, Inc.
Used with permission.

killing. Whereas war movies like *Battleground* shield audiences from the killing, Kurtzman emphasizes it, for he knows that to regard the killing of a human either too lightly or as a motive for vengeance dehumanizes us all.

In addition to differences in the depiction of killing, films and the EC war comic books differed in terms of attitudes toward death. One of the most popular films of 1955, *Battle Cry*, is—like *Sands of Iwo Jima*—a tribute to the Marines and a celebration of the valor of battle. Tellingly, the film makes this argument by presenting a minimum of battle footage; in fact, most of *Battle Cry's* 149-minute running time is devoted to either the romantic entanglements between the men and various women or to their military training and preparation. When the movie does present battle, the subject is heavily sanitized and valorized in the tradition of combat films during the war years. The battalion, under the command of Sam Huxley (Van Heflin), is referred to as "Huxley's Harlots," the "orphans" of the Marine Corps because they are given only "mop up" assignments, a form of disgrace. At one point, in fact, Huxley demands of General Snipes (Raymond Massey) that his troops be allowed to take part in the attack on Saipan. As the film makes clear—mainly through the voiceover narration of Sergeant Mac (James Whitmore)—battle is perceived as a proving ground for these men; there is no point in being trained if all they are to do is clean up after the battle takes place.

Kurtzman undermines this philosophy in "Kill," from *Two-Fisted Tales* #23 [#6] (1951), in which he presents two main characters whose thirst for battle is punished in the most brutal terms possible. The story cuts between Abner, an American soldier obsessed with his knife and a desire to use it on the enemy, and Li, a North Korean soldier who shares a similar obsession with his gun. Inevitably and in classic EC fashion, these two men meet each other on the field of combat. Li is able to shoot Abner once before his gun jams, and Abner is able to stab Li with his knife. The result is that both men kill each other and fall together into a ditch. Kurtzman uses this last panel to emphasize the waste to which the characters' obsession has led: in this long panel, both Li and Abner are drained of color as the battle rages on without them, as evidenced by a plume of smoke in the panel's upper left corner. The closing narration emphasizes a pacifist, antiwar message: "Regard no man's life cheaper than your own! Respect and cherish life and then, truly, 'Thou shalt not kill'" (6). In the world of EC comics, there is no room for the valorization of combat; when characters possess such desire to make war, they are inevitably punished. That Kurtzman addresses his theme not indirectly (by placing his characters in some distanced war) but forthrightly (by placing Abner and Li in the Korean War, raging at the time), makes his statement that much bolder.[13]

Related to the idea that battle is valorous is the idea that death in battle is noble, an idea endorsed by the many war films of this era. Not surprisingly, this idea also comes through in *Sands of Iwo Jima* and *Battle Cry*. In the former, Sergeant John Stryker (John Wayne) is shot and killed by a sniper just minutes after the Marines have taken Mount Surabachi. As the men in his platoon gather around his body, Stryker's death is linked visually with the raising of the flag and aurally with the Marine Corps Hymn. One of Stryker's antagonists throughout the film—Private Conway (John Agar)—becomes reinvigorated to carry on in the face of Stryker's death, even issuing the late sergeant's signature command, "Saddle up!" to the rest of the soldiers. Similarly, Colonel Sam Huxley's (Van Heflin) death toward the end of *Battle Cry* galvanizes the rest of the troops and forms, in the narrator's words, "our battle cry." As with Stryker's death, the Marine Corps hymn plays inspirationally in the background. What both films do in these scenes is romanticize death in battle as heroic, inspirational, and ultimately hopeful.

There is no such romanticization of death in the EC war comics. Instead, Kurtzman uses death to indicate the futility of war, and he depicts it in ways that illustrate how comic books as a medium can create an impact that rivals what is possible in film. Watching a film is largely passive because the images move at a predetermined speed that the viewer cannot control. In comics, the opposite is the case: "because we stop briefly at each [image], they each acquire greater dramatic power than they would if they were simply images in a continuously moving series of images . . . and because the pictures do not move or change in comics as we watch, we have the images before us longer than in a film, and they each therefore have greater narrative impact" (Harvey 1996 186). While skilled filmmakers can certainly control pacing, the impact of an image in a comic book is fundamentally different from those in movies because of how they are experienced.

"Hill 203," from *Two-Fisted Tales* #24 [#7] (1951), is a strong example of how panels "freeze" time to some degree in order to achieve an impact that is different from film and every bit as arresting. In this particular story, such panels deromanticize death. The story's opening presents a series of images of a soldier slumped over a machine gun (see Figure 5.14). By taking one scene and breaking it up into four separate images, the artist (Jack Davis, working from Kurtzman's layouts) forces us to closely examine the details of this dead soldier, a method that dovetails with the story's purpose,

DAWN IN KOREA! THE SUN IS RISING ON A LITTLE BIRD PERCHED UPON THE BARREL OF A MACHINE GUN! THE SUN IS RISING ON A UNITED NATIONS SOLDIER SLUMPED BEHIND THE MACHINE GUN! THE SUN IS RISING ON...

HILL 203!

WHAT HAPPENED HERE? LOOK AT THE PILE OF BURNT SHELLS, EACH AS LONG AS YOUR HAND! WHO WERE THEY FIRED AT?

WHAT HAPPENED HERE? LOOK AT THE SPENT MACHINE-GUN BARREL... THE EMPTY CARTRIDGE CASES...

WHO IS TO TELL US WHAT HAPPENED... WHAT HAS GONE BEFORE? THE SOLDIER WON'T TELL YOU! HE'S **DEAD!**

Figure 5.14. Copyright William M. Gaines, Agent, Inc.
Used with permission.

which is to decry the waste of war. This strategy is repeated on the story's final page, where we see the additional dead that populate this hill (see Figure 5.15). The narrative makes sure that each of the dead is given his space so that we understand the human cost involved in this one small piece of the war. The story also makes us confront death in one sequence of four panels where North Korean soldiers are shot by the machine gunner (see Figure 5.16). The panels show the body in various states of trauma, achieving in four panels more physical "action" than in any shooting depicted in war films of the 1940s and 1950s. Given the attention and space devoted to killing and the dead in this story, the final line, "Hill 203 has been held!" can only be read bitterly, for there is no way to justify the cost of this "victory."

But perhaps the most complicated and powerful depiction of death comes in the story "Big 'If,'" from *Frontline Combat* #5 (1952). This particular tale is often cited as a masterpiece of comic book timing, and rightly so. The story is set in Korea and opens on private Paul Maynard, who sits before a row of "devil posts," tikilike totems that dot the Korean countryside and help ward off evil spirits. As Maynard sits, he reflects on the word "if," and begins to wonder what might have happened "if" various factors had changed: if the posts "had only been a little further down the road," if a bomb "crater was only a hundred feet further away," if he "hadn't stopped to buckle [his] combat boot" (1). Like the climax of "Corpse on the Imjin," Kurtzman uses a number of moment-to-moment transitions, but this time he weaves them throughout the story to slow down and call attention to the idea of time. Why? Because, as we discover on the story's final page, Paul Maynard has been mortally wounded by a bomb, and during his last few moments, he bitterly replays for himself all of the seemingly inconsequential events that led to his fateful meeting with a chunk of shrapnel (see Figure 5.17). Kurtzman forces us to look closely at this one single death, the tragedy of which becomes multiplied to an unbearable degree when we consider the total number of dead in any war. Also, unlike Stryker and Huxley, Maynard dies alone, with neither hymns nor anyone to inspire. Thus, this particular story not only treats death in war in a more dramatic and complicated fashion than films of the time, but it raises questions about the waste of war during a time when such questions were not openly encouraged. It would take another war—the Vietnam War—to make criticism and protest of our nation's policies and leaders a viable form of public discourse.

The final difference between the war films and EC stories of this time lies in how these media viewed the most important "collateral

AND WITH THE RISING OF THE SUN, AIRPLANES RISE FROM THE SOUTH OF KOREA, SEARCHING LIKE HAWKS, PASSING OVER THE HEAPS OF DEAD CHINESE BELOW...

...ALSO PASSING OVER DEAD UNITED NATIONS SOLDIERS! FOR DEATH TREATS ALL MEN EQUALLY, AND MAKES NO DISTINCTION BETWEEN CHINESE AND AMERICANS!

THE SUN RISES ON A DEAD MACHINE GUN TEAM ON HILL 203! CORPORAL MACSWAIN!

... DUKE!

...YODONZA!

...GEORGE!

THE SUN RISES ON A FIFTY CALIBER BROWNING M2 MACHINE GUN, STILL OILED AND SHINING! THE BLUE STEELED GUN HAS OUTLIVED ITS CREW! IN THE BACKGROUND, FRESH REPLACEMENTS MOVE IN TO OCCUPY THE POSITION! LITTLE BIRD PERCHED ON THE GUN MUZZLE FLIES AWAY! *HILL 203 HAS BEEN HELD!*

Figure 5.15. Copyright William M. Gaines, Agent, Inc.
Used with permission.

Figure 5.16. Copyright William M. Gaines, Agent, Inc. Used with permission.

Figure 5.17. Copyright William M. Gaines, Agent, Inc. Used with permission.

Figure 5.18. Copyright William M. Gaines, Agent, Inc.
Used with permission.

damage" of war—foreign civilians caught in the crossfire. RKO's *One Minute to Zero* (1952) is interesting in that it opens with a sympathetic portrait of the South Koreans. The images of these people going about their daily activities unspools with a voiceover narration by Linda Day (Ann Blyth), a UN relief worker. She portrays the South Koreans as victims defending their way of life against the North Korean aggressors. The rest of the movie presents the US military as a force designed to help these people achieve their goals, articulated by Day as wanting only "to live in peace." Representing the military is Colonel Steve Janowski (Robert Mitchum), who later in the film opens fire on refugees in order to stop the communist soldiers hidden among them—an act of "necessity" that the narrative inevitably excuses. What is most notable about this film is not simply its sympathetic portrayal of Korean civilians but the ultimate limitations of that portrayal. Specifically, the film does deliver a fair amount of footage—some of it clearly archival—of Korean refugees, but the movie never allows these people to enter the narrative in any meaningful way. Instead, they are reduced to extras who must be protected by the much more powerful Americans. In this way, the film becomes little more than propaganda to justify our presence in Korea at the time.

A far more meaningful treatment of civilians caught in the middle of war comes in a host of EC stories. One of the most visually striking is "Rubble," which appeared in *Two-Fisted Tales* #24 [#7] (1951). The story focuses on the Chun family—a Korean man, woman, and small child who are trying to make a future for themselves during the unfortunate time of the Korean War. The story takes the reader through the systematic building of the Chun's house: we see him collect the stones and lay a floor, haul lumber for the house's frame, build the stone walls of the house and yard, and lay the thatch roof. Tragically, in a few panels near the story's end, all of Chun's hard work is quickly undone by the machines of war, which reduce his house and family to a pile of rubble. Visually, the layout of the page adds significantly to the story. Each page consists of two rows of three panels that illustrate the work Chun does on and a long panel at the bottom that shows the house in various stages of construction (see Figure 5.18); later, after the army comes, the final two long panels illustrate, sadly, the house's destruction. These particular images emphasize that with each destroyed building—something that appears with frightening regularity in war films—there is a story of struggle behind it. Kurtzman further emphasizes the personhood of Chun by developing him as the central character of the story: the bulk of the narrative is given over to Chun's labor and elaborate plans for his family's future. Later, when the army appears, they are faceless. Kurtzman's condemnation of war's inhumanity toward civilians is completed by the final, cruel irony: the foundation that Chun built is later used by UN forces as a base for a piece of artillery.[14]

However, the most interesting—and also one of the most subversive—of the "civilian" stories appeared in *Two-Fisted Tales* #33 [#16] (1953): "Atom Bomb." Recreating the destruction wrought on Nagasaki, the story establishes from the beginning a tone that positions the reader to sympathize with the Japanese. The narration reads, "On August 9, 1945 . . . a sunny day . . . citizens of Nagasaki, Japan, heard a radio warning . . . enemy planes over Shimbara heading west. . . . At 11:03 a.m. citizens of Nagasaki heard the VRRROOW of a B-29 banking overhead . . . and it was the last thing they heard before being blown to eternity by the ATOM BOMB!" (1). The words here put the reader in the position of the Japanese civilians, and the unironic use of "enemy" to describe the American planes underscores this role reversal. The narration is intensified by a splash page depicting the moment of impact, the visual center being a man's body just left of the center of the panel (see Figure 5.19). There are several more panels devoted to this destruction throughout the story, which is organized as the memories of an elderly woman, Tagawa. While the story ends a bit hollow on a positive note—the rebuilding of Nagasaki, the survival of Tagawa's grandson, and the narration "there is hope in Nagasaki! There is hope in the whole world!" (8)—its real achievement is to imagine the Japanese citizenry sympathetically and "raise the questions of the atomic age" (Witek 1989 39), in this case about the possibly injudicious use by America of the atom bomb. The story certainly taps into a fear prevalent in the 1950s—nuclear armageddon—but as expressed in the popular discourse of the time, this fear was always directed outward. That is, some other country would lay waste to our beloved America. That this comic taps into the threat but casts America as the unseen aggressor is a sentiment that would have never found such a direct expression in a Hollywood film of the 1950s.

Both explicitly and implicitly, all of these examples suggest that one of the reasons why the EC war comics were able to represent war in a more complicated fashion than were films of this time is that readers and viewers experience the media in very different ways. Francois Truffaut once commented "that it was impossible to make an anti-war film" (Ebert) because watching a battle unfold could not help being exciting. Comic books do not fall into this same trap because of fundamental differences between the two media. In addition to those differences already discussed, another is that the sense

ON AUGUST 9, 1945... A SUNNY DAY... CITIZENS OF NAGASAKI, JAPAN, HEARD A RADIO WARNING!... ENEMY PLANES OVER SHIMBARA HEADING WEST!... AT 11:03 A.M., CITIZENS OF NAGASAKI HEARD THE *VRRROOW* OF A B-29 BANKING OVERHEAD...AND IT WAS THE LAST THING THEY HEARD BEFORE BEING BLOWN TO ETERNITY BY THE...

ATOM BOMB!

Figure 5.19. Copyright William M. Gaines, Agent, Inc. Used with permission.

of "spectacle" does not apply to comics; as war emerges in the pages of comics, it is quiet (all sound is reproduced as text), and the pacing is determined, in part, by the reader. Because comics do not generate the same visceral excitement that film can, readers of war comics are in a position to have a much more measured response than viewers of war films. In addition, as Michael Evans contends, "The American cinema of twentieth century combat has usually been at its most powerful when it has concentrated on the small rather than the big . . . situated in a minimalist setting. In such an environment, a sense of war's social realism and its murderous immediacy can be explored with precision, and the nature of war can be revealed with detail" (87). This strength—exploring the details of war with precision in a minimalist setting—is missing from many war films of the 1940s and 1950s, or else it is largely obscured by the nature of the medium. By contrast, attention to "precise details" in a "minimalist" setting is exactly the strategy by which Harvey Kurtzman expanded the comics medium with the EC war titles.

While war comics continue to sell in far fewer numbers than other genres, they are nonetheless fascinating comic books to study and ones in which the politically subversive appears with great regularity. Since EC shut down all of its publications except for *Mad* magazine in the late 1950s, there have been many other examples of American comic books subverting the dominant views of war at different cultural moments. An early example was Warren Publishing's *Blazing Combat* (1965–66), which only lasted four issues but which featured some outstanding war stories in the EC tradition—mainly because refugees from EC like Reed Crandall, George Evans, Joe Orlando, and others found work at Warren. One notable story is Orlando and Archie Goodwin's "Landscape!" (1965), which tells the tragic story of Luong, a simple rice farmer who is caught between two equally destructive armies, one of which is unmistakably American (the soldiers' use of helicopters and flamethrowers is a dead giveaway). Another example of a subversive war comic is Greg Irons and Tom Veitch's *A Legion of Charlies* (1971), which drew (literally) graphic parallels between William Calley and Charles Manson, addressing the My Lai massacre long before the details of this event entered popular discourse about the war. More recently, Eclipse Comics released *Real War Stories* #1 (1987), the tone of which—guided by the keen editorial hand of activist and comic-book writer Joyce Brabner—certainly ran counter to Reagan era politics: one story, "A Long Time Ago and Today," makes insightful (and, for conservatives, uncomfortable) connections between US foreign policy in Central America and Spanish colonialism. This particular comic book has also been cited, in a complimentary fashion, as "get[ting] across subversive messages to kids" (Nore 12). After Eclipse went bankrupt, the publication of *Real War Stories* was taken over by Citizen Soldier, "a nonprofit organization of soldiers and veterans whose aim is to get teenagers to think before they enlist" (Nore 12). To do this, they expose the "secret history" of the military by addressing topics like "gays and lesbians in the military, misleading recruiting practices, violent training techniques, and . . . racism and sexism in the service" (Nore 12). In addition, these and other comics like Marvel's *The 'Nam* (1986–93) and Vertigo's *War Story* (2001–3) have delivered representations of war that have been both visually and morally complex.[16]

In addition to the arguments I have made throughout this chapter, another reason that I have looked backward to the 1940s and 1950s is that back then, film did not have the "literary" cachet that it does today. At that time, despite bravura examples of artistry, like Orson Welles's *Citizen Kane* (1941), film was considered an influential medium mainly because of its mass appeal. Only later did film come into its own as a bona fide form of literature worthy of reflective critical and academic study. Interestingly enough, many film scholars have focused on these early periods of the medium in order to reveal how interesting its movies were. My belief is that this period of comics—especially war comics—is also a rich and rewarding area of study. Although representations of war are dominated by the more contemporary crop of powerful films like *Apocalypse Now* (1979), *Platoon* (1986), *Full Metal Jacket* (1987), *Saving Private Ryan* (1998), and *Letters from Iwo Jima* (2006),[17] I believe the EC stories still hold up today as some of the finest examples of comic book art and narrative that the medium has ever seen, and in terms of audacity and effectiveness, they are comparable to any of these films.

Scott McCloud has warned that we should not judge an entire medium based simply upon its most popular manifestations (6). After all, how foolish would it be to dismiss the entire medium of film outright simply because one did not find *Pirates of the Caribbean 2* to be artistically redeeming? Yet this position, which seems ludicrous as stated above, is exactly the kind of thinking that most people engage in when considering comic books. The EC war titles stand as examples of comic books that were far more politically daring and relevant than their film counterparts. They stand as examples of comics' unique graphic language and serve to show how that the representational strategies of comics can be every bit as complex as those of film. They stand, in the end, as the best evidence to counter lazy film critics who wish to demean a film by using the term "comic book" as a pejorative.

Notes

1. While both media "came of age" in the twentieth century, it is worth noting that in many ways comic art developed in advance of film. David Kunzle, in his *History of the Comic Strip: The Nineteenth Century*, points out that features like close-ups and varied perspective were employed in comic art long before film (348–69). In addition, Thomas Inge reminds us in his book, *Comics as Culture*, that "uses of panning, in which the camera remains in one place but pivots to follow an action, were frequently employed by comic artists long before it became commonplace in film" (143), and that in at least one case—Winsor McCay's *Little Nemo in Slumberland*—the comic artist "resolved problems which cinematographers didn't even know yet they would have to confront with the introduction of aerial photography" (144).

2. In 1998 the American Film Institute came out with its "100 Years . . . 100 Movies" list of the greatest one hundred films of all time. *Casablanca* was number two, right behind *Citizen Kane* (1941).

3. Both of these films demonstrate the influence of economics on Hollywood's representations of the war, but it is important to note that these economic influences can be traced in the period immediately preceding American involvement in the war. Because Hollywood was dependent on turning a financial profit, they were often reluctant to make politically oriented films in the late 1930s—particularly those films which represented the Germans or Italians as villains. At this point in Hollywood's history, "European sales were particularly crucial to the continuing financial success of the studio system" (Schindler 1), and filmmakers could ill afford to represent situations or countries that would lead to the overseas banning of their films. Thus, it must be stressed that "Hollywood's boldness was inversely proportional to the extent of its German and Italian market," and only after it became clear that this market was closed to Hollywood did the studios make films that were free of European pressures (Koppes and Black 39, 34).

4. In many ways, this partnership was welcome. Throughout the studio era, particularly in its early years, the oligarchy of the studios and the existence of a central-producer system meant that the political attitudes and creative interests of the studio executives could often be felt in the studio's products. Nowhere was this more true than at Warner Bros., a studio that Hollywood historian Thomas Schatz calls "the most factory-oriented of the majors" (300). From the start of the European fighting, studio president Harry Warner was outspoken in both his opposition to Hitler and his advocacy for fighting alongside England against Germany (Koppes and Black 43). These feelings about the necessity and glory of war come out in the aforementioned *Sergeant York* and *Casablanca*, but are also felt in other Warner Bros. features like *Dive Bomber* (1941) and *Air Force* (1943). At times, Warner seemed more politically than artistically motivated in his filmmaking, at one point in 1943 agreeing to make the film *Mission to Moscow* "by direct order of the White House" (Schindler 57). And Warner was not alone; other key figures in Hollywood had a vested interest in the war: Joseph I. Breen, who ran the Production Code Administration (PCA) was the father of three sons involved in the fighting (Doherty 14) and Darryl F. Zanuck,

the production chief at 20th Century Fox, had served in the US Army Signal Corps in 1942 (Doherty 15).

5. We are mainly indebted to Paul Fussell, essayist and former World War II infantryman, for a more realistic view of battle. He writes about what he calls "the bizarre damage suffered by the human body in modern war" by stating, "You would expect front-line soldiers to be struck and hurt by bullets and shell fragments, but such is the popular insulation from the facts that you would not expect them to be hurt, sometimes killed, by being struck by parts of their friends' bodies violently detached" (270). Fussell goes on to say that "the large wartime audience never knew these things. the letterpress correspondents, radio broadcasters, and film people who perceived these horrors kept quiet about them on behalf of the War Effort. . . . By not mentioning a lot of things, a correspondent could give the audience at home the impression that there were no cowards in the service, no thieves and rapists and looters, no cruel or stupid commanders" (285–86).

6. In his enlightening study of alternative comics, Charles Hatfield identifies a key dichotomy among those members of the comics community that "hold tightly to a romanticiced position of marginality and yet court wider recognition," and he warns that scholars must "navigate this swamp of conflicting values" (xii). To some extent, I feel that my argument throughout this book is defined by this apparent contradiction, where much of the political relevance that I ascribe to comics derives from their marginal status, and yet I use that relevance as evidence for the case that this medium should be taken more seriously. As I stated in Chapter Four, however, I believe that this medium will always be vaguely disreputable. In the end, acknowledging the inevitability of comics' marginal status does not have to negate the understanding that the medium is capable of highly sophisticated narrative art; in fact, this apparent paradox is what makes comics such an interesting medium to read, discuss, teach, and write about.

7. It is important to appreciate that all of these works argued for intervention at a time when this stance was unpopular. In the case of *Confessions of a Nazi Spy*, the script ran into several problems with Joe Breen's Production Code Administration: "one faction objected strenuously, arguing that the screenplay depicted Hitler and his government unfairly" (Koppes and Black 28). Similarly, Chaplin was pressured by United Artists to abandon his project (Koppes and Black 31). As for the cover of *Captain America* #1, its history is perhaps best captured through fictionalization in Michael Chabon's novel *The Amazing Adventures of Kavalier and Clay* (2000). In this book, the two main characters create a comic book hero called the Escapist in the late 1930s. Because Josef Kavalier was a refugee from Eastern Europe and all too familiar with Hitler's danger, he puts on the cover of his first comic a picture of his hero breaking the Fuhrer's jaw. The publishers, however, balk; they tell him, "This hitting Hitler thing . . . it makes us nervous" (158). It is also important to point out that the work done by artist Jack Kirby in his and Joe Simon's *Captain America* is quite rightly hailed as a significant advancement of the comics form. In fact, along with Will Eisner's *The Spirit* and Jack Cole's *Plastic Man*, *Captain America* is commonly cited as one of the 1940s' greatest innovative developments for the medium, for with this comic Kirby begins to expand the visual possibilities of the page. He not only breaks from the standard uniform patterning of panels, but he explores more fully how to tell a story visually as opposed to relying too heavily on the

narrative. In terms of story, however, *Captain America* often succumbed to many of the same propagandistic clichés of its contemporary war films. It would take until the next decade for comic books to achieve greater political maturity.

8. The first film overall to take on the events of September 11, 2001, was *The Guys* (2002), a limited-release independent film that was adapted from a stage play.

9. In the case of *The Steel Helmet*, the film was rediscovered not because it was about the Korean War but because the film's director, Sam Fuller, was a darling of the French Auteur critics, who sang his (and the film's) praises in the pages of *Cahiers du Cinema*.

10. Kurtzman's work on these two titles and in his later development of *Mad* (1952) makes his ultimate contribution to the evolution of the comic book difficult to overstate. In assessing the impact of *Mad* on our culture, Adam Gopnik contends that "almost all American satire today follows a formula that Harvey Kurtzman thought up" (74).

11. The next decade, the 1960s, would see the creation of DC's *Enemy Ace*, a comic set during World War II that was significant not only for Joe Kubert's artwork but also for Robert Kanigher's daring choice to make his protagonist a German flying ace. Kanigher and Kubert also collaborated on the creation of Sergeant Rock in the pages of DC's *Our Army at War* in the late 1950s. This character—whose politics fell somewhere between the unabashed jingoism of the Atlas/Marvel titles and the antiwar ethos of the EC titles—nevertheless (or perhaps therefore) has the distinction of being "one of the most popular and recognizable characters to arise from the genre" (Vaughan 77).

12. The numbering for *Two-Fisted Tales* presents a bit of a problem. EC was famous for reacting quickly to marketplace demands and interests, so a common situation was that one title would be changed into another, often without any regard for genre. So, in 1950, after fourteen issues, *Gunfighter* became *The Haunt of Fear*, which started with issue #15. *Haunt of Fear* ran for three issues before it was turned into *Two-Fisted Tales*, which then began with issue #18. Later, *Haunt of Fear* was resurrected, and it began with issue #1 (von Bernewitz and Geissman 123). *Two-Fisted Tales*, however, continued its run from issue #18 (1950) until its final installment, issue #41 (1955). The pages and panels that I reference from *Two-Fisted Tales* throughout this chapter come from reprints and the EC Annuals, both published by Gemstone Publishing. In creating these reprints, Gemstone renumbered *Two-Fisted Tales* from the first issue. So, in their collection of the first five issues of *Two-Fisted Tales*, the issue numbers given are not #18–#22, but rather (and more simply) #1–#5. Each of the reprints and annuals does contain a citation that states the original issue number of the comic. When I reference the issue numbers of *Two-Fisted Tales* throughout my text, the first number is the original issue number of the comic, while the number in brackets is the Gemstone reissue number. Because *Frontline Combat* began with issue #1, this distinction is unnecessary in those cases where I cite stories from that title.

13. The story as a whole also illustrates a favorite idea of Kurtzman's: in war, all are victims of war's machinery, the "subordination of the human to the mechanical in modern warfare" (Witek 1989 42). Kurtzman emphasizes this point throughout his stories most clearly with one of his favorite compositional and layout

devices: close-ups of weapons firing, seemingly without human agency, as people in surrounding panels suffer the effects.

14. Kurtzman also attacks the thirst for battle in "War Story!" from *Two-Fisted Tales* #19 [#2] (1951), where the "savage" is not the enemy, but an American soldier. This story recounts, in the form of a "morality tale" told by an older combatant to a younger recruit, the struggles of a group of soldiers. Two of these soldiers, Dave and Duke Hunter, are identical twins. Unfortunately, the resemblance ends there: where Dave is mild and easygoing, Duke is "mean, clear through" (2). Later in the story, they overrun a group of Japanese soldiers who have captured some Americans. One of the Japanese soldiers remains alive, and because the captured Americans say that he treated them humanely, they give him medical aid. This behavior does not sit well with Duke, who sneaks into the medical tent at night to kill the man. However, due to a series of unfortunate events, Duke ends up killing his brother Dave, who had been moved to the infirmary after being wounded in an air raid. The lesson of the story is delivered unsentimentally in the story's penultimate panel: "It's a dirty job we have to do . . . but doesn't mean we have to enjoy doing it" (7). With these lines, Kurtzman undermines the idea that true men—imagined by filmmakers of the time to be people like John Wayne in *Sands of Iwo Jima* and Aldo Ray in *Battle Cry*—should seek out battle.

15. This emphasis on the damage that war wreaks on civilians appears in several other EC stories as well. One that bears mentioning is "A Baby," from *Frontline Combat* #10 (1953). This story revolves around a Korean baby who is orphaned by the bombing of invading forces. The emotion wrung from this already harrowing story is relentless and best typified by a series of five panels in which the crying child eventually discovers his dead mother (7). The perspective is manipulated here so that the child becomes larger—and therefore closer to us—with each successive panel, culminating in the final panel, where he embraces his dead mother. In the 1950s, the Hollywood imagination was incapable of conceiving of such a scene set among the enemy, let alone delivering it with such power.

16. An interesting recent example of war writing that doesn't quite count as a comic book but nonetheless calls to mind that medium is Steve Mumford's *Baghdad Journal: An Artist in Occupied Iraq* (2005). Published by alternative comics publisher Drawn & Quarterly, this magnificent book is similar to Sue Coe's journalism in that it blends the text of personal observations (rendered here in a diary format) with impressionistic illustrations. Mumford's book channels the spirit of the EC war comics insofar as it focuses on the people of Iraq and imbues them with a humanity often elided in today's media.

17. While this last film has garnered much-deserved praise for its sympathetic portrayal of the Japanese, my response is that such a portrayal is long overdue in American cinema. Kurtzman and company beat Clint Eastwood to the punch by over fifty years.

6.
ILLUSTRATING THE CLASSICS
Comic Books vs. "Real" Literature

A few years ago I was asked to speak to a group of librarians about comic books and their place in school and public libraries. Essentially, I was arguing a point that I had been making long before the idea for this book began to take shape in my mind: that comic books are a potentially powerful artistic and narrative medium, a bona fide form of "Literature." To prepare for this talk, I put together a slideshow (this was before Powerpoint put a stranglehold on the world of presentations) containing many of the same images that populate these very pages, arranged my note cards, and donned my "comic book" tie, which features a number of the more famous Marvel comics covers. The group prepared about a dozen or so promotional flyers, and emblazoned on them was my talk's somewhat aggressive title: "Deserving Respect: The Literary Art of Comic Books."

Everything went very well. The setting was comfortable, my audience was receptive and engaged, the slide projector didn't screw up, and the cookie buffet that followed the talk was lavish (it featured macaroons). The most interesting part, however, was the Q&A session that followed. Several people questioned me about what was no doubt my boldest move: to equate the perceived "low" art of comic books with the "high" art of literature. The most pointed of these questions came from one woman who began with a remark about the old *Classics Illustrated* comics—how popular they were and how much she loved them and how they just seemed to vanish—and then asked if I thought that reading comic books would lead students to seek out "real" literature (her word, not mine).

Were I able to transport myself back to that time and place, I might be tempted to quote Rudolphe Töpffer, a Swiss artist who is widely credited with having invented the comic book in 1837 and who said, in regard to comics and literature, that "with its dual advantages of greater conciseness and greater relative clarity, the picture-story, all things being equal, should squeeze out the other (literature) because it would address itself with greater liveliness to a greater number of minds, and also because in any contest he who uses such a direct method will have the advantage over those who talk in chapters" (quoted in Hoff 20). My questioner's assumptions about the lowly nature of comics were certainly not shared by Töpffer, whose position here asserts the superiority of comics over her "real" reading. What actually happened, though, was that I stammered out a response about how reading comics was challenging and reward-ing in its own right. She nodded politely, but I don't think that she quite bought it. Her words continued to work their way around my mind, however, and in many ways I consider this final chapter to be a more fitting response to her question about the relationship between comic books and literature.

In each of the previous chapters I have attempted to show that comic books are worthy subjects for literary study in that they are every bit as complicated, revelatory, and relevant as more accept-able types of art. By positioning different comic book genres against the literatures of memoir, journalism, and film, I have attempted to show that comics creators can achieve artistic and political feats that are unique to the medium and thus unavailable to authors of these more respected forms. My approach in this chapter is somewhat dif-ferent. In the preceding chapters, my conceit of using "vs." in the title headings has been largely tongue-in-cheek, but here the intimation of conflict is more warranted, for—as the questioner in my audience implied—comic books are often cast in an oppositional relationship to "good" or "real" literature. In this chapter I examine what happens when comic book and literary worlds collide—a situation that has recurred fairly steadily since 1921, when a work of literature (Johann Wyss's *Swiss Family Robinson*) was first adapted into comics (Jones 9). In the years since then, there have been many more adaptations of the "classics" into comic books, and I focus on sever-al of the more prominent of these—including, of course, the comic book series that has served as the template for all such adaptations, *Classics Illustrated* (1941–71). From my perspective as a staunch advocate for the sophistication of comics, these literary adaptations have gone through a distinct evolution, ranging from paradoxical self-effacement of the comics medium, to embracing the unique for-mal and stylistic elements that comics have to offer, to asserting comics' own status as important literature that challenges popular conceptions of what it means to be "literary."

For students of my generation, the number one stress reliever for paper writing was (and perhaps still is) Cliffs Notes. These tidy little black and yellow booklets—available for just about every piece of reading in the high school English curriculum—contained everything a nervous student under the gun to write an essay could desire: plot synopses, historical contexts, character analyses, theme and symbol identification, and other elements that help students make sense of fiction. What better way, a high school senior might wonder, to understand the labyrinthine story of William Faulkner's *The Sound and the Fury*? Or the social conventions satirized by Jane Austen in *Pride and Prejudice*? Or the historical underpinnings of Nathaniel Hawthorne's *The Scarlet Letter*?[1] But long before Cliffs Notes and similarly packaged "help aids" became a cottage industry (and scourge of English teachers everywhere), many students of an earlier generation relied on a different kind of short cut: the Gilberton Company's line of *Classics Illustrated* comic books. After all, where else could one find a nearly seven-hundred page novel like Herman Melville's *Moby Dick* boiled down to just under fifty pages—complete with pictures, too? The popularity of these books was significant: over the course of its thirty years, the Gilberton Company printed and reprinted more than 160 titles; in addition, these titles would eventually "appear in 26 languages in 36 countries" (Jones 7).

Because of their popularity, no doubt, these comics were a source of controversy for the education-minded. As Donna Richardson points out, the controversy often revolved around a question very similar to the one voiced following my talk: "Did the comic format succeed in getting young readers to pick up the original works, or did the comics merely help students avoid tough reading assignments?" (82). Predictably, the jury was split. In his 1960 study comparing the Robert Louis Stevenson novel *Treasure Island* to its *Classics Illustrated* incarnation, educator Robert Emans defines the sides of the debate as it emerged in the 1940s. According to Ivah Green, writing in *Nation's Schools*, comics were a "solution to our problems of how to make learning painless and lasting" (quoted in Emans 253). On the other side was R. Ronson, who wrote in *National Parent–Teacher* that comic books were a "narcotic kind of reading [that] is contributing in no small measure to our deplorable national illiteracy" (quoted in Emans 253).[2] Ronson's position had a lot of traction in the anticomics fervor of the times, and his criticism was echoed by none other than Fredric Wertham, whose *Seduction of the Innocent* (1954) helped pave the way for the oppressive Comics Code discussed in Chapter One. Though some educators and critics sought to draw a distinction between "bad" and "good" comics, Wertham contended that "'good' comic books are at best weeds" (313) and that comic book versions of classics "do active harm by blocking one of the child's avenues to the finer things of life" (311).

I call attention to this debate because no discussion of comic book adaptations of literature can avoid it; after all, whether or not comic books can lead youngsters to the "classics" is the "central question" surrounding these comics (Richardson 82). My answer to this question is that the question itself is flawed, invested as it is in the belief that comic books constitute "low" art. Approaching *Classics Illustrated* and other comic books of this type from this perspective and with the aim of examining how the adaptation stacks up against the original does not, in the end, afford any real insight into the complexity of comics as an art form.[3] So while Ruth Stein provides a thorough comparative analysis between Mark Twain's *Huckleberry Finn* and various abridged versions, including the *Classics Illustrated* edition, her conclusion that the copies are "watered down and distorted" (1163) is largely beside the point. It goes without saying that transferring a several-hundred-page novel to a forty-eight-page comic book will necessarily "distort." But I am less interested in making specific comparisons between the source materials and their comic book adaptations than I am in discussing how comic books are positioned artistically in relation to that source material. That is, to what extent do the authors of comic book adaptations make a space for comic books as important literary creations in their own right?

Adapting "classic" works of literature into comic books was the brainchild of Albert Kanter, and the very features that make his line of comics so interesting—and paradoxical—can be traced back to the motivations that inspired his project in the first place. Like many immigrants who came to the US in the early twentieth century, Kanter (who hailed from Russia) was interested in capturing a portion of the great wealth that the new country promised. In his early years, he worked as a seller of cooking utensils, real estate, and surplus books (Sawyer 1–2). Having endured the Great Depression and its hardships, Kanter was attentive to different money-making opportunities, and the growing popularity of comic books in the 1940s was not lost on him (Jones 7). Somewhat opposed to his desire to capitalize on the popularity of comic books was his concern that these books were becoming too popular with his own children at the expense of what he considered to be more suitable reading. Thus did he come up with the idea to make money from comics by "'wooing' youngsters to great books" (Sawyer 2, 4).

The oft-repeated charge against *Classics Illustrated*—that they would replace the classics in young readers' lives—is ironic, therefore, given that such a circumstance was completely at odds with Kanter's intent, best captured by the exhortation that concluded each issue: "Now that you have read the *Classics Illustrated* edition, don't miss the added enjoyment of reading the original, obtainable at your school or public library." Kanter wanted his readers to seek out "real" books, not comic books. And in fact, he sought to differentiate his own titles from the other comics on the newsstand and drugstore racks.

He accomplished this objective in various ways. First, his comic books were much longer: the first issues weighed in at sixty-four pages, which was much longer than the industry standard of around thirty-two pages; when the page total was later reduced to fifty-six and then to forty-eight, the *Classics Illustrated* titles were still longer than other comics.[4] Second, there was no advertising in *Classics Illustrated*; any pages that were not devoted to the adaptation were given over to short educational essays on the author or some historical event. Third, reprints were readily available, unlike other comic books, which, once they sold out were gone forever (or at least until comic book shops and eBay came along); the *Classics Illustrated* comics, by contrast, often went through several printings and could be ordered via a handy list on the back cover of each book. Fourth, *Classics Illustrated* cost a full nickel more than other titles, and finally, the use of painted covers for new issues and reprints beginning in 1951 "was supposed to render the Classics as a cultured comic that more closely reflected the original works on which they were based" (Sawyer 9–10).

Kanter did not develop such differences because he wanted to create a new kind of comic book; his interest was far less in the comics than in promoting the classics, so he sought to efface the comics medium whenever possible. One such denial took place in the naming of his product. When the Gilberton Company released its first adaptation—*The Three Musketeers* in October of 1941—the title on the cover was *Classic Comics*, a name that would remain until 1947, the year in which Kanter excised the "Comics" part of the name and rechristened the line as *Classics Illustrated*, the moniker by which most people remember them. When this change occurred, beginning with *Mysterious Island* (issue #34), the editors included a blurb that read, in part, "The name 'Classics Illustrated' is the better name for your favorite periodical. It really isn't a 'comic' . . . it's the illustrated, or picture, version of your favorite classics" (quoted in Jones 72).[5]

This rejection of the medium was also evident in the aftermath of the creation of the Comics Code and its enforcer, the Comics Magazine Association of America (CMAA). Ascribing to the newly established and oppressive code meant joining the CMAA, but the Gilberton Company refused—not as an anticensorship protest, but out of the belief "that [their] adaptations of literary classics were not comic books" (Nyberg 117).[6] In the end, Kanter's negative feelings about the comic book medium and the subordination of his products to their more esteemed source material established that the *Classics Illustrated* comic books' "essential endeavor [was] to make themselves obsolete" (Witek 36).

This paradoxical attitude—to simultaneously use and efface the comic book medium—also plays out in the artwork over the course of the *Classics Illustrated* series. Generally, readers who preferred the exploits of Batman to those of D'Artagnan avoided their "literary" cousins, for they "bore too little resemblance to comic books" (quoted in MacPherson). Yet artistically speaking, this perception is not wholly warranted. In actuality, the Gilberton Company employed many talented artists, including Louis Zansky, Henry C. Kiefer, Alex Blum, Lou Cameron, and Norman Nodel. These artists were joined by several others with impressive résumés, including individuals who did fine work for EC in the 1940s and 1950s like Joe Orlando, Reed Crandall, George Evans, and one of the most infamous of the horror artists, Graham Ingels. In addition, comic book readers of the 1960s who counted their change and the days until the next issue of *The Fantastic Four*, *X-Men*, or *The Hulk* appeared would no doubt be dumbfounded to know that even their beloved Jack Kirby—Marvel's head artist, whose work significantly changed the look of mainstream comic books—had done work for *Classics Illustrated*.

As skilled draftsmen, these and other artists were familiar with the graphic language of comics, and they demonstrated as much in the visual construction of their panels. One important element in a panel is composition—the arrangement of details within the panel. Robert Webb's adaptation of Mary Shelley's *Frankenstein* is noteworthy for its interesting compositions throughout, particularly in the scene where Justine is wrongly hanged for a murder committed by the monster (see Figure 6.1). Webb uses the gallows' vertical beams to create two smaller panels within the larger whole—one to frame Justine's hanging body in the foreground on the left and the other to frame Victor, who feels responsible for the deaths that have resulted from his creation, in the background on the right. The effect of this framing is to highlight these two individuals, and the size differences between the figures—Justine's lifeless form is much larger than Victor—serve as a visual interpretation of how Justine's death overwhelms the spiritually diminished Victor.

Another element of panel construction is perspective. In his

Figure 6.1. Copyright 2007 First Classics Inc. All rights reserved.
By permission of Jack Lake Productions, Inc.

Comics and Sequential Art—a remarkable exegesis on the visual language of comics—Will Eisner argues that "the viewer's response to a given scene is influenced by his position as a spectator" (1985 89). As an illustration of this point, artist Joe Orlando enhances the interpretation of Charles Dickens's *A Tale of Two Cities* by giving the reader a "street's eye" view of the action, consciously placing the viewer amidst the French revolutionaries (see Figure 6.2). This placement brings the viewer nearer to the action and renders the riot more vivid and threatening—a strategy highlighted by the appearance of a victim's arm in the bottom center of the panel. Coupled with the text, which reads in part, "Mobs killed 1,100 defenseless prisoners," Orlando's use of perspective allows us to judge the revolutionaries without being quite able to escape them.

Along with construction of individual panels, the arrangement of these panels on a page—or the "layout"—is an important "controlling device" (Eisner 1985 41). Over the course of the *Classics Illustrated* run, many artists used interesting visual combinations of panels to

FOUR DAYS PASSED BEFORE DR. MANETTE RETURNED. DURING THAT TIME THERE WAS AN ATTACK UPON THE PRISONS. MOBS KILLED 1,100 DEFENSELESS PRISONERS.

Figure 6.2. Copyright 2007 First Classics Inc. All rights reserved.
By permission of Jack Lake Productions, Inc.

tell their story. Throughout his adaptation of Robert Louis Stevenson's *Dr. Jekyll and Mr. Hyde*, for example, artist Lou Cameron continually alters panel sizes and employs shifting visual perspectives in order to effectively pace the narrative and heighten the effects of Stevenson's tale of terror. In one two-page spread where Jekyll transforms into Hyde, Cameron's visual mastery is evident (12–13). On the left page, Cameron begins the sequence with a large "establishing" panel that fills the entire top half of the page. In this panel, Cameron depicts Jekyll, inside his laboratory, working with his chemicals. Beneath this panel and filling out the rest of the page is a row of three narrow, vertical panels in which Jekyll drinks and reacts to his potion. Because of their dimensions, these panels tightly frame Jekyll's body and are an effective visual illustration of this particular moment, for "narrow panels . . . create a crowded feeling [and] enhance the rising tempo of panic" (Eisner 33). On the next page, Cameron delivers the transformation in bits and pieces through separate panels: a close-up of Jekyll's face; Jekyll, now much shorter, from behind; a closeup of a misshapen, hairy hand; a shaded image of a body slumped on the floor; and finally, a tight close-up of Hyde's visage. The images are helped along—arguably unnecessarily—by text boxes documenting the changes at the top of each panel. The penultimate panel contains a thought balloon in which we read, "Now I am once more free from that righteous old doctor. I shall go out and taste of life as Henry Jekyll has never dared dream" (13). Here, Hyde's thoughts allow him to emerge as a character from the preceding visual spectacle. The page's final panel is a long shot that frames Hyde's shadowed figure. Had this panel appeared without the context of the previous panels, we might read the diminutive figure in the center as an image of loneliness; however, given the preceding images and the story they tell, we read it instead as ominous.

Despite these and other instances of visual flair, the art in *Classics Illustrated* generally suffered from "officially sanctioned blandness" (Richardson 81). One reason is the series used what was known in the early days of the industry as a "shop." These shops were "comic book factories" where writers and artists, under the direction of the shop owner, could meet the growing demand for comic books by using "assembly line methods" (Harvey 1996 17). Because each shop used a specific group of writers and artists, the comic books that rolled out of its doors often had a distinctive, uniform style. One of the most famous of these shops—the "Iger" shop, named after its founder, Jerry Iger—began to do work for the Gilberton Company. Beginning in 1945 with Issue #23, Charles Dickens's *Oliver Twist*, the Iger Shop oversaw production of *Classics Illustrated* and continued to do so for nine years, their work amounting to almost one hundred issues (Jones 37). The result of this arrangement and its legacy was a certain "house style" that some critics have derided as "workmanlike" and "endlessly the same" (Richardson 81).

One element of Gilberton's house style involved the text design, and in particular the lettering and word balloons. I discussed in Chapter Two the importance of hand-lettering to the comic book memoirist, for it "more closely approximates the nuances of the human voice than does mechanically produced type" (Witek 23). One of the trademarks of the *Classics Illustrated* is this "mechanical" lettering style that conveys a stiffness in all of the elements requiring text: narration, dialogue, and thoughts. Virtually any comic in the line serves as an example of this trait, which was often echoed and intensified by the "squarish" word balloons. Even these balloons' "tails"—those appendages that denote the speaker—are drawn with straight edges. These effects create an odd formality to this comic in particular and to the line as a whole.

Such formality extended to the layout as well. It is important to point out that many of the flourishes discussed earlier involved action sequences and were, by and large, the exception to the rule. Even Jack Kirby's art—so dynamic in mainstream comics such as *Captain America*, *The Fantastic Four*, and *X-Men*—was handcuffed by the uniform and conservative house style, here "evident in the almost universal prescription of square or rectangular panels with straight-edged borders" (Jones 113). In Kirby's adaptation of Edward Bulwer-Lytton's *The Last Days of Pompeii*, for example, there is a sequence describing the various physical matches—such as jousting and boxing—that took place in the in the arena. Unlike Kirby's mainstream work, which would tell a story visually by employing flourishes such as shifting perspective, panel size variance, and the simulation of motion, this particular sequence is a series of uniform images that rely on the information in the text boxes to tell the story (37). Although Kirby's flair for depicting the physical body in action is evident, his capabilities as an artist were not served well by the restrictive house style of *Classics Illustrated*.

This situation proved especially challenging in the adaptations of Shakespeare. In general, a theatrical setting creates a uniformity of perspective; the nature of the proscenium is that spectators remain a constant distance from the action throughout. For prolific house artists like Alex Blum and Henry C. Kiefer—who had an acting background (Jones 50)—this constant distance between reader and subject perfectly suited their style. Unfortunately, such uniformity creates remoteness in a comic book. In Blum's adaptation of *Hamlet*, for example, it is admirable that entire speeches—including Hamlet's monologues—are kept intact (and even helpfully glossed). However, the visual delivery of these speeches is stagnant. In the scene of Hamlet's "to be or not to be" soliloquy, Blum creates a full-page panel in which we see Ophelia in the foreground, Hamlet in the center, and Polonius on the background, behind a curtain (13). On the page, the word balloon containing Hamlet's speech fills a full quarter of the space, and the reader's attention is monopolized by the text at the expense of the visual. In fact, the visual accomplishes little more than to establish staging; the storytelling duties fall completely to the text. While this situation works in a written copy of the play, it creates flatness in a comic book insofar as the images—the lifeblood of the comics form—are woefully underappreciated.

The larger problem, however, is that all of the art tended toward realism, giving an overwhelming sense of uniformity to the series as a whole. As I discuss throughout this book, a key element of comics' graphic language is the artistic style and its function as an expressive device. Chapters Two and Four discuss this idea within the contexts of the memoir and journalism, respectively, and a main argument in both chapters is that the art becomes an outgrowth of an individual creator's perspective, marking those stories as the imaginative product of that particular creator and no other. That is, the art becomes a sign of individuality. Yet it is precisely this individuality that is absent from the *Classics Illustrated* line, which sought a certain look that was informed by Kanter's desire to distance himself from the comic book form and, therefore, to appear respectable. His artists adapted a stylistically diverse group of writers that included Cervantes, Twain, Dostoyevsky, the Brontë sisters, Dickens, Stowe, Hugo, and others, but in the majority of cases the art does little to convey subtle and not-so-subtle differences among these writers' styles. The result is that both comic book and "literature" get shortchanged: the comic book is denied full expression of its signifying capabilities, and "literature" loses its stylistic diversity as the unique features of each writer are downplayed in favor of consistency.

Later comic book adaptations of literature would not completely suffer this same fate. Gilberton may have closed up shop in 1971, but its project was resurrected in a few different forms, and what is most notable about these reincarnations is that they embrace—to varying degrees, to be sure—the comic book medium as one that can tell a story with power and artistry. One of the first reappearances of this genre came in 1976 with issue #1 of *Marvel Classics Comics*. Like the *Classics Illustrated*, these comics carried no advertising and were longer than the standard comic; in Marvel's case, the length was a hefty fifty-two pages. Unfortunately, aside from Gil Kane–drawn covers, the first several issues look and read like second-rate knock offs of the Gilberton products—mainly because they were. The first twelve *Classics Comics* were actually from the disappointing series *Pendulum Classics*; Stan Lee purchased and repackaged several of these issues to no one's admiration (Jones 190). Beginning with issue #13, however, Marvel began to produce the adaptations itself, and future "stars" of the comic book industry like Doug Moench and Chris Claremont often wrote the scripts while a stable of capable artists provided the visual renderings.

The results were mixed. On the one hand, these newer versions embraced a looser, more dynamic visual style that employed devices such as erratically shaped word balloons, sound effects, and a far less "gridlike" layout style (see Figures 6.3–6.5); in short, the *Classics Comics* were not afraid to look like comic books. On the other hand, as was the case with the original *Classics Illustrated*— and maybe even more so—the style of artwork from issue to issue is unnervingly consistent, again creating a false sense of stylistic consistency among the source material writers. So, while the *Marvel Classics Comics* embrace their "comic bookness" more so than the *Classics Illustrated*, they still fail to fully explore the medium's potential to create art.

Despite the appeal that *Classics Comics* might have held for readers of mainstream comic books, they never caught on, and the series folded after thirty-six issues. The real advance in terms of comic books carving out a space for themselves as a legitimate artistic medium came in the early 1980s, when Oval Projects, Ltd. produced graphic novel adaptations of three of Shakespeare's tragedies: *Macbeth* (1982), *Othello* (1983), and *King Lear* (1984). What immediately sets these editions apart from the *Classics Illustrated* comics is that they retain the complete text of each play. So, unlike the editing and rewording that appeared in *Classics Illustrated* versions of *Hamlet*, *Macbeth*, and *A Midsummer Night's Dream*, the main task undertaken by Oval Projects was to adapt the plays in strictly visual terms. In his adaptation of *Othello*, artist Oscar Zarate is adept at using every square inch of a panel, filling them with lush colors and ornamentation that make the play come alive. One of the most striking segments occurs when Othello is called before the Senate to answer charges that he has somehow bewitched Desdemona into marrying him. Othello makes his case to the Duke of Venice, the senators, and Brabantio, claiming that he wooed her only by telling tales of his youth and adventures. As he recounts this storytelling—and indirectly, his adventures—Zarate fills the panels with images of the strange sights Othello has witnessed (16–17).

Similarly effective is Ian Pollack's adaptation of *King Lear*. Pollack's boldest stroke is the union of a surreal drawing style with a highly expressionistic use of watercolors. In his depiction, the characters are drawn in ways that emphasize their inner selves; thus, Cordelia and France are open-faced and earnest, while Edmund, the bastard, has a cold, sloping face and predatory eyes (4, 123). Pollack uses his art to underscore the play's concerns about the importance of and problems with perception. The art makes clear to the reader what is often hidden from the other characters: their true natures. The play is also about madness and emotion, and these are qualities that Pollack grounds visually with his impassioned brush-

Figure 6.3. Image appears courtesy of Marvel Comics, Inc.

Figure 6.4. Image appears courtesy of Marvel Comics, Inc.

Figure 6.5. Image appears courtesy of Marvel Comics, Inc.

work—particularly in the scenes of Lear on the heath (67). In these two books, the art shares the stage, as it were, with the text of Shakespeare's play.

Building on such celebration of comic book art as a viable medium for literary adaptation, Berkley/First Publishing revived the *Classics Illustrated* line in 1990—but with noticeable differences. Although less successful than the original *Classics Illustrated* (the revival lasted only twenty-nine issues and did not enjoy even a fraction of the first series' sales), these books represented an advancement of the original concept. Besides the *Classics Illustrated* imprint and a penchant for the same source material, one important difference was that the new books were printed in a square-bound prestige format, and thus looked far less disposable than the originals. One might argue that this type of binding is simply a continuation of Kanter's desire to make his product look as little like a comic book as possible. However, the changed binding should be viewed in the larger context of comic books at this particular point in their history: specifically, the rise of the "graphic novel" during the late 1980s as a more respectable type of comic book—but still a comic book—and the attempt of publishers to channel this respectability by giving their books a binding suitable for placement on a bookshelf. That is, rather than effacing the medium, the book design here is meant to elevate it. Also consistent with this move to elevate the status of the lowly comic book is the added attention paid by the new *Classics Illustrated* to those responsible—the artists. In the originals, one is lucky to find a small "illustration by" credit on the first page; more often than not, the people who wrote and drew the comic books were anonymous—an anonymity further reflected in the general lack of distinction from issue to issue. In the new line, not only were the artists' names featured prominently on the cover, but these individuals also received their own biographical notes at the end of each book.

Another interesting shift between the original and the revamped line was in the editors' direction to the reader regarding the source material. Whereas the whole point of the Gilberton issues was to get young readers to get to their local library and do some "real" reading, the new versions suggest that their comic books possessed some value of their own. Specifically, while the mission statement printed on the inside cover of each issue states that they are "not substitutes for the original," it also declares that the comic books could "stand on their own merits." Further, the statement offers praise for the comic book form by informing the reader that the book in hand was "produced by some of the world's most talented writers and artists"—as opposed to the original *Classics Illustrated* covers, which praised only the writers—and that these comics "reflect those individual styles that made the original works great—not just the stories, but the nuances as well." The assumption here is that the comic book form is capable of capturing the "nuances" of great literature. This was not an assumption that Albert Kanter would have shared.

But the most significant change between the original and the revamped series is the art. Unlike its forebears, the new *Classics Illustrated* line celebrates the comic book aesthetic by emphasizing dynamic art by prominent comic book artists like Kyle Baker, Bill Sienkiewicz, Jill Thompson, Peter Kuper, and others. A cursory glance at the covers of these new versions—all drawn by the artists themselves—is enough to get a sense of the diverse artistic styles that appear within. While the uniform painted covers of the old line bespoke staid consistency, the new covers promise visual excitement and difference. The acknowledgment of the importance of comic art is further reflected in the editors' attempts to match certain artists with particular source material and, in effect, to use the artistic style as a visual expression of a writer's prose style. On the whole this matching is quite effective. Jill Thompson's delicate watercolors capture the solemnity of Nathanial Hawthorne's *The Scarlet Letter*; Michael Ploog's broad, comedic linework evokes the humor of Mark Twain's *Adventures of Tom Sawyer*; and Peter Kuper's geometric, almost woodcutlike rendering of his characters emphasizes the dehumanization of the working class that Upton Sinclair wrote of in *The Jungle*.

One of the most startling of these pairings is Bill Sienkiewicz's adaptation of *Moby Dick*. Sienkiewicz's version is heavily atmospheric and imbues Melville's tale with a palpable sense of dread. In the scene at the Whaleman's Chapel, for instance, Sienkiewicz both captures the mood of the scene and at the same time makes a strong case for comics as a unique and powerfully expressive medium. In this particular scene, Sienkiewicz's use of heavy brown and yellow tones creates a distinct atmosphere and helps locate the story in the past (4). Also interesting is the way in which Sienkiewicz uses different colors of text boxes to differentiate between Ishmael's narration and Father Mapple's sermon. And just as the novel *Moby Dick* is a pastiche of sorts in which Melville hangs on the main narrative various essaylike digressions about the history and nature of whaling, so too does Sienkiewicz indulge in different artistic styles to reflect the different writing styles (19).

The dynamism of the art in the new *Classics Illustrated* comic books is reflected in the layouts as well. Unlike the original line, these versions remain ungoverned by a "house style"; instead, the

Figure 6.6. Copyright 2007 First Classics Inc. All rights reserved.
By permission of Jack Lake Productions, Inc.

artists create breakdowns based on their unique vision of the book
in question. Steven Grant and Tom Mandrake's adaptation of *Hamlet*
is a good example of how comic book artists use layout to "open up"
a story. As discussed earlier, such an objective was not a goal in the
original *Classics Illustrated* version, where the proscenium was often
preserved to the detriment of the comic book. In the case of *Hamlet*,
the artists fully exploit the fact that comics can, visually, take the
reader anywhere; we are not confined to one spot, as we would be
when watching a play. In the scene when Hamlet first confronts his
uncle and mother, for example, Grant and Mandrake eschew traditional panels in order to emphasize the psychological drama (see
Figure 6.6). Here, we are given close-ups of Claudius and Gertrude
as they respond to Hamlet's entrance. That they are not confined by
panels and instead seem to be crowding Hamlet to the side of the
page is a visual expression of their dominance over him. The long
horizontal panel that follows—an extreme close-up of Hamlet's
eyes—brings us closer to that character than is possible in a con-

ventional theatrical production. The specific effect in *Hamlet* is that the churning inner drama of Shakespeare's characters is reflected by the visual narrative; the more general effect of *Hamlet* and the other new *Classics Illustrated* adaptations is that the unique elements of this medium are recognized as important storytelling devices. Through their emphasis on individual, stylized art and expressive layouts, these books celebrate the capabilities of the comic book form and help establish the literary and artistic value of that medium.

More recently, comic book creators have continued to take up this cause in the graphic novel, which has become the chosen vehicle for literary adaptations. Such titles include David Zane Mairowitz and Robert Crumb's *Introducing Kafka* (1993); the "Neon Lit" series that featured Paul Karasik and David Mazzucchelli's adaptation of Paul Auster's *City of Glass* (1994) and Bob Callahan and Scott Gillis's adaptation of Barry Gifford's *Perdita Durango* (1995); Gareth Hinds's *Beowulf* (2000)[7]; and Peter Kuper's *The Metamorphosis* (2003). By virtue of their attention to the creative use of visual art, these graphic novels celebrate the ability of comics to translate substantial works of literature, but none embrace this position more fully than the "Puffin Graphics." This series of paperback-sized graphic novels features visually diverse comic book adaptations of the usual suspects (e.g., *Frankenstein*, *The Call of the Wild*, *The Red Badge of Courage*). Like the Shakespeare graphic novels and the revamped *Classics Illustrated* series, the Puffin Graphics provide strong visual adaptations of "classics" by using artists who have both individual styles and a strong sense of visual storytelling. In Gary Reed and Frazer Irving's adaptation of *Frankenstein*, these skills are exemplified by Irving's atmospheric shading; in Reed and Becky Cloonan's adaptation of *Dracula*, Cloonan's distinctive style of exaggerating facial features plays up the characters' "monstrosity." In addition, the illustrators employ extreme variety in their page layouts throughout. All in all, these are solid adaptations that are served well by the added length of the graphic novel, for the additional space gives the adaptors more room to stay true to the original story.

But the feature that most firmly marks the Puffin Graphics as a celebration of the comic book medium comes at the end of each adaptation, in a "Making of" section. These parts of each book— which run upwards of twenty-five pages—provide readers with information about how the book in hand was created. Or, more specifically, how prose was broken down visually into panels and pages. Included in these sections are examples from the artists' "sketchbooks" as they develop a visual conception for each character, explanations of "pencils" and how they are transformed into final art, and presentations of rough panel and page layouts. These sections do something that Albert Kanter would have never dreamed of for his *Classics Illustrated* line: they acknowledge the artistry that goes into the creation of a comic book, and in so doing they affirm the value of that form as a complex storytelling medium.

One of the Puffin Graphics, Arthur Byron Cover and Tony Leonard Tamai's adaptation of *Macbeth*, does something even more remarkable in terms of the juxtaposition between comic books and "literature": it begins to articulate an argument not simply for the comic book medium's formal sophistication, but for that medium's literary value in its own right. Despite the fact that most recent examples of comic book adaptations explore the possibilities of the comic book form, such possibilities are presented strictly in terms of adaptation. That is, the point they establish is that the formal elements of comics are capable of adapting something "literary." As such, the comic book remains subservient to the original source material. The Puffin Graphic *Macbeth*, however, retells Shakespeare's tragedy by transporting the play into the world of Japanese manga. Set in an alternative world where characters ride winged dragons and interact with intelligent robots, Shakespeare's themes remain the same but are transplanted into a distinctly comic book world. Tamai's artistic style is informed by several conventions commonly associated with manga: distinctive facial features, excessive emotion, pointed word balloons, the use of "speed lines," and frenetic, text-free layouts (see Figures 6.7 and 6.8). By transporting *Macbeth* in this way, Cover and Tamai are not using comics simply as a vehicle for adaptation—a position that privileges the source material; instead, they meld the two forms together in a way that places both comic books and "literature" on the same level.

Arguing that comic books are both a literature in their own right and much more than an "easy-to-read" format for kids is a position that many comic book creators have taken. These creators aim to expose an artificial split between so-called "high" and "low" culture, where "literature" is a clear example of the former and comic books of the latter. One comic book that has addressed this dubious split is Neil Gaiman's *Sandman* (1987–96), which remains one of the medium's most literate and engaging series, garnering a great number of critical and commercial rewards over its run.[8] Describing this marvelous and imaginative series in a few sentences is inevitably reductive, but in essence *Sandman* chronicles the lives of the Endless, seven siblings who preside over various facets of existence: Destiny, Death, Desire, Despair, Delirium, Destruction, and Dream. The

Figure 6.7. From *William Shakespeare's Macbeth: The Graphic Novel* adapted by Arthur Byron Cover, illustrated by Tony Leonard Tamai. Copyright 2005 by Byron Preiss Visual Publications. Used by permission of www.penguin.com.

Figure 6.8. From *William Shakespeare's Macbeth: The Graphic Novel* adapted by Arthur Byron Cover, illustrated by Tony Leonard Tamai. Copyright 2005 by Byron Preiss Visual Publications. Used by permission of www.penguin.com.

ostensible focus of the series is this last character—known also as "Sandman"—and the intrigues that he and his siblings find themselves enmeshed in through various planes of existence, including our own world. As readers of *Sandman* would be quick to point out, however, the series is more accurately a celebration of stories and storytelling. As Dream intones in *Sandman* #19 (1990), "Things need not have happened to be true. Tales and dreams are the shadow-truths that will endure when mere facts are dust and ashes, and forgot" (21). In celebrating the value of stories, Gaiman interweaves disparate narrative traditions including various mythologies, different religious traditions, history, popular culture, and—most relevant to my purposes here—Shakespeare.

Gaiman introduces Shakespeare into his comic with *Sandman* #13 (1990). As a subplot to this issue's main narrative, Dream encounters young "Will Shaxberd" as a struggling playwright who is consumed with envy over his friend Christopher Marlowe's gift with words. Intrigued, Dream strikes a bargain with Will: in return for literary abilities that will "spur the minds of men" (13), Shakepeare must write two plays for Dream. These plays turn out to be *A Midsummer Night's Dream*—which is dramatized in *Sandman* #19—and *The Tempest*—the writing of which is the subject of *Sandman* #75 (1996), the series' final issue. These two plays—filled as they are with dreams, stories, and magic—find a perfect complement in the larger themes of *Sandman*. While neither issue can be considered an adaptation as such—at least not in the *Classics Illustrated* sense—both issues convey the essential plots and ideas of the plays. What is more significant, however, is how Gaiman uses the themes of the plays to serve the larger *Sandman* narrative. In *Sandman* #19, Dream asks that Shakespeare and his acting troupe perform *A Midsummer Night's Dream* to a private audience that happens to include King Auberon and Queen Titania of the Faerie Kingdom—two important characters in the play. During the performance, Dream reveals that the play is meant to repay a debt that he owes to the two. As he tells them, "They shall not forget you. That was important to me: that King Auberon and Queen Titania will be remembered by mortals, until this age is gone" (21). Here, Shakespeare's play serves mainly as an element in the relationship between Gaiman's own characters.

In *Sandman* #75, Gaiman's portrait of Shakespeare at the end of his career dovetails with the end of the series and the death of Dream, which occurs in *Sandman* #69. Events in *Sandman* #75 take place several hundred years earlier than Dream's demise, but they form an instructive moment in that character's history. When

Shakespeare asks him why he wanted a play such as *The Tempest*, Dream responds, "I wanted a tale of graceful ends. I wanted a play about a King who drowns his books, and breaks his staff, and leaves his kingdom. About a magician who becomes a man. About a man who turns his back on magic" (35). Readers of the series recognize that Dream is giving voice to his own desires, which (at the time) he believes will never come to pass. For readers of *Sandman*, this recognition in the series' last issue is poignant, and we see Prospero's final speech in *The Tempest* as an explanation of the motivations that have driven Dream throughout the comic book's run.

Gaiman's achievement in these issues is really quite radical: he uses the themes of a timeless play for his comic book character, and what is more, he recasts these themes so that they partially emanate from this character. In effect, Gaiman appropriates the most sacrosanct figure in English literature to serve the needs of his comic book. To Gaiman, all stories are valuable no matter their origin, and his fascination with Shakespeare reveals his own democratic spirit regarding what constitutes the "literary." In discussing the theory that Shakespeare was not the original author of his plays, Gaiman admits to anger at "the underlying assumption that the plays had to be written by someone with property and a title, that they couldn't be the work of a 'normal' person" (quoted in Bender 224–25). Similar literary pretensions are reflected in the notion that great literature could not possibly emerge in the comic book, and Gaiman contributed seventy-six issues of *Sandman* as evidence to the contrary.[9] Despite his "theft," Gaiman remains respectful of Shakespeare, creating in him a complexity worthy of the playwright's own characters. Gaiman's two Shakespeare issues—as well as the series as a whole, with its connections to mythology, theology, and folklore—demonstrate a true union of "high" and "low" art insofar as the source material takes a subsidiary role within the larger comic book narrative.

Sandman is not the only mainstream title to challenge perceptions of what is "literary." In his *League of Extraordinary Gentlemen, Vol. I* (2000) and *Vol. II* (2003), Alan Moore continues Gaiman's project to bridge the "high" and "low" divide, but his approach is somewhat different. Where Gaiman focuses on a well-known and respected writer in order to subsume his play's themes into his own narrative, Moore reimagines famous fictional characters in terms of comic book formulas. This strategy undermines any literary pretensions that those characters may lay claim to, and through it Moore argues that comic books are every bit as literary as the novels that traditionally enjoy that distinction. The *League* books center on a small group of characters assembled to fight menaces that threaten the world. In this way, Moore's league calls to mind another league—DC Comics' Justice League of America—and conforms to the conventions of the "team superhero story: a handful of members of disparate personality and abilities are brought together from their various fictional narratives to face a threat that could not be faced alone" (Klock 100). The main difference is that the setting for the *League* books is late-nineteenth-century England, and the characters wear, instead of capes, a literary pedigree from classic British literature (and, for that matter, from *Classics Illustrated*). The roster includes Alan Quartermain (from several H. Rider Haggard novels, including *King Solomon's Mines*), Mina Harker (from *Dracula*), Henry Jekyll/Edward Hyde (from *Dr. Jekyll and Mr. Hyde*), Hawley Griffin (from *The Invisible Man*), and Captain Nemo (from Jules Verne's *20,000 Leagues under the Sea*). Interacting with these characters are several other literary personages, including Edgar Allan Poe's August Dupin, Sir Arthur Conan Doyle's Professor Moriarty, Edgar Rice Burroughs's John Carter (of Mars), and Wells's Dr. Moreau.

Through his use of these characters, Moore makes a statement about the problematic connotations of "high" and "low" art and how these perceptions are ever-shifting. He sets the stage for this statement by applying a key feature of comic books—that the characters cohabitate a common "universe"—to the world of literature. Thus, Mina Harker can interact with Edward Hyde in much the same way as Batman can make a guest appearance in a Superman comic. Moore has fun with the possibilities here. In *League*'s second volume, Moore retells *The War of the Worlds* but revises that novel so that his team is at the forefront of battling the Martians. In Moore's revision, characters from two other Wells novels play key roles: Griffin betrays the team and his fellow countrymen in order to help the alien invaders, and Dr. Moreau creates the supervirus that eventually destroys them. In this way, Moore reconceives the world of literature as a grand "comic book" universe.

This move, however, is not idle play; rather, it is a clear strategy that forces us to reevaluate the very idea of what it means to be "literary." Specifically, the books from which these characters hail are today recognized as classics, but that was not always the case: writers like Haggard, Wells, Verne, and the others that Moore borrows from here were mainstays of Victorian pulp literature, that "relatively disreputable fiction" (Wolk 9). That is to say, at the time of their publication, these books were popular with readers but certainly not taught in British classrooms. Appealing as they did to a wide range of (mainly young) readers and embarking on adventure, mystery, and horror, these writers' characters were, for all intents and pur-

Figure 6.9. Copyright 2000 R. Sikoryak. Used with permission.

poses, the comic book heroes of their day,[10] and Moore cleverly makes this situation literal in his books. Taken together, his two *League* books underscore "the failures of the dominant high-low culture paradigm by reminding us that the high culture of this century was the pop culture of the last" (Klock 102).

Moore's objective to challenge the literary pretensions that build a wall between comic books and "literature" is also shared by Robert Sikoryak, who brilliantly satirizes the stodginess of *Classics Illustrated*. Sikoryak's "low" art adaptations of "high" art have appeared in the Art Spiegelman–edited *Raw* magazine and in three anthologies from Drawn & Quarterly Publications: *Drawn & Quarterly* 3 (2000), *Drawn & Quarterly* 4 (2001), and *Drawn & Quarterly* 5 (2003). In his stories, Sikoryak adapts literary classics in the form of well-known and recognizable comics. His pieces have included "Inferno Joe" (Dante's *Inferno* retold through a series of Bazooka Joe comics), "Good Ol' Gregor Brown" (Kafka's *Metamorphosis* reimagined as a series of *Peanuts* strips), "Ras Kol: Crime and Punishment" (Dostoyevsky's psychological novel filtered through a 1950s Batman comic), "Little Pearl: Red Letter Days" (Hawthorne's *The Scarlet Letter* as it might play out in *Little Lulu*), and "The Heights" (Emily Brontë's *Wuthering Heights* recast as an EC horror comic).

No small part of Sikoryak's achievement is technical, as he is an undisputed master of imitation. Were it not for the bizarre story lines, one could easily mistake his renderings of the Caped Crusader as having been done by quintessential *Batman* illustrator Dick Sprang (see Figure 6.9). Similarly, his visual evocations of John Stanley and

Irving Tripp's *Little Lulu* and of EC's *Tales from the Crypt* are impeccable (see Figures 6.10 and 6.11). Sikoryak's ability to inhabit these diverse artistic styles is emblematic of the esteem with which he holds classic comic art, and even a cursory look at his adaptations attests to the visual richness of the form. Of course, the revamped *Classics Illustrated* series with its emphasis on diverse, energetic art also showcased this richness. But unlike that series, which called attention to the importance of art in the comic book, Sikoryak's adaptations call attention to the importance of comic book art. It is, perhaps, a subtle distinction, but one that is worth making: the former celebrates the formal aspects of the medium while the latter celebrates the specific history of the medium. Thus, it is impossible to read, say, Sikoryak's "Little Pearl" without being aware of the *Little Lulu* comics. Every panel of Sikoryak's work reminds readers of a piece of comic book history even as they move through the plot of a recognizable story from Western literature. As such, it becomes impossible to separate these two worlds.

And this is what truly sets Sikoryak's work apart from that of *Classics Illustrated*: his combination of literature and comics does not subordinate the latter to the former; instead, the literature is just as much informed by the comics as vice versa. In effect, Sikoryak creates adaptations that reward versatile and eclectic readers who are as familiar with the family and character dynamics in Hawthorne as in *Little Lulu*. Here and elsewhere, Sikoryak's pairings are brilliantly appropriate. For example, the two-bit moralizing that is part and parcel of the Bazooka Joe comics resonates mightily when recast as Dante's epic poem about sinners and sinning. Moreover, in "The Heights," Sikoryak reveals that both *Wuthering Heights* and *Tales from the Crypt* are about the passion of human nature and the chaos to which its expression often leads. Also, in "Ras Kol," Sikoryak lays bare the deep thematic bond between Dostoyevky's Raskolnikov and Batman: both characters attempt to impose their own sense of morality and justice on what they see as an unfair world.[11]

Sikoryak's most pointed pairing, however, is "Good Ol' Gregor Brown." Here, the story of *The Metamorphosis*—in which Gregor Samsa awakes one morning to find himself transformed into a giant cockroach—is heavily informed by the cadences that Charles Schultz brought to *Peanuts*. One strip in the story takes place completely in the dark; the only visuals are Gregor's (Charlie Brown's) thought balloons, a strategy that echoes numerous *Peanuts* strips, right down to the final panel: a "sigh." Also, Sikoryak implicitly argues that Kafka's and Schultz's main characters are at the very least spiritual cousins; who better, after all, to evoke the dehumanized, exis-

Figure 6.10. Copyright 2001 R. Sikoryak. Used with permission.

Figure 6.11. Copyright 2003 R. Sikoryak. Used with permission.

tential woe of Kafka's Gregor Samsa than Charlie Brown, who suffers numerous indignities at the hands of his playmates? Sikoryak forces us to question our artistic judgment. Why, after all, is Kafka any more "literary" than Schultz? Don't both writers capture the human condition in indelible, illuminating ways? For readers who are willing to listen, Sikoryak provides an important lesson about literary value: it is often accorded less on merit than on prejudice, and we disdain certain forms at the expense of our own enrichment. Sikoryak understands the perceived gulf between "literature" and comic books, so by making his stories equally dependent on a knowledge of both "high" and "low" art, and by interweaving those two types of art so thoroughly, he undermines those labels altogether.

An important concept that mutually supports and is supported by these labels is the literary "canon," which might be defined as "the commonplace book of our shared culture, the archive of those texts and titles we wish to remember" (Gates 44). The world of academia—and especially literary studies departments—has been ground zero for debates about the canon, and such debate has been productive in that many more writers who were previously relegated to the margins are now being taught in classrooms across the country. Simply put, the canon is a largely theoretical construct that is nevertheless important because it "defin[es] what is 'central' and what is 'marginal'" (Lauter ix). The problem here is that deciding the issue of literary merit is not an objective process. After all, "literary canons do not fall from the sky. They are constructed and reconstructed by people, people of particular stations in life, people with certain ideas and tastes and definable interests and views of what is desirable" (Lauter 261).

Looking over the list of comic book adaptations that I discuss in this chapter, one can get an immediate sense of how exclusionary the canon can be, for on this list there are no serious challenges to the traditional Western canon. By and large, the authors of the books adapted by *Classics Illustrated* and others are "educated white males of European descent" (Richardson 81). Though women writers like the Brontë sisters or Harriet Beecher Stowe occasionally sneak in, these titles—even the recent ones—sorely lack writers from underrepresented groups. In the case of *Classics Illustrated*, it is possible to see that its roster of writers "to some degree mirrored the canon endorsed by high school and college English departments . . . that reflected the cultural assumptions of the period" (Jones 48–49). But this somewhat limited canon has persisted in the more recent comic book adaptations, all of which are firmly situated in our more diversity-minded present day. To understand the persistence of such a traditional canon in comic book adaptations, one need look no further than economics: many more males than females read comics, so the stories that have been adapted have been, by and large, those stories that appeal mainly to boys.

The work of comic book creators like Gaiman, Moore, and Sikoryak assaults the canon, but the assault is less on the content of the canon than on the very idea of it. Or more specifically, on the assumptions of canon-makers that "literature" embodies only certain forms, and that comic books are certainly not one of them. But comic book creators who use the form with imagination and insight have the ability to complicate the very nature of how we award literary merit. All of the incarnations of the comic book that I have discussed throughout this book—*Eightball* #22 and *Love and Rockets* in Chapter One, the memoirs of Chapter Two, *Maus* of Chapter Three, the examples of comic book journalism in Chapter Four, the EC war comics in Chapter Five, and several of the comic book adaptations of literature that I have discussed in this chapter—help to upend the notion of "literature" as an inviolable model that must adhere to certain dimensions. What we are in need of is a new model of the "literary," and I here return to my opening chapter and its attempts to reconsider what we talk about when we talk about "literature"—a subject that has great significance for me as a writer and reader, certainly, but also as a teacher.

Whenever I meet someone for the first time and tell him or her that I am an English teacher, the response is almost always the same: "English was my worst subject." It always concerns me that this subject that I love so much is a source of dread for so many, and in order to help prevent my own students from making this same declaration in their future, I spend some time at the beginning of each semester finding out something about their attitudes toward literature. When I ask them to define "literature," the responses are revealing. Certain remarks are consistent from semester to semester: literature makes us think about big ideas, literature is difficult, literature is boring, literature is something that people have decided was good or important. This last answer intrigues me the most insofar as it reveals my students' sense of removal from the canon that I have been discussing. In their view, decisions about literary quality are made by others—the omnipresent "They," from whom so many important decrees flow.

As a way of provoking my students to think more deeply about the alleged sanctity of this canon and how artistic value is accorded to particular media, genres, or titles, I give them comic books to read. Because they are not typically considered "literary" and therefore raise larger questions about literary merit and the canon, comic books make an ideal subject for my purposes. My students and I can talk about what makes something "literary" more freely than when we discuss Hemingway's *The Sun Also Rises* (1926) or even Toni Morrison's *Beloved* (1987), for those works already occupy some mystical station in my students' minds as works whose importance is beyond question. But not so with comic books. Instead, these works invite such questioning, especially when students must reconcile their enjoyment of reading comics with the value—and work—of reading literature. In asking and answering these questions—the central one being, perhaps, "What is literature?"—students and all readers can begin to look beyond labels and articulate what constitutes true art to them.

What is at stake in such questioning? A brief history of comics reveals that inaccurate perceptions of comics—such as the previously discussed, erroneous idea that they contribute to juvenile delinquency—has given way to far more troubling results. That is, not only have comic books been subjected to censorship, but they have also suffered from a lack of public support in these attacks. There are many reasons for this situation: the primary audience for comic books is juveniles, and censorship is often carried out in the name of "protecting" young minds; comic book creators and publishers often lack the funds to mount a proper defense; and, most significantly, comic books are not considered to be "literature" (Hermes 24). Combating such views of comic books—that they were juvenile and unchallenging—was exactly what I had in mind when I introduced comic books into my classroom and first conceived of this book. If literature is an art that brings about new understanding and insight—as I believe it to be—then comics certainly fit the bill.

My hope for this book is that it will do something that the many existing works of fine comics scholarship and history have not: provide a close analysis of this very interesting (and growing) medium as it relates to other important artistic media and genres in order to our expand our definitions of literature. My further hope is that this book persuades those who regard comics either uncritically or not at all to consider the complexity of this medium. With the emergence of classes and programs focusing on comics art, and with the growing interest in this medium among libraries, publishers, bookstores, and the press, this rich literature is slowing getting its due. And if you are reading this book (and you don't happen to be one of my friends upon whom I've foisted a draft, demanding feedback), then take it as a further sign that there are others who believe in the maturity, complexity, and artistry of comics.

Notes

1. Or so goes the rationalization, anyway. Before proceeding any further, I must fulfill my obligation as a teacher of literature by voicing my strong opposition to the use of Cliffs Notes. Too many students see these pamphlets as substitutes for reading the original. I'd like to further declare that my record as a student in high school and college is unblemished; never did I stoop so low as to resort to Cliffs Notes. Graduate school, however, with its oral exams based on gargantuan reading lists, is another matter entirely.

2. For a more complete picture of the debate over the educational value of comic books during the 1940s, see Amy Kiste Nyberg, *Seal of Approval: The History of the Comics Code* (1998).

3. Such studies might, however, yield insight into how comic books function as cultural artifacts. That is, an interesting avenue of study would be to examine how a given historical and cultural climate might have impacted the adaptation of a specific title.

4. This page reduction had another effect on the series: the existence of issues with different interior art. There are a substantial number of issues that, when reprinted, contained different art than the original, and potential collectors of *Classics Illustrated* comics should be aware of these different versions, lest they spend money on a particular issue believing it to contain the work of a certain artist when it actually features that of another. Complicating matters is the fact that the Gilberton Company did not provide new publication information in their reprints until the early 1960s. Fortunately, a complete listing of these different versions has been compiled by William B. Jones Jr. in his *Classics Illustrated: A Cultural History, with Illustrations* (2002). As a general rule, the interior art tends to correspond with the covers, where the "first" art appeared with line-drawn covers and the "second" art appeared with the painted covers. In cases where I reference art in issues of *Classics Illustrated* with multiple versions, I indicate in my "Works Cited" list if the issue that I discuss contains the second version of interior art.

5. One of the circumstances that helped bring about the end of *Classics Illustrated* came in the early 1960s when the US Postal Service decided that they should no longer qualify for second class mailing status because the publications "were books, not periodicals" (Sawyer 14). It seems strangely karmic that Kanter's holding the "comic book" at arm's length should, in the end, help put him out of business.

6. On the surface, this move suggests a certain "maverick" attitude on the part of Kanter, but that estimation is unwarranted. In actuality, Kanter tended to avoid controversy generated by his comic books. When certain titles came under fire, Kanter responded by dropping them from production, leading to "gaps" on subsequent reorder forms. One example is emblematic of this situation: in *Seduction of the Innocent*, Wertham noted the distinct parallels between his *bête noire*—the crime comic—and the *Classics Illustrated* version of *Great Expectations* (issue #43); what he found particularly lurid was the cover and first eight pictures, all of which depicted the graveyard scene between Pip and Magwitch and which causes Wertham to ask, "Am I correct in classifying this as

a crime comic?" (311). As a result of such negative attention, *Great Expectations* had only two printings and remains one of the most difficult *Classics Illustrated* to find (as well as one of the most valuable).

7. This work originally appeared serially as three separate comic book issues before being collected into a graphic novel edition. The other titles mentioned in this list all appeared originally as graphic novels.

8. All told, Neil Gaiman and *Sandman* won just about every industry award available, including a grand total of nine Eisner Awards (the comic book industry's equivalent of the Oscars). *Sandman* #19 (*A Midsummer Night's Dream*, which I discuss in this chapter) also "won the 1991 World Fantasy Award for Best Short Story, making it the first monthly comic ever to win a literary award" (Bender 260).

9. Although the final issue of *Sandman* was numbered at seventy-five, there are actually seventy-six issues. An issue published in September of 1991—*The Song of Orpheus*—appeared as *The Sandman Special* and did not receive a number (Bender 264).

10. This analogy is especially true of Alan Quartermain, whose exploits could be enjoyed by young readers through many different books and stories by Haggard. Mina even comments at one point that she "grew up reading of his exploits" (Moore 17), and her statement is not unlike what one might hear from an adult comic book fan reflecting on Batman or Spider-man.

11. As an added bonus, the story recasts Robin as "Sonny," the crossdressing son of a drunk whom Raskol attempts to help. As comic book aficionados well know, Robin (and other young partners, for that matter) has long been the target of critics who wish to read the older hero/young sidekick dynamic in homoerotic terms.

LIST OF ILLUSTRATIONS

WORKS CITED

Adams, Timothy Dow. *Telling Lies in Modern American Autobiography*. Chapel Hill: University of North Carolina Press, 1990.

Alvi, Dana. "24 C. Polish National Libel." *Polish-American Public Relations Committee Website*. September 5, 2000. <http://www.geocities.com/CapitolHill /Senate/8844/24c.htm>

Améry, Jean. *At the Mind's Limits*. 1980. New York: Schocken Books, 1986.

Arlen, Michael J. "Notes on the New Journalism." *The Reporter as Artist: A Look at the New Journalism Controversy*. Ronald Weber (ed). New York: Hastings House, 1974. 244–54.

Arnett, Peter. "Hill 875." *Reporting Vietnam: American Journalism 1959–1975*. Milton J. Bates et al (eds). New York: Penguin Books, 2000. 267–69.

Atlas, James. "The Age of the Literary Memoir is Now." *The New York Times Magazine*. 12 May 1996: 25–27.

Avisar, Ilan. *Screening the Holocaust*. Bloomington, IN: Indiana University Press, 1988.

———. "Holocaust Movies and the Politics of Collective Memory." *Thinking about the Holocaust after Half a Century*. Ed. Alvin Rosenfeld. Bloomington, IN: Indiana University Press, 1997. 38–58.

B., David. *Epileptic*. 2004. New York: Pantheon Books, 2005.

Bagge, Peter. "The Second Coming of Alan Keyes." *Hate Annual #1*. Kim Thompson (ed). Seattle: Fantagraphics Books, Inc., 2001.

Bang, Molly. *Picture This: How Pictures Work*. 1991. New York: SeaStar Books, 2000.

Barks, Carl. *The Carl Barks Library of Walt Disney's Comics and Stories in Color #13*. Prescott, AZ: Gladstone, 1993.

Barlow, John. "Visual Literacy and the Holocaust." *Remembering for the Future: The Impact of the Holocaust on the Contemporary World (Theme II)*. Oxford: Pargamon Press, 1988.

Barry, Lynda. *One Hundred Demons*. Seattle: Sasquatch Books, 2002.

Basinger, Jeanine. *The World War II Combat Film: Anatomy of a Genre*. New York: Columbia University Press, 1986.

"Bataan!" *Battle #32*. New York: Foto Parade, Inc., 1954.

Bechdel, Alison. *Fun Home*. New York: Houghton Mifflin, 2006.

Bender, Hy. *The Sandman Companion*. New York: Vertigo/DC Comics, 1999.

Benfer, Amy. "Real Women." *Salon.com*. 20 February, 2001. Accessed August 17, 2006 <http://archive.salon.com/mwt/feature/2001/02/20/her nandez/index.html>

Benton, Mike. *The Comic Book in America*. Dallas: Taylor Publishing Company, 1993.

Berger, Alan. "Ashes and Hope: The Holocaust in Second GenerationAmerican Literature." *Reflections of the Holocaust in Art and Literature*. Ed. Randolph L. Braham. New York: Columbia University Press, 1990. 97–116.

Berger, John and Jean Mohr. *Another Way of Telling*. 1982. New York: Vintage Books, 1995.

Bergmann, Martin S. and Milton E. Jucovy. *Generations of the Holocaust*. New York: Basic Books, Inc., 1982.

Blum, Alex A. et al. *Classics Illustrated #99: Hamlet*. New York: The Gilberton Company, Inc., 1952.

Boynton, Robert (ed). *The New New Journalism: Conversations with America's Best Nonfiction Writers on Their Craft*. New York: Vintage Books, 2005.

Bresler, Robert J. "The Death of Hollywood's Golden Age and the Changing American Character." *USA Today*. March 1997: 64–7.

Brooks, Peter. *Reading for the Plot: Design and Intention in Narrative*. 1984. New York: Vintage Books, 1985.

Brown, Chester. "Helder." *The Little Man: Short Strips 1980–1995*. Montreal: Drawn & Quarterly Publications, 1998. 47–67.

———. *I Never Liked You*. Montreal: Drawn & Quarterly Publications, 1994.

———. *The Playboy*. Montreal: Drawn & Quarterly Publications, 1992.

———. "Showing Helder." *The Little Man: Short Strips 1980–1995*. Montreal: Drawn & Quarterly Publications, 1998. 68–101.

Brown, Jeffrey. *Clumsy*. Marietta, GA: Top Shelf Productions, 2002.

Bruss, Elizabeth. *Autobiographical Acts: The Changing Situation of a Literary Genre*. Baltimore: The Johns Hopkins University Press, 1976.

Capote, Truman. *In Cold Blood*. 1966. New York: Random House, 1994.

Cameron, Lou et al. *Classics Illustrated #13: Dr. Jekyll and Mr. Hyde* [second interior art]. New York: The Gilberton Company, Inc., 1953.

Carr, David. *Time, Narrative, and History*. Bloomington, IN: Indiana University Press, 1991.

Chabon, Michael. *The Amazing Adventures of Kavalier and Clay*. New York: Picador USA, 2000.

Claremont, Chris et al. *Classics Comics #14: The War of the Worlds*. New York: Marvel Comics Group, 1976.

———. *Classics Comics #17: The Count of Monte Cristo*. New York: Marvel Comics Group, 1977.

Cloonan, Becky and Gary Reed. *Dracula: The Graphic Novel*. New York: Puffin Books, 2006.

Clowes, Daniel. *Eightball #22*. Seattle: Fantagraphics Books, Inc., 2001.

———. "Just Another Day." *Twentieth Century Eightball*. Seattle: Fantagraphics Books, Inc., 2002. 44–47.

———. "The Stroll." *Twentieth Century Eightball*. Seattle: Fantagraphics Books, Inc., 2002. 17–21.

Coe, Sue. "Liverpool's Children." *The New Yorker*. 13 December, 1993: 102–7.

———. "The Sweatshop, 1994." *The New Yorker*. 7 November, 1994: 229–33.

———. *Dead Meat*. New York: Four Walls Eight Windows, 1995.

Coe, Sue and Holly Metz. *How to Commit Suicide in South Africa*. New York: RAW Books & Graphics, 1983.

Collier, David. *Portraits from Life*. Montreal: Drawn and Quarterly, 2001.

"Commitment to the Struggle: The Art of Sue Coe." *Brown University Website*. October 20, 2003. <http://www.brown.edu/Facilities/David_Winton_Bell_Gallery/coe.html>

Conroy, Frank. *Stop-Time*. 1967. New York: Penguin Books, 1977.

Couser, G. Thomas. *Altered Egos: Authority in American Autobiography*. New York: Oxford University Press, 1989.

Crumb, Robert. "I Remember the Sixties!" *Crumb Family Comics*. San Francisco: Last Gasp, 2000. 158–62.

Crumb, Robert and Aline Kominsky-Crumb. "Let's Have a Little Talk." *The Complete Dirty Laundry*. San Francisco: Last Gasp, 1993. 7.

———. "Our Lovely Home." *The Complete Dirty Laundry*. San Francisco: Last Gasp, 1993. 103–11.

Daniels, Les. *Comix: A History of Comic Books in America*. New York: Bonanza Books, 1971.

———. *Marvel: Five Fabulous Decades of the World's Greatest Comics*. New York: Harry N. Abrams, Inc., 1991.

Davis, Francis. "Storming the Home Front." *The Atlantic Monthly*. March 2003: 125–32.

Davis, Jack et al. "Grounds . . . for Horror!" *Tales from the Crypt #13.* 1952 (as #26). West Plains, MO: Gemstone Publishing, 1995. 1–8.

Davison, Al. *The Spiral Cage.* London: Titan Books, 1990.

De Fuccio, Jerry and Jack Davis. "Silent Service." *Two-Fisted Tales EC Annual Volume 3* [Issues #28-#32/#11-#15]. West Plains, MO: 1996.

Deitch, Kim. "Ready to Die." *Details* May 1999: 146-51.

Des Pres, Terrence. *The Survivor: An Anatomy of Life in the Death Camps.* New York: Washington Square Press, 1977.

Doherty, Catherine. *Can of Worms.* Seattle: Fantagraphics Books, Inc., 2000.

Doherty, Thomas. "Art Spiegelman's Maus: Graphic Art and the Holocaust." *American Literature* March 1996: 69–84.

———. *Projections of War: Hollywood, American Culture, and World War II.* New York: Columbia University Press, 1993.

Dower, John W. *War without Mercy: Race & Power in the Pacific War.* New York: Pantheon Books, 1986.

Drechsler, Debbie. *Daddy's Girl.* Seattle: Fantagraphics Books, Inc., 1995.

Dreifus, Claudia. Interview with Art Spiegelman. *The Progressive.* November 1989: 34–37.

Eakin, Paul John. *How Our Lives Become Stories: Making Selves.* Ithaca: Cornell University Press, 1999.

———. "The Referential Aesthetic of Autobiography." *Studies in the Literary Imagination* 23.2 (1990): 129–45.

Ebert, Roger. Rev. of *Elephant,* dir. Gus Van Sant. *The Chicago Sun-Times* online. November 7, 2003. http://www.suntimes.com/ebert/ebert_reviews/200311/110701.html>

Eisner, Will. *Comics and Sequential Art.* Tamarac, FL: Poorhouse Press, 1985.

———. Introduction. *To the Heart of the Storm.* 1991. New York: DC Comics, 2000.

Emans, Robert. "*Treasure Island*: The Classic and the Classic Comic." *The Elementary School Journal* 60.5 (1960): 253–57.

Epstein, Helen. *Children of the Holocaust.* 1979. New York: Penguin Books, 1988.

———. *Where She Came From: A Daughter's Search for Her Mother's History.* New York: Penguin Books, 1998.

Evans, George et al. *Classics Illustrated #136: Lord Jim.* New York: The Gilberton Company, Inc., 1957.

Evans, Michael. "The Serpent's Eye: The Cinema of Twentieth-Century Combat." *Quadrant.* January 2001: 85–93.

"The Face of the Enemy." *War Comics #8.* New York: USA Comic Magazine Corp., 1952.

Felman, Shoshana and Dori Laub. *Testimony: Crises of Witnessing in Literature, Psychoanalysis, and History*. New York: Routledge, 1992.

Friedländer, Saul. *When Memory Comes*. 1978. New York: The Noonday Press, 1991.

Fussell, Paul. *Wartime: Understanding and Behavior in the Second World War*. Oxford: Oxford University Press, 1989.

Gaiman, Neil. *Sandman #13*. New York: DC Comics, Inc., 1990.

———. *Sandman #19*. New York: DC Comics, Inc., 1990.

———. *Sandman #75*. New York: DC Comics, Inc., 1996.

Gates, Henry Louis. "Whose Canon Is It, Anyway?" *The New York Times Book Review*. 26 February 1989: 3, 44–45.

Gergen, Kenneth. *An Invitation to Social Construction*. London: Sage Publications, Ltd., 1999.

Giddins, Gary. "Seduced by Classics Illustrated." *Give Our Regards to the Atomsmashers: Writers on Comics*. Ed. Sean Howe. New York: Pantheon Books, 2004. 78–94.

Gilmore, Leigh. *The Limits of Autobiography: Trauma and Testimony*. Ithaca: Cornell University Press, 2001.

Gloeckner, Phoebe. "Minnie's Third Love." *A Child's Life and Other Stories*. Berkeley, CA: Frog Ltd., 2000. 70–81.

Gold, Herbert. "On Epidemic First Personism." *The Reporter as Artist: A Look at the New Journalism Controversy*. Ronald Weber (ed). New York: Hastings House, 1974. 283–87.

Gopnik, Adam. "Kurtzman's Mad World." *The New Yorker*. 29 March 1993: 74.

Gossman, Lionel: "History and Literature: Reproduction or Signification." *The Writing of History: Literary Form and Historical Understanding*. Ed. Robert Canary and Henry Kozicki. Madison, WI: The University of Wisconsin Press, 1978. 3–39.

Goulart, Ron. *Over 50 Years of American Comic Books*. Lincolnwood, IL: Publications International, Ltd., 1991.

Grant, Steven and Tom Mandrake. *Classics Illustrated: Hamlet*. New York: Berkley/First Publishing, 1990.

Grealy, Lucy. *Autobiography of a Face*. 1994. New York: Harper/Perennial Books, 1995.

Green, Justin. "Binky Brown Meets the Holy Virgin Mary." *The Binky Brown Sampler*. San Francisco: Last Gasp, 1995. 9–52.

Grossman, Lev. "The Trouble with Memoirs." *Time*. 23 January 2006: 58–62.

Hajdu, David. "Comics for Grown-Ups." *The New York Review of Books Online*. September 15, 2003. <http://www.nybooks.com/articles/16515>

Halberstam, David. *The Fifties*. New York: Villard Books, 1993.

Harrison, Kathryn. *The Kiss*. 1997. New York: Bard Books, 1998.

———. *Thicker Than Water*. 1991. New York: Harper Perennial, 1992.

Hartsock, John C. "'Literary Journalism' as an Epistemological Moving Object within a Larger 'Quantum' Narrative." *Journal of Communication Inquiry* October 1999: 432–47.

Harvey, Robert C. *The Art of the Comic Book: An Aesthetic History*. Jackson, MS: The University of Mississippi Press, 1996.

———. "Attacking the Attack Dogs: Walt Kelly's Finest Hour." *Pogo, Volume 10*. Seattle: Fantagraphics Books, Inc., 1998. i–x.

Hass Aaron. *In the Shadow of the Holocaust: The Second Generation*. Ithaca: Cornell University Press, 1990.

Hassell, Bravetta. "The Bold Outlines of a Plot." *Washington Post*. 16 July 2006: D1.

Hatfield, Charles. *Alternative Comics: An Emerging Literature*. Jackson, MS: The University of Mississippi Press, 2005.

Hellmann, John. *Fables of Fact: The New Journalism as New Fiction*. Urbana, IL: The University of Illinois Press, 1981.

Hermes, Will. "Drawing the Line: A New Wave of Censorship Hits Comics." *Utne Reader*. November–December 1995: 22–24.

Hernandez, Gilbert. "Human Diastrophism." *Blood of Palomar*. Seattle: Fantagraphics Books, Inc., 1989. 13–117.

———. *Poison River*. Seattle: Fantagraphics Books, Inc., 1994.

———. "Poseur." *Luba in America*. Seattle: Fantagraphics Books, Inc., 2001. 118–25.

Hernandez, Jaime. *Chester Square*. Seattle: Fantagraphics Books, Inc., 1996.

———. "Flies on the Ceiling." *Flies on the Ceiling*. Seattle: Fantagraphics Books, Inc., 1991. 1–15.

———. *Ghost of Hoppers*. Seattle: Fantagraphics Books, Inc., 2005.

Hernandez, Los Bros. *Tears from Heaven*. Seattle: Fantagraphics Books, Inc., 1988.

Herr, Michael. *Dispatches*. 1977. New York: Vintage Books, 1991.

Hirsch, Marianne. "Family Pictures: *Maus*, Mourning, and Post-Memory." *Discourse* 15.2 (1992–93): 3–29.

Hoff, Gary R. "The Visual Narrative: Kids, Comic Books, and Creativity." *Art Education* 35.2 (1982): 20–23.

Hollowell, John. Fact and Fiction: *The New Journalism and the Nonfiction Novel*. Chapel Hill, NC: The University of North Carolina Press, 1977.

Hornschemeier, Paul. "Of This Much We Are Certain." *Autobiographix.* Ed. Diana Schutz. Milwaukie, OR: Dark Horse Books, 2003: 91–98.

Inge, M. Thomas. *Comics as Culture.* Jackson, MS: University of Mississippi Press, 1990.

Irving, Frazer and Gary Reed. *Frankenstein: The Graphic Novel.* New York: Puffin Books, 2005.

James, Caryn. "Putting the Unimaginable to Imaginative New Uses." *The New York Times.* 1 March 1992.

"James Frey and the *A Million Little Pieces* Controversy." 26 January. *Oprah.com.* May 12, 2006. <http://www2.oprah.com/tows/slide/200601/20060126/slide_2006012 6_350_113.jhtml>

Jameson, Fredric. *The Political Unconscious: Narrative as Socially Symbolic Act.* Ithaca, NY: Cornell University Press, 1981.

Jensen, Jay. "The New Journalism in Historical Perspective." *Liberating the Media: The New Journalism.* Charles Flippen (ed). Washington, DC: Acropolis Books, Ltd., 1974. 18–28.

Jones, Gerard. *Men of Tomorrow: Geeks, Gangsters, and the Birth of the Comic Book.* New York: Basic Books, 2004.

Jones, William B., Jr. *Classics Illustrated: A Cultural History, with Illustrations.* Jefferson, NC: McFarland & Company, Inc., 2002.

Kane, Kathryn. *Visions of War: Hollywood Combat Films of World War II.* Ann Arbor, MI: UMI Research Press, 1982.

Katin, Miriam. "Oh, to Celebrate!" *Drawn & Quarterly, Volume 4.* Montreal: Drawn & Quarterly Publications, 2001. 138–49.

Kauffman, Bruce. "Journalists Sound Off on Media Coverage." *North County Times* 5 May 2002. Oceanside edition: B1+.

Kihl, H. J. et al. *Classics Illustrated #39: Jane Eyre.* New York: The Gilberton Company, Inc., 1962.

Kirby, Jack et al. *Classics Illustrated #35: The Last Days of Pompeii* [second interior art]. New York: The Gilberton Company, Inc., 1961.

Klock, Geoff. *How to Read Superhero Comics and Why.* New York: Continuum International Publishing Group, Ltd, 2002.

Kochalka, James. *American Elf.* Marietta, GA: Top Shelf Productions, 2004.

Koppes, Clayton R. and Gregory D. Black. *Hollywood Goes to War: How Politics, Profits and Propaganda Shaped World War II Movies.* Berkeley, CA: University of California Press, 1987.

Krakauer, Jon. *Into the Wild.* New York: Random House, 1996.

Kundera, Milan. *Immortality.* 1991. New York: Harper Perennial, 1992.

Kunzle, David. *The History of the Comic Strip: The Nineteenth Century.* Berkeley, CA: University of California Press, 1990.

Kuper, Peter. *Classics Illustrated: The Jungle*. New York: Berkley/First Publishing, 1991.

Kurtz, Howard. "NY Times Uncovers Dozens of Faked Stories by Reporter." *Washington Post*. 11 May, 2003, F edition: A1.

Kurtzman, Harvey. "Big 'If.'" *Frontline Combat EC Annual Volume 1* [Issues #1–#5]. 1952. West Plains, MO: Gemstone Publishing, 1996.

———. "Corpse on the Imjin." *Two-Fisted Tales EC Annual Volume 2* [Issues #23–#27/#6–#10]. 1952. West Plains, MO: Gemstone Publishing, 1995.

———. "Kill." *Two-Fisted Tales EC Annual Volume 2* [Issues #23–#27/#6–#10]. 1951. West Plains, MO: Gemstone Publishing, 1995.

———. "Rubble." *Two-Fisted Tales EC Annual Volume 2* [Issues #23–#27/#6–#10]. 1951. West Plains, MO: Gemstone Publishing, 1995.

Kurtzman, Harvey and Jack Davis. "Enemy Assault." *Frontline Combat EC Annual Volume 1* [Issues #1–#5]. 1951. West Plains, MO: Gemstone Publishing, 1996.

———. "Hill 203." *Two-Fisted Tales EC Annual Volume 2* [Issues #23–#27/#6–#10]. 1951. West Plains, MO: Gemstone Publishing, 1995.

———. "Korea." *Two-Fisted Tales EC Annual Volume 3* [Issues #28–#32/#11–#15]. West Plains, MO: Gemstone Publishing, 1996

———. "Silent Service." *Two-Fisted Tales EC Annual Volume 3* [Issues #23–#27/#11–#15]. 1953. West Plains, MO: Gemstone Publishing, 1996.

Kurtzman, Harvey and John Severin. "The Caves." *Frontline Combat EC Annual Volume 2* [Issues #6–#10]. 1952. West Plains, MO: Gemstone Publishing, 1997.

Kurtzman, Harvey, John Severin, and Bill Elder. "Buzz Bomb." *Two-Fisted Tales EC Annual Volume 2* [Issues #23–#27/#6–#10]. 1952. West Plains, MO: Gemstone Publishing, 1995.

———. "The Landing." *Frontline Combat EC Annual Volume 2* [Issues #6–#10]. 1952. West Plains, MO: Gemstone Publishing, 1997.

———. "War Story." *Two-Fisted Tales EC Annual Volume 1* [Issues #18–#22/#1–#5]. 1951. West Plains, MO: Gemstone Publishing, 1994.

Kurtzman, Harvey and Wally Wood. "Atom Bomb." *Two-Fisted Tales #16* [#33]. 1953. West Plains, MO: Gemstone Publishing, 1996

———. "A Baby." *Frontline Combat EC Annual Volume 2* [Issues #6–#10]. 1953. West Plains, MO: Gemstone Publishing, 1997.

———. "Iwo Jima." *Frontline Combat EC Annual Volume 2* [Issues #6–#10]. 1952. West Plains, MO: Gemstone Publishing, 1997.

Langer, Lawrence. *The Holocaust and the Literary Imagination*. New Haven, CT: Yale University Press, 1975.

——— (ed.). *Art from the Ashes: A Holocaust Anthology*. Ed. Lawrence Langer. New York: Oxford University Press, 1995

Lauter, Paul. *Canons and Contexts*. New York: Oxford University Press, 1991.

Lay, Carol. "Pinups & Playmates." *Salon.com*. October 22, 2003. <http://www.salon.com/health/sex/urge/1999/07/31/pinups/index1.html>

Lehmann-Haupt, Christopher. "Taking Risk to Its 'Logical' Extreme." Rev. of *Into the Wild* by Jon Krakauer. *New York Times*. 4 January, 1996. Late edition: C17.

———. "Seeing with New Eyes in a World of Exotic Obsession." Rev. of *The Orchid Thief* by Susan Orlean. *New York Times*. 4 January 1999: E8.

Lejeune, Philippe. *On Autobiography*. Minneapolis: University of Minnesota Press, 1989.

Leroy. Letter. *Love and Rockets Vol. II #2*. Summer 2001: 8.

Levi, Primo. *Survival at Auschwitz*. 1958. New York: MacMillan, 1961.

———. *The Reawakening*. 1965. New York: MacMillan, 1987.

———. *The Drowned and the Saved*. New York: Random, 1989.

Long, Rob. "Reality Bites." *National Review*. 13 February 2006: 30–31.

Lounsberry, Barbara. *The Art of Fact: Contemporary Artists of Nonfiction*. New York: Greenwood Press, 1990.

Lutes, Jason. "Rules to Live By." *Autobiographix*. Ed. Diana Schutz. Milwaukie, OR: Dark Horse Books, 2003: 23–28.

MacPherson, Ken. "When Comic Books Were Food for Thought." *Globe and Mail*. 11 March 2002.

Malcolm, Janet. *The Journalist and the Murderer*. New York: Random House, 1990.

Matt, Joe. *Fair Weather*. Montreal: Drawn & Quarterly Publications, 2002.

———. *Peepshow: The Cartoon Diary of Joe Matt*. Princeton, WI: Kitchen Sink Press, 1991.

———. *The Poor Bastard*. Montreal: Drawn & Quarterly Publications, 1997.

McCarthy, Mary. *Memories of a Catholic Girlhood*. New York: Harcourt, Brace Jovanovich, Inc., 1957.

McCloud, Scott. *Understanding Comics*. 1993. New York: Harpercollins, 1994.

McGrath, Charles. "Not Funnies." *The New York Times Magazine.* 11 July 2004: 24–33, 46, 55–56.

"A Million Little Lies." 4 January 2006. *The Smoking Gun.* May 12, 2006. <http://www.thesmokinggun.com/archive/0104061jamesfrey1.html>

Moore, Alan and Kevin O'Neill. *The League of Extraordinary Gentlemen, Vol. I.* La Jolla, CA: America's Best Comics, 2000.

Moore, Judith. *Fat Girl.* 2005. New York: Plume Books, 2006.

Murphy, Bernadette. "Addict's Memoir: Loathe It or Love It." *The Los Angeles Times.* 20 May 2003: E1.

Murphy, Robert. *The Body Silent.* 1987. New York: W.W. Norton, 1990.

Nelson, Sara. "Don't Shoot the Storyteller." *Publisher's Weekly.* 16 January 2006: 5.

Newfield, Jack. "The 'Truth' about Objectivity and the New Journalism." *Liberating the Media: The New Journalism.* Charles Flippen (ed). Washington, DC: Acropolis Books, Ltd., 1974. 59–65.

Nodel, Norman et al. *Classics Illustrated #138: Journey to the Center of the Earth.* New York: The Gilberton Company, Inc., 1957.

Nore, Gordon. "Beyond Superman." *The Progressive.* November 1992: 12.

Nyberg, Amy Kiste. *Seal of Approval: The History of the Comics Code.* Jackson, MS: The University of Mississippi Press, 1998.

O'Brien, Tim. *The Things They Carried.* 1990. New York: Penguin Books, 1991.

Olney, James. "'I Was Born': Slave Narratives, Their Status as Autobiography and as Literature." *The Slave's Narrative.* Eds. Charles T. Davis and Henry Louis Gates, Jr. Oxford: Oxford University Press: 1985. 148–74.

"Oprah's Book Club." *Wikipedia: the Free Encyclopedia.* August 28, 2006. <http:// http://en.wikipedia.org/wiki/Oprah's_Book_Club>

Orenstein, Peggy. "A Graphic Life." *The New York Times Magazine.* 5 August 2001: 26–29.

Orlando, Joe et al. *Classics Illustrated #6: A Tale of Two Cities* [second interior art]. New York: The Gilberton Company, Inc., 1956.

Orlean, Susan. *The Orchid Thief.* New York: Ballantine Books, 1998.

Pekar, Harvey. "Austere Youth." *The Best of American Splendor.* New York: Ballantine Books, 2005: 14–21.

———. "*Maus* and Other Topics." *The Comics Journal.* December 1986: 54–57.

———. *Our Cancer Year.* New York: Four Walls Eight Windows, 1994.

———. *The Quitter.* New York: DC Comics, 2005.

Ploog, Michael. *Classics Illustrated: The Adventures of Tom Sawyer.* New York: Berkley/First Publishing, 1990.

Polenberg, Richard. *War and Society: The United States 1941–1945.* New York: J.B. Lippincott Company, 1972.

Pollack, Ian and William Shakespeare. *King Lear.* New York: Ravette Books, Ltd., 1984.

Pustz, Matthew. *Comic Book Culture: Fanboys and True Believers.* Jackson, MS: The University of Mississippi Press, 1999.

Quindlen, Anna. "How Dark? How Stormy? I Can't Recall." *The New York Times on the Web.* 11 May 1997. *The New York Times.* October 23, 2006. <http://www.nytimes.com/books/97/05/11/ book-end/bookend.html>

Rall, Ted. *To Afghanistan and Back.* New York: NBM Books, 2002.

Ray, Robert. *A Certain Tendency of the Hollywood Cinema, 1930–1980.* Princeton, NJ: Princeton University Press, 1985.

Rhett, Kathryn. Introduction. *Survival Stories: Memoirs of Crisis.* Ed. Kathryn Rhett. 1997. New York: Anchor Books, 1998. 1–14.

Richardson, Donna. "Classics Illustrated." *American Heritage.* May/June 1993: 78–85.

Robinson, Leonard Wallace. "The New Journalism: A Panel Discussion with Harold Hayes, Gay Talese, Tom Wolfe and Professor L.W. Robinson." *The Reporter as Artist: A Look at the New Journalism Controversy.* Ronald Weber (ed). New York: Hastings House, 1974. 66–75.

Rosenfeld, Alvin. *A Double Dying: Reflections on Holocaust Literature.* Bloomington: Indiana University Press, 1980.

———. *Imagining Hitler.* Bloomington: Indiana University Press, 1985.

———. "Holocaust Fictions and the Transformation of Historical Memory." *Holocaust and Genocide Studies* 3.3 (1988): 323–36.

Rust, Michael. "Read About Why I Love Me and How Much I've Suffered." *Insight on the News.* 2 June 1997: 19–20.

Rybak, Deborah Caulfield. "Taking Liberties: Memoir Writers Walk a Wavy Line Between Reality and Invention." *The Star Tribune: Newspaper of the Twin Cities.* 27 July 2003: 1E.

Sabin, Roger. *Adult Comics: An Introduction.* London: Routledge, 1993.

———. *Comics, Comix & Graphic Novels.* London: Phaidon Press, Ltd., 1996.

Sacco, Joe. "Christmas with Karadzic." *Zero Zero #15.* Kim Thompson (ed). Seattle: Fantagraphics Books, Inc., 1997. 4–24.

———. "The War Crimes Trials." *Details* (September 1998): 260–65.

———. *Palestine.* 1994, 1996. Seattle: Fantagraphics Books, Inc., 2001.

———. *Safe Area Gora☐de.* Seattle: Fantagraphics Books, Inc., 2001

———. Lecture. Palomar College. San Marcos, CA. April 29, 2002.

Sackett, Susan. *The Hollywood Reporter Book of Box Office Hits*. New York: Billboard Books, 1996.

Sarris, Andrew. *The American Cinema: Directors and Directions, 1929–1968*. Chicago: The University of Chicago Press, 1968.

Sarup, Madan. *An Introductory Guide to Post-structuralism and Postmodernism*. Athens: The University of Georgia Press, 1993.

Satrapi, Marjane. *Persepolis*. New York: Pantheon Books, 2003.

Sawyer, Michael. "Albert Lewis Kanter and the Classics: The Man Behind the Gilberton Company." *Journal of Popular Culture* 20.4 (1987): 1–18.

Schatz, Thomas. *The Genius of the System: Hollywood Filmmaking in the Studio Era*. New York: Pantheon Books, 1988.

Schindler, Colin. *Hollywood Goes to War: Films and American Society, 1939–1952*. London: Routledge & Kegan Paul Ltd., 1979.

Schoolman, Martha. Rev. of *Midnight in the Garden of Good an Evil* by John Berendt. *Booklist* (15 October 1993): 413–14.

Schwarz-Bart, André. *The Last of the Just*. 1960. New York: Atheneum, 1985.

Seth. *It's a Good Life, If You Don't Weaken*. Montreal: Drawn & Quarterly Publications, 1996.

Shamsavari, Sina. Letter. *Love and Rockets Vol. II #4* (Summer 2002): 31.

Sienkiewicz, Bill. *Classics Illustrated: Moby Dick*. New York: Berkley/First Publishing, 1990.

Sikoryak, Robert. "Good Ol' Gregor Brown." *Raw 2.2*. New York: Penguin Books, 1990. 178–79.

———. "The Heights." *Drawn & Quarterly 5*. Montreal: Drawn & Quarterly, 91–99.

———. "Little Pearl: Red Letter Days." *Drawn & Quarterly 4*. Montreal: Drawn & Quarterly, 2001. 67–79.

———. "Raskol." *Drawn & Quarterly 3*. Montreal: Drawn & Quarterly, 2000. 89–99.

Sklar, Robert. *Movie-Made America: A Cultural History of American Movies*. New York: Random House, 1975.

Slater, Lauren. *Lying: A Metaphorical Memoir*. 2000. New York: Penguin Books, 2001.

Smith, Andrew. "Comics Go with Public Opinion During Wartime." *Memphis Commercial Appeal* 30 March 2003: F6.

Smith, David Gaddis. "9/11 Report Gets a Comic-book Version." *San Deigo Union Tribune*. 6 August 2006: F7.

Smith, Sedonie. "Construing Truths in Lying Mouths: Truthtelling in

Women's Autobiography." *Studies in the Literary Imagination* 23.2 (1990): 145–64.

"Snow." *Battle #32*. New York: Foto Parade, Inc., 1954.

Sontag, Susan. *On Photography*. 1977. New York: Anchor Books, 1989.

Spiegelman, Art. *Breakdowns*. New York: Nostalgia Press, Inc., 1977.

———. *The Complete* Maus. CD-ROM. New York: Voyager, 1994.

———. "A Jew in Rostock." *The New Yorker*. 7 December, 1992: 119–21.

———. Lecture. Indiana University. Bloomington, IN, 10 March 1992.

———. *Maus I: My Father Bleeds History*. New York: Pantheon Books, 1986.

———. *Maus II: And Here My Troubles Began*. New York: Pantheon Books, 1991.

———. "Symptoms of Disorder/Signs of Genius." *Binky Brown Sampler*. By Justin Green. San Francisco: Last Gasp, 1995. 4–6.

———. "WORDS, Worth a Thousand." *The New Yorker*. 20 & 27 February 1995: 196–99.

Stein, Ruth. "The ABC's of Counterfeit Classics: Adapted, Bowdlerized, and Condensed." *The English Journal* 55.9 (1966): 1160–63.

Steyn, Mark. "Why Should He Have to Live What He Writes?" *Maclean's*. 6 February 2006: 50–51.

Stone, Laurie. "Recalled to Life." *Close to the Bone: Memoirs of Hurt, Rage, and Desire*. Ed. Laurie Stone. New York: Grove Press, 1997.

"Sturgeon's Law." *Cool Jargon of the Day*. November 7, 2005 <http://www.jargon.net/jargonfile/s/SturgeonsLaw.html>

Swiebocka, Teresa. *Auschwitz: A History in Photographs*. Engl. ed. Jonathan Webber and Connie Wilsack. Bloomington, IN: Indiana University Press, 1990.

Tamai, Tony Leonard and Arthur Bryon Cover. *Macbeth: The Graphic Novel*. New York: Puffin Books, 2005.

Thompson, Craig. *Blankets*. Marietta, GA: Top Shelf Productions, 2003.

Thompson, Hunter S. *Fear and Loathing: On the Campaign Trail '72*. 1973. New York: Warner Books, 1983.

Thompson, Jill and P. Craig Russell. *Classics Illustrated: The Scarlet Letter*. New York: Berkley/First Publishing, 1990.

Turrentine, Jeff. "A Rough Road to Sobriety." *The Los Angeles Times*. 18 May 2003: R16.

Twain, Mark. "No Earthquake." *Twainquotes*. September 25, 2003. <http://www. twainquotes.com/18640823.html>

Uslan, Michael. Introduction. *America at War: The Best of DC War Comics.* New York: Simon and Schuster, 1979. 5–12.

Vansant, Wayne. *The Red Badge of Courage: The Graphic Novel.* New York: Puffin Books, 2005.

Vaughan, Don. "Four-Color Combat." *Military Officer.* March 2003: 72–78.

Villani, Carmen. Letter. *Washington Post.* 25 July 2006: A14.

Von Bernewitz, Fred and Grant Geissman. *Tales of Terror!* Seattle: Fantagraphics Books, Inc., 2000.

"War Is Certainly Hell to Film." *The Economist.* 8 August, 1998: 69–70.

Ware, Chris. *Quimby the Mouse.* Seattle: Fantagraphics Books, Inc., 2003.

Warner, John et al. *Classics Comics #20: Frankenstein.* New York: Marvel Comics Group, 1977.

Webb, Robert H. et al. *Classics Illustrated #26: Frankenstein.* 1945. New York: The Gilberton Company, Inc., 1958.

Weber, Ronald. "Some Sort of Artistic Excitement." *The Reporter as Artist: A Look at the New Journalism Controversy.* Ronald Weber (ed). New York: Hastings House, 1974.

Wertham, Fredric. *Seduction of the Innocent.* New York: Rinehart & Company, Inc., 1954.

White, Hayden. *Tropics of Discourse.* Baltimore: The Johns Hopkins University Press: 1978.

Wiesel, Elie. *Night.* 1958. New York: Bantam, 1982.

Witek, Joseph. *Comic Books as History: The Narrative Art of Jack Jackson, Art Spiegelman, and Harvey Pekar.* Jackson, MS: The University of Mississippi Press, 1989.

―――. "The Dream of Total War: The Limits of a Genre." *Journal of Popular Culture* (Fall 1996): 37–45.

Wolff, Tobias. *Old School.* 2003. New York: Vintage Books, 2004.

Wolin, Jeffrey. *Written in Memory: Portraits of the Holocaust.* San Francisco: Chronicle Books, 1997.

Wolk, Douglas. "The Comic Book Was Better." *New York Times.* 13 July 2003: AR9.

Woodward, Joe. "The Literature of Lies." *Poets and Writers* May/June 2006: 10–11.

Young, James. *Writing and Rewriting the Holocaust: Narrative and the Consequences of Interpretation.* Bloomington, IN: Indiana University Press, 1988.

———. *The Changing Shape of Holocaust Memory.* New York: The American Jewish Committee, 1995.

———. "The Holocaust as Vicarious Past: Art Spiegelman's *Maus* and the Afterimages of History." *Critical Inquiry* Spring 1998: 666–90.

Zarate, Oscar and William Shakespeare. *Othello.* New York: Workman Publishing, 1983.

INDEX

*Page numbers in **bold** indicate illustrations*